The CHURCH At RISK

Ernestine M. Hill

Star Bible Publications
Fort Worth, Texas 76182

© *Copyright 1995 Ernestine M. Hill*

ISBN 1-56794-082-X

Dedications

The writings contained in this book are lovingly dedicated:

1. To the service of our Lord, who died that the lost might be saved.

2. To the preservation of belief in His word and the maintenance of purity in the doctrines and practices of His church.

3. To the memory of all those in past ages who played a part in the preservation of God's word for future generations.

4. To all those of the present and future generations whose lives are and shall be devoted to this sacred cause.

All scripture citations are taken from the American Standard Version.

Acknowledgments

My first and greatest benefactor is God, to whom I offer my deep gratitude and praise for having provided me with a lifetime of association with hundreds of fellow-Christians among an assortment of congregations. I have been closely associated with thriving, growing churches whose members worked together in harmony, striving to fulfill their divinely given mission. I have also been associated briefly with a few churches which were hampered by jealousy and mistaken ideas of Christian doctrine and by backbiting friction within. I have lived during the period when the church was distinguished for its rapid growth as well as during a period with almost no growth. I have witnessed the results of those dangers which constantly threaten the church. Consequently my observations and experiences have prompted me to sound a warning against those forces which threaten the church today and place at risk the preservation of the purity of the church in both doctrine and practice, and in so doing put at risk the souls of countless individuals.

I am also extremely grateful to my daughter, Jean, who has tirelessly typed my writings; to my Christian friend, Gail Christian, and my daughter, Jerry, who have spent many hours of proof-reading the manuscript for technical errors; and to David Christian, for his art work on the book cover.

Table of Contents

Chapter		Page
ONE	THE CHURCH — WHO NEEDS IT?	1
TWO	WHICH CHURCH — DOES IT MATTER?	9
THREE	ONLY ONE WAY OF ENTRY INTO JESUS' CHURCH	29
FOUR	IDENTIFYING CHARACTERISTICS OF JESUS' CHURCH	43
FIVE	THE DEMAND FOR CHANGE IN CHURCH WORSHIP	57
SIX	BIBLE ILLITERACY	97
SEVEN	GOD'S BLUEPRINT FOR A CHRISTIAN WOMAN	115
EIGHT	CHRISTIANS AND THE WORLD	147
NINE	CHURCH LEADERSHIP	165
TEN	THE TEACHING MINISTRY	209
ELEVEN	EVERYBODY IS AT RISK:? YOU DON'T HAVE TO BE!	239
TWELVE	THE CHURCH AND POLITICS	257

CHAPTER ONE

THE CHURCH — WHO NEEDS IT?

"For no prophecy ever came by the will of man: but men spake from God, being moved by the Holy Spirit" (II Pet. 1:21).

The messages herein to be considered are addressed to persons who firmly believe that God exists and that the Bible is His inspired Word. There are multiple evidences as to the reality of God's existence, as well as numerous confirmations that the Bible was written by divine inspiration, and therefore contains God's will for humanity. However, proof of these truths is not the purpose or within the scope of this writing. If you do not accept these two facts as the premise, you will likely have no interest in the matters to be considered. On the other hand, if you do believe that the God of the Bible exists and that this book contains His directions for mankind as to how to be pleasing to Him, I urge you to think seriously on the following matters as to the way in which they relate to you personally.

This country was founded by people who voluntarily exposed themselves to many dangers, privations and hardships in order to achieve for themselves and their posterity freedom from political and religious oppression. Until very recently, almost all American citizens believed strongly in the existence of God and the divine inspiration of the Bible. A vast majority of American citizens still holds these beliefs. These are not the people found in street gangs, in prisons, and among other trouble-makers of society. These are the people who, for the most part, enjoy stable homes, the people who go about the business of life with diligence and energy trying to improve the quality of their own lives and that of others. These people believe in the existence of God because all of their natural surroundings proclaim the necessity of the existence of a supreme, all powerful and provident Creator. They believe that the Bible is the divinely-given-instruction book produced and preserved by their Creator to instruct them as to the best way of life. Evidences of these two basic truths are so abundant and well documented by historical facts, archeological findings, and human experiences that this writer is proceeding on the premise that the reader already has a firm conviction of God's existence and the authority of His written word, the Bible.

With these truths in mind, let us note the precarious spiritual position in which every individual must find himself—a situation of which many today are only vaguely aware, if at all cognizant of it. Let us begin with the story of the very beginning of the human race.

God Sets The Stage

When God created the earth, He made every part of it in a state of perfection and loveliness. Every tree, plant and form of life was one of beauty and usefulness for the people whom God planned to live on the earth. The waters and atmosphere were pure, providing perfectly for all the needs of mankind. God, Himself, is a perfect Being, and it was in His own image that He made Adam, who was to be the father of the whole human race. God created, from Adam's own body, a wife, who was to be a helper and companion, that together they might populate the earth.

God placed Adam and his wife Eve in a garden, the likes of which no other man has ever seen, or will see again on this earth. This garden contained every kind of fruit-bearing tree and shrub unique for its beauty or for its usefulness for man and beast. Every kind of animal life useful or appealing to humanity was there. The result was a friendly and luxurious environment which would contribute to man's well-being and happiness. There was also in the garden a tree of life. Eating the fruit from this tree provided sustenance for continuing life throughout eternity.

It was God's desire to provide a people who would live forever as His completely loyal and loving subjects, happy to serve Him as their Lord and Master, King of their realm, for whom no one was capable of challenging their love, obedience and loyalty.

God did not make these first earthly inhabitants to be mere robots, programmed to serve Him as slaves, held captive in servitude by unseen chains and no opportunity to live their lives otherwise. Instead, God made Adam and Eve free moral agents—masters of their own decisions and eternal fate. In order to enable them to have free choice, they must be given the opportunity to choose another master to whom they would give allegiance rather than to their Creator. For this reason God placed another tree in the midst of that garden. This strange tree was the tree of the knowledge of good and evil. God even allowed Satan, the arch-enemy of God and everything good, to enter the garden to enable man to exercise his free choice. Satan and other of his angel followers had been cast out of heaven because of their rebellion against God (Rev. 12:7-9). Satan gladly exercised his wiles of deception upon Eve. He presented the alternative to heeding the words of God.

God had prepared Adam and Eve to be ready for such temptation by warning them, "You may eat the fruit of the trees of the garden, but you shall not eat of the fruit in the midst of the garden. If you do so, you will die."

Perfection Becomes Corrupted

Taking the form of a serpent, Satan presented his tempting invitaion to Eve. He suggested that she put aside God's warning and yield to the urge to eat of the forbidden fruit before her. The very sight of the fruit was not only appealing to her physical appetite, as a beautiful luscious delicacy, but it seemed even more desirable because, according to the serpent's words, eating it would make Eve like God Himself, knowing good and evil. She had beheld God's beauty, wisdom and power. She viewed His wondrous creation all about her. She had even heard Him speak directly to Adam and herself in the garden. She wanted to be like Him. Here, she thought, was being offered that opportunity. The longing to satisfy these desires of the flesh overshadowed and made her disregard God's warning. She yielded to the temptation and ate the fruit, giving it to Adam who also ate of it. Thus it was that they brought sin into the perfect world of God's creation. The earth was no longer a place of perfection.

God is a perfect Being. He will not tolerate sin. It is incompatible with His very Being.

Adam and Eve had sinned. They had shown lack of perfect trust in God's word. They were no longer completely loyal to God's supremacy. They had disregarded God's word and accepted the words of Satan.

The devil's temptation contained some truth as is usually the case, but it also contained a lie as usual. As a result of eating the fruit, Adam and Eve learned that both good and evil exist and to this degree they were like God, but they also learned that this worked toward their disadvantage because that knowledge did not prevent God's warning from being fulfilled. God had said that eating of that fruit would cause them from that moment to become subject to death. They were removed from the garden.

The earth with its human inhabitants was now no longer a place of perfection. If Adam and Eve had been loyal and obedient to God, they could have remained in a completely desirable and beautiful environment forever sustained by the fruit of the wonderful tree of life, but after their sin, they were driven from the garden and found themselves in a place where necessities of physical life required toil, suffering and pain. No longer surrounded by luxurious and plentiful foods, they found thorns and thistles. Once friendly animals became beasts of prey. Adam and Eve knew that after toils, problems, and suffering, eventually death and judgment before God must come.

God's words tell us that

"... as through one man sin entered into the world, and death through sin; and so death passed unto all men, for that all sinned" (Rom. 5:12).

"for all have sinned, and fall short of the glory of God" (Rom. 3:23)

All men includes you and me. None of us can escape from our inheritance from our first forefather. That inheritance is a fleshly nature, easily tempted to sin. None of us has the capacity within ourselves alone to live a life of absolute complete perfection. Adam and Eve put the eternal fate of you and me—all humanity at risk in the final day of judgment.

The Universality of Sin

From that time forth, men and women have had to constantly wrestle with fleshly temptations confronting them through Satan and his evil fallen-angel cohorts. After Adam and Eve sinned, God directed that early man offer sacrifices of certain animal and plant life in recognition before Him of their guilt and of His supremacy, but these offerings could not atone completely for their guilt. They were only symbolic. As time continued, and after many generations had been born and passed from the earth, the earth's entire population became so completely evil that God knew that through them He could never accomplish His purpose. He saw only one righteous man, Noah. God instructed Noah how to make an ark in which he and his family could be saved when God would send a flood of such proportions that all human and animal life upon the earth's land would be totally destroyed, except for Noah's family and certain animals which Noah was to place inside the ark.

As the long years passed, during which Noah and his sons constructed the ark, Noah preached to others, hoping to bring them to repentance and reformed lives, but his words fell on scornful hearts and heedless ears. Therefore, when the promised flood occurred, in all the world, **there was only one place of safety and escape from God's wrath.**

Noah and his three sons built the ark according to the explicit directions given by God. All human, land animals and creatures of the air upon the earth were destroyed during the flood except those within the ark, which provided a place of complete safety during the forty day deluge and the year required for the land to be fit again for man's habitation. It is likely, when the waters of the flood began to rise high and rain continued falling, that many people outside the ark beat upon its sides and pled for entry. How they must have wished they had listened to Noah! But it was too late for their salvation. Their fate was already sealed by their refusal to listen to Noah and heed his warning to repent while they had time.

Centuries later, the inspired writer to the Hebrew Christians pointed to the great importance of faith in the lives of the early patriarchs. He wrote:

> "By faith Noah, being warned of God concerning things not seen as yet, moved with godly fear, prepared an ark to the saving of his house; through which he condemned the world, and became heir of the righteousness which is according to faith" (Heb. 11:7).

Noah's salvation within the ark is a fitting symbolism of the Christian salvation within the church as pointed out in the writing of Peter, another divinely-inspired New Testament writer. He told of the patience of God, who

> "...waited in the days of Noah, while the ark was a preparing, wherein few, that is, eight souls, were saved through water" (I Pet. 3:20).

Peter continued writing to show that as the **ark was the only place of safety** for those living in Noah's time, the church into which one enters through faith, repentance and baptism, **is the only place of safety for those living in the present Christian Dispensation.** Peter continued:

> "And corresponding to that, baptism now saves you—not the removal of dirt from the flesh, but an appeal to God through a good conscience - through the resurrection of Jesus Christ, who is at the right hand of God, having gone into heaven, after angels and authorities and powers had been subjected to Him" (I Pet. 3:21,22).

The church established by Jesus is depicted in the New Testament under various figures of speech. It is called His body, His family, His kingdom, His bride. The church is the totality of all those who have obeyed, and all of those who will yet obey, the gospel as it was proclaimed by Jesus' apostles during their ministries to Him and in their divinely inspired writings.

As the ark provided the only place of safety during God's visitation of His punishment on the wicked of Noah's time, so the church will provide the only place of safety when the final reckoning of God will cause all of the world's inhabitants—past, present and future to stand before Christ to be judged on the basis of their earthly lives. Those who have refused allegiance to Him, either purposely or by neglect, shall be sentenced to eternal damnation. Those who have taken advantage of His loving offer of salvation through obedience to the gospel, and thus have been added to the body or church of our Lord and have lived faithful lives in His service, shall receive His approval and admission into His heavenly abode.

The apostle Paul with Silas and Timothy made reference to this coming event in a letter to Christians in Thessalonica, who were suffering persecution for their Christian faith and activities.

> "For after all it is only just for God to repay with affliction those who afflict you, and to give relief to you who are afflicted and to us as well when the Lord Jesus shall be revealed from heaven with His mighty angels in flaming fire, dealing out retribution to those who do not know God and to those who do not obey the gospel of our Lord Jesus. And these will pay the penalty of eternal destruction, away from the presence of the Lord and from the glory of His power, when He comes to be glorified in His saints on that day, and to be marveled at among all who have believed—for our testimony to you was believed" (II Thess. 1:6-10).

Christ's followers will not be saved "by the church," but rather because they are "in the church." It was God, not the ark, that saved Noah. And it will be by the grace of God in providing Jesus as the sacrifice by whom forgiveness and eternal salvation will be obtained, that those in the church will be saved.

It must be understood that the church is not a building of stone and mortar, but it is composed of individuals who have, by faithful obedience and trust in God, accepted the offer of His grace. Jesus said:

> "Come to Me, all who are weary and heavy-laden, and I will give you rest. Take My yoke upon you, and learn from Me, for I am gentle and humble in heart; and you shall find rest for your souls" (Matt. 11:28,29).

After Jesus' church was established, according to the record found in Acts, chapter 2, those who responded to the opportunity to take upon themselves the yoke of Christ became the "saved" (Acts 2:47) who constitute His church.

Writing to fellow-Christians, Peter explained the concept of Christ's church as a spiritual entity composed of individuals. Having spoken of Christ, our Lord, as a

> "...living stone, rejected by men, but choice and precious in the sight of God" (I Peter 2:4).

Peter continued:

> "You also, as living stones, are being built up as a spiritual house for a holy priesthood, to offer up spiritual sacrifices acceptable to God through Jesus Christ" (I Peter 2:5).

The church which embodies all who are saved will be set forth more fully in subsequent chapters, but the point of emphasis presently is the fact that every soul is at risk of eternal condemnation unless proper spiritual provision is made by that individual in placing his soul in the only place where safety can be found. In answer to "Who needs the church?," the only acceptable answer is: every individual who seeks a life on this earth of true fulfillment and hopes for an eternity of real happiness in the presence of God—at the same time being rescued from the eternal destruction to which all others are destined.

Hearts Need Cleansing!

> When typhoid germs are in a well, to paint the pump does not purify the water. The only thing to do is to clean out the well. Sins unforgiven will condemn one even though he adorns his life with a multitude of good deeds. The thing to do is clean out the heart. God provided a way to do this through His Son.
>
> — Selected

CHAPTER TWO

WHICH CHURCH - DOES IT MATTER?

"And I also say unto thee ... I will build my church; and the gates of Hades shall not prevail against it" (Matt. 16:18)

Do you attend religious services regularly? Do you believe this is necessary or important? Why? Are you a church member? If so, to what church do you belong? Why do you attend that particular church? Is it because you were brought up in a family which accepted that faith? Is it because you married a person of that faith? Is it because you visited the services at that church and felt comfortable to be a part of that group? Is it because a friend invited you and you enjoyed the services and association? Is it because you thought you should "go to church" somewhere and you searched among various groups to find the one you found most compatible with your personal beliefs? These questions are posed for your consideration because there are many persons attending all kinds of churches, purporting to be Christian, where persons attend because of one or more of the various reasons suggested.

To become a member of a church for any of the above reasons indicates that one considers all organizations calling themselves "Christian" as acceptable to God, and that choosing between them is an option of personal choice, and that each teaches truths, the acceptance and practice of which will result in eternal salvation. The prevalence of this idea is evident and is fostered by the oft-seen statement in newspaper religious sections admonishing people to "attend the church of your choice." The intention of such expressions may come from a worthy motive, but the premise that any church which you may choose is acceptable to God is entirely false.

All of the various so-called Christian denominations, as well as so-called non-denominational churches, claim to base their beliefs on the Bible. Nevertheless, various doctrines espoused by one denomination are often directly opposed to the teaching on the same subjects by another denomination. Common reasoning indicates that both viewpoints cannot be right. Both cannot come from divine revelation, the only source of truth regarding Christ's church.

If all cannot be right, certainly some must be wrong. It is impossible for all to be right, but it is possible for all churches of today to be wrong. Therefore, it should be evident that the reasons suggested as to why people attend where they attend are fallacious bases for determining where and how one should worship. It should also be evident that if all churches must agree as to proper doctrine and practice, that will result in only one church that is acceptable to God. Therefore, all churches will believe and practice the same teachings. This is a truth evident through the process of reasoning, as well as the truth proclaimed in God's word. In the New Testament, reference to the church is made under many figures of speech. For instance, the church is often called the body, of which Christ is the head. Paul told the Ephesians:

> "For the husband is the head of the wife, as Christ also is the head of the church, being himself the saviour of the body" (Eph. 5:23).

Paul further instructed:

> "There is one body, and one Spirit, even as also ye were called in one hope of your calling; one Lord, one faith, one baptism, one God and Father of all, who is over all, and through all, and in all" (Eph. 4:4-6).

Just as there is only one head (Christ) there is only one body. To think of a head with many bodies would be ludicrous.

All necessary information about that one body, the one church, is provided in the Bible. It is common for men to take a part of what the Bible says on a given subject and misapply or misinterpret the Bible's teachings on the subject. Often one or two passages are taken as the basis of one's doctrine, without consideration of other passages bearing on the same subject. Thus, persons become advocates of unscriptural doctrines. Every passage given in the Bible on one subject must be considered and harmonized before a person can arrive at the true Bible teaching on that subject. Many people, without careful personal study, accept erroneous doctrines propounded by various teachers and thus, many denominations result, and different contradictory beliefs are promoted. Safety in making the proper decision as to the right church cannot rely on the teaching of men, because men are fallible, regardless of their good intentions. This truth is emphasized repeatedly in the scriptures.

By divine inspiration, the wise king Solomon declared:

"There is a way which seemeth right unto man;
But the end thereof are the ways of death" (Prov. 14:12).

To Jeremiah God revealed the same truth, that of man's inability to please God by following human judgment. Jeremiah wrote:

"O Jehovah, I know that the way of man is not in himself; it is not in man that walketh to direct his steps" (Jer. 10:23).

Early in Jesus' ministry, in anticipation of the church which He was soon to establish, Jesus admonished His followers regarding the way of salvation. He emphasized that there are only two ways of life. One of these ways involves certain difficulties and therefore requires much self-discipline, but it will finally lead to the greatly desired happy and eternal destination.

The other way of life may appear, for the present, to be much more inviting. It consists of many paths or roads to follow. Others, traveling these highways of life, may appear to be happy. Their pursuits may seem attractive, inviting, and promising great things that appeal to the physical tastes and desires of humanity. Nevertheless, though these paths may be deceptively strewn with apparent beauty and promise of fulfillment of man's needs, Jesus declared that all of these paths, or roads, lead to one final destination of eternal destruction. Hear Jesus' own plain declaration of these truths and His exhortation regarding the two ways of life:

> "Enter ye in by the narrow gate: for wide is the gate, and broad is the way, that leadeth to destruction, and many are they that enter thereby.
>
> For narrow is the gate, and straitened the way, that leadeth unto life, and few are they that find it" (Matt. 7:13,14).

We need to explore the Bible to determine exactly what the Bible teaches regarding the one true church, or one way to salvation.

During Jesus' earthly ministry, people often gathered about Him to hear Him speak. Many of them listened eagerly to His words, hoping that He was the long-promised Messiah. But among the Jewish religious leaders there was much antagonism and censure motivated by jealousy and misunderstanding of the scriptures. At one time Jesus questioned His disciples, saying, "Who do men say that the Son of man is?"

They answered, "... Some say John the Baptist; some Elijah; and others Jeremiah, or one of the prophets."

Jesus responded, "But who say ye that I am?"

It was Simon Peter who quickly answered, "Thou art the Christ, the Son of the living God."

Jesus was pleased with Peter's words, and pronounced upon Peter a blessing. Then Jesus made a solemn and determined pronouncement of two things: He was going to build His church and nothing, not even the gates of Hades, could prevent it. Also, He announced the very fundamental truth or foundation upon which His church would be built. He said to Peter:

> "And I also say unto thee, that thou art Peter, and upon this rock I will build my church; and the gates of Hades shall not prevail against it" (Matt. 16:18).

Many people have been confused by this statement because of the two references in the original Greek text to rocks. These persons interpret the passage to say that Jesus' church would be founded on Peter. This fallacious interpretation, propounded by religious teachers and accepted by the masses—who had no personal access to the scriptures —resulted during the Middle Ages in the ultimate establishment of the

Catholic hierarchy with the Pope as its head. However, the true meaning of the passage is quite evident when one notes and understands the original writing in the Greek language. The Greek words, from which this English translation was made, are "Petros" and "petra." "Petros" refers to Peter, the disciple's name. "Petros" means a small rock or pebble. "Petra," the rock on which Jesus said He would build His church, refers to a large substantial ledge of rock. In truth, the church was not to be built on Peter, but rather on the truth of Peter's confession, when he said to Jesus "Thou art the Christ, the Son of the living God." In plain words, Peter was professing faith in Jesus' claim that He was truly God's Son. Further study of the New Testament reveals that this belief in Jesus' divinity is the basis or foundation on which the church was built and on which it stands today.

When Jesus declared that nothing could prevent His building the church—not even "the gates of Hades," He meant death itself. Jesus did indeed die, and through His death on the cross, He entered the Hadean world, the abode of departed spirits, but He overcame death and rose triumphantly from the grave. After that, He built His church just as He had promised, as is witnessed in the New Testament writings.

Note that this was to be "His" church. It was to belong to Him. Just before ascending into Heaven, Jesus made this affirmation:

"... All authority hath been given unto Me in heaven and on earth" (Matt. 28:18).

Since the church belongs to Christ, and He has all authority both in heaven and on earth, it is fitting that He, and He alone, should make the rules and establish the pattern of that church which was to belong to Him.

Note that when Jesus said "I will build my church," He did not say "I will build my churches." He built only one and only that one will receive the blessings promised to the faithful.

The time was drawing near when Jesus' church would be established. Early in the evening of the night when Jesus was to be betrayed into the hands of His enemies by Judas, Jesus and His apostles had gathered in an upper room in Jerusalem to observe the annual Jewish Passover meal. Judas had departed on the way to do his dastardly deed of betraying His Lord. Just before Jesus and the eleven remaining disciples were to depart to go to the garden of Gethsemane, Jesus prayed a very fervent prayer to His heavenly Father, regarding Jesus' great desire for unity among the believers who would constitute His church after it was established. Read Jesus' prayer as recorded by John in his gospel record, chapter 17. Note the explicitness and fervency for unity as Jesus prayed:

> "I manifested thy name unto the men whom thou gavest me out of the world; thine they were, and thou gavest them to me ..." (John 17:6).

> "I pray for them; I pray not for the world, but for those whom thou hast given me; for they are thine" (John 17:9).

> "... Holy Father, keep them in thy name which thou hast given me, that they may be one, even as we are" (John 17:11).

> "Neither for these only do I pray, but for them also that believe on me through their word; that they may all be one; even as thou, Father, art in me, and I in thee, that they also may be in us; that the world may believe that thou didst send me. And the glory which thou hast given me I have given unto them; that they may be one, even as we are one" (John 17:20-22).

Note that Jesus spoke in His prayer of the reason why He so greatly desired unity among His followers:

> "I in them, and thou in me, that they may be perfected into one, that the world may know that thou didst send me, and lovedst them, even as thou hath lovedst me" (John 17:23).

The church that Jesus said He would build was established ten days after Jesus ascended into Heaven, there to remain until the judgment day when He will appear, but not as the Savior, as was His purpose when He first came to earth. His second appearance will be as the supreme judge of all mankind, who have ever lived. See II Thess. 1:7-10.

The wonderful incidents relating to the establishment of the church are recorded in Acts, chapter two.

Because of the divisions now existing among those who claim to be and think that they are Christians, the world is confused. How sad that Jesus' prayer, though it was answered in the first century for a time, is now ignored by those who fail to study for themselves the word of God concerning Jesus' church. Instead these people look to organizations which profess to be true followers of Christ, but who themselves are following the precepts of men who mistakenly profess to be expounding divine truth. Yet, instead of following only Holy Spirit inspired teaching as found in New Testament writings, these persons and churches follow man-made creeds, and worship in ways of their own choosing.

Some years after the church had its beginning, the apostle Paul established a congregation of the church of our Lord in the Grecian city of Corinth. After laboring there for eighteen months, he left, continuing his missionary efforts in other places. After some time, the Corinthian Christians came in contact with other gospel preachers. Among them was Apollos who worked in Corinth for a time.

While elsewhere, Paul learned of some problems that had developed in Corinth. Very concerned, he wrote a letter to the church. This letter appears as "I Corinthians," now a part of the New Testament. One of the problems in Corinth was division among the Christians there. Paul wrote to them.

> "Now this I mean, that each one of you saith, I am of Paul; and I of Apollos; and I of Cephas; and I of Christ" (I Cor. 1:12).

Earnestly, Paul exhorted them to reason:

> "Is Christ divided? was Paul crucified for you? or were ye baptized into the name of Paul?" (I Cor. 1:13).

In the denominational world there are many religious groups which profess to be Christian. Nevertheless they wear names not found in the New Testament, are organized differently from the church of the New Testament, incorporate items of worship that do not conform to New Testament command or example, engage in items of worship not divinely authorized, or who fail to include items divinely authorized. The unity which Jesus earnestly desires and for which He prayed, even at the brink of a cruel death, is sadly missing. This lack of unity among churches claiming to be Christian has resulted in grave confusion and disbelief among those people of the world who need to hear the gospel of salvation. When they hear different messages and different doctrines from different people, all of whom claim to have the message of Christ, the result, too often, is disbelief and rejection of Christ and the salvation He offers. Jesus foresaw this possibility and because of it was impelled to pray for unity in order that the world may believe. Imagine the huge impact Christ's church could make against Satan and his cohorts if all who profess Christianity were united in their message and efforts to lead the lost to salvation! What a better place this world would be and how many more lost souls would be saved!

The primary purpose of any religion is to achieve a pleasurable existence after death. If a religion promises this falsely, it is worse than useless because it not only can't deliver what it promises, but it prevents one from having chosen the true religion which can deliver what it promises. It is only through the way made available by Jesus that any one can obtain eternal salvation. Jesus said of Himself:

> "... I am the way, and the truth, and the life; No one comes to the Father but through Me" (John 14:6).

If you have chosen to have your name added to some particular church membership because of any such questions as those posed at the beginning of this discussion, you are likely among those who, not only are helping to put the one true church at risk for this and future generations, but your own eternal soul may be in grave danger of being lost eternally. In order to assure your eternal safety, you need to study your Bible diligently in order to learn how to recognize from among the many churches which profess to follow Christ, that group of Christians who seek to follow only the explicit teachings of the apostles relative to the church Jesus built and its peculiar identifying characteristics.

WHY THERE ARE SO MANY DENOMINATIONS

APOSTASY

There was a great apostasy of the church which took place after the death of all of Jesus' twelve apostles.

We learn from the divinely-given history of the early church, as recorded in the book of "Acts," that the preaching of the gospel was so widespread even during the apostles' ministry that the gospel had been spread throughout practically all of the known world even in Paul's day (Col. 1:23).

Apostasy is simply the forsaking of those explicit instructions and principles divinely revealed in God's word. Even as Paul spread the gospel, the Holy Spirit caused Paul again and again to warn the early disciples against false teachers who would lead the church away from the truth—such particular warnings are found repeatedly throughout the New Testament. Note Acts 20:28-30 and II Thess. 2:7-10.

After the death of all of the apostles, there was no divine guidance for the church except the new Testament writings, and these writings were in the possession of only a few church leaders. The sacred writings could be reproduced only by handwritten copies. Making these copies was time consuming and expensive. Therefore, it was quite a long time before they were gathered together, and until then few persons, if any, had all of the writings. Most members of the church had to depend on what they were taught by their leaders.

During the days of the apostles and the establishment of the church, most of the known world was under the dominion of the Roman Empire.

Persecution of the church — 64-100 A.D. — Although Jewish religious leaders persecuted the church during the early days after its establishment, at first the Romans did not object to Christianity because they thought it was a part of Judaism. But after the destruction of Jerusalem, they saw that Christianity was a separate and distinct religion. It opposed all heathen religions which the Romans sanctioned. It also opposed emperor-worship, which was demanded by Roman emperors. These and other reasons caused the Roman government to persecute Christianity. After much of Rome burned in 64 A.D., the

Emperor Nero was accused of starting the fire. To protect himself he falsely accused Christians. This brought about a terrible persecution. Thousands of Christians suffered torture and death.

Emperor Domitian began another siege of persecution of Christians about 90 A.D. Most historians agree that the apostle John was then still alive, the last living apostle. He was banished to the island of Patmos. There he was divinely inspired to write "Revelation" shortly before his death. "Revelation" completed the New Testament. Thus ended the period of divine inspiration and miracles.

The Persecuted Church — 100-313 A.D. — There were many outbreaks of persecution against Christianity during the second and third centuries. The Roman government wanted to destroy this religion. Bibles and church buildings were burned. Christians were enslaved, tortured and martyred. This persecution helped maintain the purity of the church by keeping the insincere and half-hearted out of it. But in spite of Christian sincerity and devotion, errors in doctrine and practice began to develop.

1. **Unscriptural Church Organization** — The churches were without possession of the New Testament books except that copies of separate books were in the hands of a few church leaders. If everyone had been content to be guided in all matters of faith and practice by consideration of what these books contained, and by these alone, all would have been well. But soon after the death of the apostles, un-inspired men began to make changes. Among the first departures from the New Testament order was the distinction between bishop and elder. This began some time in the second century. "In the New Testament, as we have seen, there are two classes of officers in each church, called, respectively, elders or bishops, and deacons. After we cross the limit of the first century, we find that with each board of elders there is a person to whom the name bishop is specially applied."[1] "Gradually, each city bishop took the oversight of all the churches in the country near him. The higher the rank of the city, the more influence had the bishop. The bishops of Antioch, Alexandria and Rome became very prominent

---

[1]*History of the Christian Church*, B.P. Fisher, p. 51

because these cities were regarded as having been seats of the apostles in an important sense. The term 'archbishop,' which was first applied to all city bishops, was finally applied to these alone. They were eventually called primates or patriarchs."[2]

2. **Unscriptural Name** — During the second century the church began to call itself *Catholic*, meaning universal. Although the church was divinely intended to be universal in its scope, men do not have the right to give the church any name other than those given in the scriptures. Human names, applied to religious bodies, help to maintain division among believers in Christ.

3. **Unscriptural Creed** — Creed comes from the Latin *credo*, meaning *I believe*. A religious creed is a summary of principles or ideas believed. The New Testament is the only God-given creed of Christianity. The rise of sects and false teaching caused the church to think it necessary to prepare a "rule of faith," or a short written statement of the main facts of Christianity, so "The Apostles' Creed" was written. This was a document of human origin. It was the forerunner of various human creeds and was another step of apostasy.

4. **Unscriptural Doctrines** —

(a) The practice of infant baptism was begun early in the third century. This was unscriptural because the New Testament teaches that belief must precede baptism. Infants cannot believe the gospel. At first, when infant baptism began to be practiced, it was by immersion.

(b) Infant baptism was related to another unscriptural doctrine, the belief in *total depravity*, or the idea that children are born in a state of sin, and that if they die without baptism, their souls will be lost.

(c) The *substitution of pouring for immersion* first took place in 251 A.D. This was in a case of illness, where it was thought that the patient could not be immersed. This was called a clinic case. For a time, substitution of pouring for immersion was allowed only in clinic cases. Many church leaders opposed this, for all knew that the baptism

---

[2] *The Eight Leading Churches*, G.K. Berry, p. 18

taught and practiced by the apostles was by immersion. Nevertheless, pouring gradually became common and later led to sprinkling.

The Imperial Church — 313-476 A.D. — In 312 A.D. Constantine and Mazentius were battling for the imperial crown of the Roman Empire. Constantine, not then a Christian, claimed to have seen in the sky a shining cross with the Latin words meaning *By this sign thou shalt conquer.* He was victorious and, therefore, professed Christianity. In 313 A.D. Constantine issued an edict officially ending all persecution of Christians. Christianity became the state religion. The general results of this union of church and state were not good. One of Constantine's successors decreed that all Roman subjects must accept Christianity. Thus, many people who had no Christian convictions became Christian in name. Christianity became a popular religion, but the moral purity, Godly faith and sweet humility of early Christianity gave way to insincerity and hypocrisy. There were still some humble and God-fearing Christians, but the moral tone of the church as a whole was gradually falling as the tide of worldliness swept higher.

In an effort to escape the worldly influences in the church, some persons retired individually or in groups to live as hermits in secluded places. Thus began the movement that finally resulted in the establishment of monasteries where monks or nuns shut themselves apart from the world. Though their motives were good, this was not God's plan of a way of life for His people.

The clergy, or church officers, became a favored class. The church received public funds, formerly devoted to heathen worship. The clergy thus became well supported and received many special privileges from the government. Desire for financial gain, social influence and political power caused many worldly, ambitious men to seek offices in the church. This speeded further departure of the church from New Testament teaching in church organization, in worship and in daily living.

1. **Church Organization** — To deal with various problems arising in the church, Councils were held. Bishops of the various districts met and enacted laws for the church. **This idea of human authority to make laws for the church is entirely foreign to the New Testament.** Constantine established a new capital at Constantinople. In the centuries that followed, there was much rivalry between the

bishops at Rome and Constantinople. For a time the title *Papa* (Pope) was applied to various bishops, but by the sixth century this title was reserved exclusively for the bishop at Rome. The term meant *father* in Latin. Note that Jesus commanded His followers to call no man by that name in a religious sense. See Matt. 23:8-10.

    2.   **Church Worship** — The influence of unconverted and untaught members of the church is seen in the pagan practices brought into the worship. During the fifth century pictures and images began to be used. "About 400 A.D. saint worship and the veneration of sacred places and relics began to appear, at first as memorials of saints and martyrs, gradually growing into reverence, and then into worship. The adoration of the virgin Mary was substituted for the worship of Venus and Diana. The Lord's Supper became a sacrifice instead of a memorial, and the preachers came to be priests."[3]

The Medieval Church — 476-1453 A.D. Invading Asiatic tribes overran the western boundaries of the Roman Empire and seized territory for many years. In 467 A.D. Rome itself was captured. The eastern part of the Roman Empire continued for nearly a thousand years after the fall of Rome. The divided empire, together with the rivalry between the bishops at Constantinople and Rome, eventually led in 1054 A.D. to a division of the Catholic Church, into Greek Catholic and Roman Catholic. These have never since been united. We shall notice particularly the development and influence of the Roman church.

Most of the conquering tribes of the western empire became Christians. For four centuries after the fall of Rome, Europe's civil affairs were very unsettled. Authority was divided and rulers changed often. But the church remained an established and enduring institution. The fall of the imperial power at Rome gave the pope many opportunities to increase his powers over the state. In 800 A.D. Pope Leo III crowned Charlemagne Emperor of the Holy Roman Empire. In name, he ruled over all Europe. In fact, his rule was limited to Germany, and even there he did not always maintain control. "For many centuries during the earlier history of the empire, there was strong rivalry, and sometimes

---

[3]*Brief History of the Christian Church*, Wm. Stuart, p. 39

open war, between the emperors and the popes; emperors striving to rule the church, popes striving to rule the empire."[4] Between 1073 and 1216 A.D. the pope had almost absolute power, not only over the church, but also over the nations of Europe.

Another movement which influenced world affairs was begun in 610 A.D. when Mohammed began his career in Arabia. He founded the Mohammedan religion. It was based upon a belief in one God, Allah. Jesus was accepted as a prophet comparable with Adam and Moses, but was considered above all of them. Mohammed united all the scattered Arabian tribes under his religion and authority. He was succeeded by caliphs, who soon conquered Palestine and Syria and then began a siege of Europe. If the forces of Charles Martel had not won the victory at Tours, France in 732 A.D., all of Europe might have been overcome by the Mohammedans, as was the Eastern Empire. Constantinople fell in 1453 A.D. The desire of Christians to free the Holy Lands from Mohammedan rule led to the Crusades between 1095 and 1271 A.D. These so-called Holy Wars failed to accomplish their chief purpose, but they set in motion influences that resulted in the political development of Europe and the decline of papal power.

Note the increased corruptions of church doctrine and practice during this period. *Centralization of power in the pope* was a complete departure from the New Testament plan of church organization, whereby each congregation was to be independent, its only officials elders and deacons. *The moral purity of Christianity was almost wholly corrupted.* Many of the popes led lives of almost unbelievable immorality and sin. The sale of indulgences (buying the right to sin), forbidding the clergy the right to marry, and the requirement of personal confesson contributed to immorality. In the *titles conferred upon the pope and display of reverence required toward him*, the system of papery became a fulfillment of Paul's prophecies in II Thess. 2:4. The pope is addressed as Lord God the Pope, Vicar of the Lord Jesus Christ on earth. The *New Testament form and spirit of worship were corrupted by idolatrous rites* in connection with images, pictures, signs and symbols. *Introduction of musical instruments into the worship was a further digression* from New

---

[4] *The Story of the Christian Church*, J.L. Hurlbut, p. 124

Testament instruction. "Pope Vatalianus in 568 introduced the organ into Roman churches to accompany the songs."[5] As the powers of the papacy increased, *reliance upon the scriptures decreased.* In 1229 the inquisition was organized. This was the court of the Roman Catholic Church. Its purpose was to find and punish all whose beliefs differed from established doctrines of the church. Its treatment of those it condemned or even suspected was cruel and inhuman. Mere possession of the Scriptures was enough to bring one to trial before the court. Thus the New Testament faith and practice of Christianity were supplanted by the apostate system of religion foretold by Paul and other New Testament writers.

THE REFORMATION

First Movements Toward Religious Reform

Gradually a few thinkers began to realize, at least in part, how far the church had apostatized. In southern France about 1170 members of a group known as Puritans encouraged the reading of the New Testament and opposed the acceptance of tradition as religious authority. They were opposed to the Roman Catholic church, for it forbade its laymembers to read the scriptures, and most of its doctrines were based on tradition alone. At the pope's command, almost all of these Puritans were put to death.

About the same time Peter Waldo led a group in Italy to see some of the errors of Roman Catholic doctrine. His followers were called Waldensians. They were bitterly persecuted by the Catholics, but there are still small groups of Waldensians in Italy.

In England John Wyclif led the movement for reform. He opposed the authority of the pope and the Catholic doctrine of transubstantiation. (This is the belief that the elements of the Lord's supper actually become the body and blood of Christ.) The pope opposed Wyclif and for a time his life was in constant danger. He translated the New Testament and part of the Old Testament into English. He has been called "The morning star of the reformation."

---

[5]London Encyclopedia, Vol. XV, p. 280

John Huss in Bohemia read and preached Wyclif's teaching. The pope excommunicated Huss. Later he was unfairly tried, condemned and burned, but his life and teaching exerted a great influence toward the Reformation.

Results of The Reformation — 1453-1648

There was widespread protest and revolt against the Roman Catholic teachings and practices The movement for reform spread over all Europe. The Reformation resulted in the establishment of various churches which refused the authority of the papal powers at Rome.

Several circumstances encouraged the Reformation movement: (1) There was a general renewal of interest in literature, art and science. This led to more study of Greek and Hebrew, which led in turn to a study of the Scriptures. (2) In 1455 Gutenberg invented the printing press. Until that time, all books were written by hand and were, therefore, very expensive. The price of a Bible amounted to a whole year's salary of the average worker. The printing press made books more plentiful and much cheaper. The Bible was the first book printed on Gutenberg's press. Many people then read the New Testament for the first time. They began to see the difference between the New Testament church and the church of their day. Various men took the lead in proclaiming the corruptions of the Catholic church and the reforms that were needed. The reformers' teachings spread rapidly as they were circulated in books and pamphlets among the people. This gave rise to a general spirit of independence and a desire for reform.

There were many outstanding leaders in the movement for reform. We can mention only a few, and these briefly. The foremost figure of the Reformation was Martin Luther. He was a Catholic monk and a teacher in the University of Wittenberg, Germany. His conflict with papal authority began in 1517. At that time efforts were being made to build St. Peter's church at Rome. John Tetzel was going through Germany selling "indulgences." These were certificates signed by the pope. They promised full pardon of sins to those for whom the indulgences were bought. Even the forgiveness of sins which people planned to commit in the future was promised. Tetzel claimed that indulgences could be bought for friends, living or dead. Regarding the dead, he said, "At the very instant that the money rattles in the bottom of the chest, the soul escapes from purgatory and flies liberated to heaven ... The Lord our God no longer reigns. He resigned all power to the pope."[6]

Luther bitterly opposed Tetzel's work. On October 31, 1517, Luther nailed to the church door in Wittenberg a list of 95 statements against the unscriptural authority of the pope and practices of the Roman Catholic church. Luther spent the remainder of his life (29 years) in defending the stand he had taken. During much of this time his life was in great danger from the pope. Luther's work resulted in the establishment of the Lutheran church, though he did not desire this. He said, "I pray you to leave my name alone and not to call yourself Lutherans, but Christians."[7] Luther did not recognize all the evils in the Catholic church, but he recognized and opposed many of them.

In 1529, through the influence of Catholic rulers, certain laws were passed that limited the preaching of Luther's followers to certain regions in Germany. Luther and others protested. For this reason they were called Protestants. Since then, all religious bodies that teach against Catholicism have been regarded as Protestant.

At the same time that Luther began his reform in Germany, Ulric Zwingli was doing a similar work in Switzerland. He was slain in 1531. His fight for Protestantism was taken up by John Calvin in Switzerland. He became the founder of the Presbyterian church. His teaching involved five particular doctrines, none of which are taught in the New Testament. Since many modern denominations accept parts of his doctrines, they have been listed on the next page for you to examine.

In England, Henry VIII wanted to divorce his wife and marry another. For this he could not get permission from the pope. The king finally declared England free from papal control. A separate church was organized with the king as its head. This was called the Church of England, or later the Episcopal Church in America. Henry VIII was not a reformer. He merely substituted the king instead of pope as head of the church. Reformers in England were William Tyndale, John Rogers,

---

[6]*Restoration Handbook*, L.G. Thomas, p. 54
[7]*Life of Luther*, Michelot, p. 262

John Hooper and others. John Wesley worked in both England and America. He established the Methodist church. There is some dispute regarding the founder of the Baptist church, but this denomination developed in England around the middle of the seventeenth century.

In summarizing the chief results of the Reformation, let us note its accomplishments: (1) It freed the Protestant churches from all papal authority. (2) It encouraged an attitude of looking to the Bible as the source of authority in religion. (3) It brought about a wide circulation of the Bible, making it accessible to all. But the Reformation did not restore to the world the full New Testament plan of doctrine and practice.

FIVE BASIC POINTS OF CALVINISM

T OTAL DEPRAVITY. The guilt of sin rests upon each soul as soon as it enters the world.

U NCONDITIONAL ELECTION. Man can do nothing to influence his future destiny.

L IMITED ATONEMENT. Christ's atoning sacrifice was only for those whom God had already chosen to save.

I RRESISTIBLE GRACE. The Holy Spirit operates directly upon the hearts of those whom God has already chosen to be saved.

P ERSEVERANCE OF THE SAINTS. Individuals whom God has predestined to salvation cannot sin so as to be lost.

(Note: The first letters of each point of doctrine spell TULIP, making it easier to remember the five points)

THE RESTORATION

Protestant denominations and Catholicism were brought to America by settlers from Europe. Catholic countries led in the colonization of Central and South America, also in Canada, while Protestant nations led in the establishment of the colonies that later became the United States.

The actual restoration of the New Testament church, in its purity and simplicity, was brought about by the efforts of several men. Each of these was gradually led by independent study to see the errors of his earlier beliefs and practices.

In 1801 Barton W. Stone was among other Presbyterian preachers who took part in a great revival at Cane Ridge, Kentucky. Over 20,000 people attended this meeting. Salvation through faith and repentance was preached. This was not in keeping with the written creed to which these preachers belonged. Stone and four others withdrew from their former religious connections and decided to take the Bible as their only authority. They began to organize churches and call them Christian.

James O'Kelly in North Carolina soon left the Methodist church, and Abner Jones in Vermont left the Baptist church. Both of them believed that Christ's church should have no creed but the New Testament and should wear no name but Christ's. They and others united with Barton W. Stone.

The two men who had perhaps the widest influence in restoring New Testament teachings and practices were Thomas Campbell and his son, Alexander. They belonged to the Seceder branch of the Presbyterian church, but they became convinced through study of the scriptures that Christians should accept the New Testament as the only guide and authority in religion. The Campbells opposed human creeds and human names for the church. Thomas Campbell originated the expression: "Where the Bible speaks, we speak; where the Bible is silent, we are silent." He recognized this as a sound principle to follow. But at first he did not realize all the changes he would have to make in observing this principle. It finally led him and Alexander to see that infant baptism was wrong and that only immersion of penitent believers is scriptural baptism.

Walter Scott, another Presbyterian who studied his Bible carefully, took his stand with the Campbells. Both Thomas and Alexander gave Scott credit for being the first among them to note the scriptural order of the terms of salvation: faith, repentance, baptism, remission of sins and the gift of the Holy Spirit.

After some years of enlightening experiences, these various leaders in the Restoration movement realized that they were in agreement in teaching and practice, so they joined themselves to the same common cause.

Restoration Movement is the term generally used in referring to the influences set in motion by the activities of Stone, the Campbells, Scott and others. The result of this movement was not the establishment of another denomination, for none of these men established a church. Their work accomplished the restoration of the doctrines and practices of the early church as set forth in the New Testament. Since the Restoration period the church of Christ in America has always sought to maintain the same position as did the church in the first century. In the church of Christ, terms of entrance, organization, worship, faith and practice are the same as in New Testament times.

> "Truth forever on the scaffold, wrong forever
>   on the throne —
> Yet that scaffold sways the future, and behind
>   the dim unknown,
> Standeth God within the shadow, keeping
>   watch upon His own."
>
> — James Russell Lowell

CHAPTER THREE

ONLY ONE WAY OF ENTRY INTO JESUS' CHURCH

"Enter ye in by the narrow gate: for wide is the gate, and broad is the way, that leadeth to destruction, and many are they that enter thereby. For narrow is the gate, and straitened the way, that leadeth unto life, and few are they that find it" (Matt. 7:13,14)

"... I am the way, and the truth, and the life; no one cometh to the Father, but by me" (John 14:6).

During Jesus' earthly ministry, His disciples, Peter, James and John, were granted a revelation like no other human has ever experienced. They went one night with Jesus to a secluded mountain top. There they saw Jesus as He was never seen before on earth, nor ever shall be seen again by mortal man until the end of time. No longer would these loving disciples see Jesus as an itinerant preacher and prophet, a humble Nazarene, hated and persecuted by their highest religious officials. Now Jesus appeared before the three apostles in shining celestial glory. His glowing countenance surpassed the brightness of the noonday sun. Even His clothing beamed with dazzling brilliant whiteness. Talking with Jesus were Moses and Elijah, though long departed from this world.

The ever-impulsive Peter, overcome by the wonders of the occasion, quickly proposed building three tabernacles to honor Jesus, Moses and Elijah. But immediately overhead, out of the darkness of night, a bright cloud appeared, and the voice of God, Himself, proclaimed Peter's error in equating Jesus with Moses and Elijah. The sovereign God of the universe solemnly announced and commanded:

"... This is my beloved Son, in whom I am well pleased; hear ye him" (Read Matt. 17:1-5)

In times past God had commanded His people to hear the instructions of Moses and Elijah, but a new era was dawning. The Christian Dispensation was very soon to supplant that dispensation when Moses was God's lawgiver and when the prophet Elijah pronounced God's will for man. During this new dispensation, Christ was to bring about a new relationship between God and man. Through Christ was to be provided **the only way** of access to forgiveness of past sins and provision for a blissful eternity. As God commanded on that eventful night, we must look only to Christ for eternal salvation. The majestic words of our heavenly Father continue to reverberate throughout the entire New Testament and throughout all remaining time.

"Hear Him! Hear Him! Hear Him!"

On one occasion, Jesus told His disciples:

"Truly, truly, I say to you, he who does not enter by the door into the fold of the sheep, but climbs up some other way, he is a thief and a robber" (John 10:1).

"I am the door; by me if any man enter in, he shall be saved..." (John 10:9).

"I am the good shepherd: the good shepherd layeth down his life for the sheep" (John 10:11).

These words exclude every way of reaching heaven, eternal abode of the Father, except the way provided by Jesus through His sacrifice upon the cross. This excludes future blessings through any other person, whether Buddha, Mohammed, Joseph Smith, Mary Eddy Baker, or anyone but Jesus, the Christ. Of Him, Luke wrote:

"And in none other is there salvation: for neither is there any other name under heaven, that is given among men, wherein we must be saved" (Acts 4:12).

Jesus, "The way, the truth, the life," came to dwell on this earth in fleshly form for a period of less than 34 years. His ministry, involving close association with His apostles, lasted only about three and one-half years, during which time these men saw Jesus' miracles and heard His teachings, thus being totally convinced that Jesus was the promised Messiah, the very Son of God. Jesus' apostles loved Him deeply. When, on the eve of His betrayal, He told them that He was going away to a place where they could not accompany Him, they were confused and sorrowful, but He made them a consoling promise. He said:

> "And I will pray the Father, and he shall give you another Comforter, that he may be with you for ever, even the Spirit of truth: whom the world cannot receive; for it beholdeth him not, neither knoweth him: ye know him; for he abideth with you, and shall be in you" (John 14:16,17).

> "But the Comforter, even the Holy spirit, whom the Father will send in my name, he shall teach you all things, and bring to your remembrance all that I said unto you" (John 14:26).

Note that He whom the Father was to send is called "the Comforter," "the Spirit of truth," and "the Holy Spirit."

It is important to note that this promise of future miraculous revelation was made by Jesus **only** to the apostles, not to all Christians of that time or to those of future generations. This information was to come by the direct agency of the Holy Spirit, the third member of the God-head. When this revelation would be received, it would be not only the fulfillment of Jesus' promise to His apostles, but also the fulfillment of a prophecy previously given through John, the Baptist. When John's disciples were wondering if he was the promised Messiah,

> "John answered, saying unto them all, I indeed baptize you with water; but there cometh he that is mightier than I, the latchet of whose shoes I am not worthy to unloose: he shall baptize you in the Holy Spirit and in fire" (Luke 3:16).

Forty days after Jesus was resurrected, the eleven apostles were gathered on Mt. Olivet, which was near Jerusalem. Jesus appeared to them there.

> "and, being assembled together with them, he charged them not to depart from Jerusalem, but to wait for the promise of the Father, which, said he, ye heard from me" (Acts 1:4).

Jesus was referring to His promise, on the night of His betrayal to send "another Comforter," "the Spirit of truth," "the Holy Spirit." Jesus further explained His promise by foretelling how the promise was to be fulfilled.

"for John indeed baptized with water; but ye shall be baptized with the Holy Spirit not many days hence" (Acts 1:5).

After thus directing the apostles, Jesus ascended into heaven. As the apostles continued to gaze heavenward, two men stood by them in white apparel. They promised that Jesus would return in like manner as the apostles had seen Him ascend; thus they were comforted.

The apostles returned to Jerusalem. They waited for ten days, during which time, at God's direction, Matthias was selected to replace the departed Judas as the twelfth apostle. At the end of ten days, all of the promises mentioned above were fulfilled. The apostles were baptized with the Holy Spirit. By inspiration, Luke records the manner in which this occurred:

"And when the day of Pentecost was now come, they were all together in one place. And suddenly there came from heaven a sound as of the rushing wind, and it filled all the house where they were sitting. And there appeared unto them tongues parting asunder, like as of fire; and it sat upon each one of them. And they were all filled with the Holy Spirit, and began to speak with other tongues, as the Spirit gave them utterance" (Acts 2:1-4).

At this time multitudes of Jews from all over the world had come to Jerusalem to observe the Jewish annual celebration of the Passover. The sound as of a violent rushing wind and the sudden voices of the apostles speaking brought together a great crowd of people. Representatives of at least fourteen different areas of the world were present, in addition to Jews from all over Palestine. Included in the assembly were also officials of the Jewish court and others who had been responsible for Jesus' crucifixion.

The strange sound as of a violent rushing wind, accompanied by no wind, and the sound of twelve men speaking caused confusion and amazement among the hosts of people within the temple court. They recognized that all of the speakers were from Galilee, the northern province of Palestine. Yet, every person listening heard the words as if they were spoken in his own language.

Then, Peter, standing up with the other eleven apostles, took the lead in speaking to explain that the strange happenings were fulfillment of the prediction of the prophet Joel spoken hundreds of years earlier. Peter proceeded to talk to the multitude about Jesus. Those present from other lands may not have known much about Jesus' ministry, but the Palestinian Jews were well acquainted with the strange occurrences of recent days relating to Jesus. Peter continued to speak to the huge audience, held captive by their initial curiosity, but gradually they became spellbound by Peter through whom the Holy Spirit convincingly set forth the truths concerning Jesus' divinity. Peter was proclaiming the first gospel sermon. The proofs that the same Jesus, who had been crucified and resurrected, was truly and without question the Son of God were so plainly portrayed that Peter's hearers were completely overwhelmed with the realization of their heavy burden of guilt. They cried out, "Brethren, what shall we do?" They longed for surcease of guilt and release of their souls from the condemnation of God. They saw the enormity of their sins in the rejection, persecution and crucifixion of the very Son of God. They were strongly convicted of their sin and thoroughly convinced that Jesus was divine. No wonder that they cried out for help! "What shall we do?" How could such tremendous guilt be removed?

Seeing that the questioners now believed that the person they had crucified was, indeed, the divine Son of God, Peter answered their question of despair:

> "And Peter said unto them, Repent ye, and be baptized every one of you in the name of Jesus Christ unto the remission of your sins; and ye shall receive the gift of the Holy Spirit" (Acts 2:38).

"Can it be true?," each listener must have thought in surprise. "Can the rejection, even the crucifixion of God's Son, as well as all of my other former sins, be forgiven solely by my recognizing Jesus as divine, repenting of all the many sins I have already done, and being immersed in water according to the divine authority of Jesus? Can these actions make me entirely free from guilt?"

Then came the greatest consolation of assurance. Each questioner admitted to himself his belief in the truth he had heard, saying in his heart, "Undoubtedly, I believe that this Jesus whom I helped to be crucified was indeed the Son of God; I do wholeheartedly repent of all the sins I have committed in the past. I must avail myself of this wonderful way of redemption from the burden weighing so heavily on my conscience. And even more, this will result in my receiving the promised gift of the Holy Spirit."

Hastily, the guilt-ridden Jews began to respond, one by one, to Peter's instruction. That very day about three thousand persons obeyed the gospel's injunctions. Having already believed that Jesus was truly God's Son, these people sincerely repented of their sins and were baptized, one by one, as enjoined by the words of the Holy Spirit delivered through Peter.

Rejoicing over the obedience of the believers present on that occasion, Peter continued to speak for the benefit of all future generations of humanity, including you and me. He continued:

> "For to you is the promise, and to your children, and to all that are afar off, even as many as the Lord our God shall call unto him" (Acts 2:39).

In other words, Peter was not announcing only to his present audience the terms set by our Lord, by which sinners can receive forgiveness and the gift of the Holy Spirit. Peter said this same "way" of salvation is a promise to all future generations. It is "the way" available to all humanity. Any person may become the beneficiary of this promise who will hear the gospel, believe it, and obey it, just as was done by about three thousand persons who heard Peter's sermon on the day that the first gospel sermon was delivered.

Previous to this event, and after Jesus' resurrection, He had appeared to the apostles on a Galilean mountain. There he announced His complete divine authority and gave His apostles a very important commission. He declared:

"...All authority hath been given unto me in heaven and on earth. Go ye therefore, and make disciples of all the nations, baptizing them into the name of the Father and of the Son and of the Holy Spirit: teaching them to observe all things whatsoever I commanded you: and lo, I am with you always, even unto the end of the world" (Matt. 28:18-20).

Thus upon the apostles was placed the obligation of making known to humanity the truths everyone needs to know in order to be saved eternally.

Likewise, the same obligation to proclaim the gospel message that was given to the apostles rests upon all of those today who hear, believe and obey that gospel. This duty of all Christians is evident from Jesus' words to the apostles, "teaching them (those who obey the gospel) to observe all things whatsoever I commanded you."

The inspired writer says that after the three thousand responded to Peter's words on the first day of Pentecost following Jesus' resurrection:

"... they continued stedfastly in the apostles' teaching and fellowship, in the breaking of bread and the prayers" (Acts 2:42).

Thus, the church of our Lord was established. Each person, having believed that Jesus was the Christ, the Son of God, having repented of all past sins, and having been immersed in the waters of baptism, was a Christian, a citizen of Christ's earthly kingdom, a child of God, a member of Christ's church.

Luke concluded the relation of these happenings with these words:

"And day by day, continuing stedfastly with one accord in the temple, and breaking bread at home, they took their food with gladness and singleness of heart, praising God, and having favor with all the people. And the Lord added to them day by day those that were saved" (Acts 2:46,47).

Note that, according to the inspired words of Luke, those who believed Jesus to be the Son of God, who then repented of their sins and were baptized "were being saved." That is, they were being saved from paying the God-ordained penalty for sin. Their forgiveness at that time, however, covered only the guilt of their past sins. Further instructions were given and later recorded in the New Testament instructing these first Christians, and those of all future generations, in the way their continuing lives should be conducted in order to remain in that condition of freedom from the guilt of sin.

It is evident from the incidents just discussed that all who obey the gospel instruction to believe, repent and be baptized, have thereby become a part of Christ's family, the church. No one can join the Lord's church as a simple matter of choice among many churches any more than a newborn baby has the privilege of deciding among many families which family he wishes to join. A child of God must be born into Christ's family through the same process as did Peter's hearers on the day of Pentecost.

One is spiritually reborn through the process of obeying the gospel. When one responds to the gospel message with a firm belief in the divinity of Jesus, and acting out of conviction of past sins, repents and is baptized in the name of the Father, the Son and the Holy Spirit, that soul experiences the new birth. This is the spiritual new birth of which Jesus, during His ministry on earth, told Nicodemus:

> "Jesus answered and said unto him, Verily, verily, I say unto thee, Except one be born anew, he cannot see the kingdom of God" (John 3:3).

There is a popular phrase "born-again Christian." This is a misnomer. No Christian exists except one who has been "born again."

Later, Paul was writing on the same subject to Christians in Rome. He reminded them of how they, when laden with all the sins of their former lives, had through obedience to the gospel message which exhorted them to believe, repent and be baptized, experienced the new birth, thus becoming new creatures in Christ.

> "We were buried therefore with him through baptism unto death: that like as Christ was raised from the dead through the glory of the Father, so we also might walk in newness of life. For if we have become united with him in the likeness of his death, we shall be also in the likeness of his resurrection; knowing this, that our old man was crucified with him, that

the body of sin might be done away, that so we should no longer be in bondage to sin; for he that hath died is justified from sin" (Rom. 6:4-7).

Consider again what Jesus said in the early days of His earthly ministry.

"Enter ye in by the narrow gate: for wide is the gate, and broad is the way, that leadeth to destruction, and many are they that enter in thereby. For narrow is the gate, and straitened the way, that leadeth unto life, and few are they that find it" (Matt. 7:13,14).

All of these early Christians, through hearing and obeying the gospel as preached by Peter in that first gospel sermon, discovered and entered "the narrow gate" which opened "the narrow way that leads to life." In doing so they turned away from the broad way, in which they had been traveling, and determined to continue in the narrow way which they had entered. Oh, if only more, who seek salvation, would heed the words of Jesus!

Do not be deceived by the various religious organizations whose members claim and even truly believe that they are Christians, yet their doctrines and practices alter those of the church which Jesus built. All religious groups professing Christianity, who teach that sinners receive forgiveness and become Christians in some way other than by the New Testament examples and teachings, should study the Word of God more carefully and take heed to the Biblical warning

"There is a way which seemeth right unto a man;
But the end thereof are the ways of death" (Prov. 14:12).

Accepting as true Jesus' declaration that there is only one way, that it is a "narrow way," and that "those who find it are few," should motivate every individual to search for that way. Note that you, whoever you are, are either now included among those who are walking in that narrow way, or else you are in the broad way. There are no other ways. If you are a member of a church which professes to be a Christian church, have you measured the particular beliefs and practices of that church in relation to the distinctive characteristics of the church that Jesus built as revealed in the New Testament writings?

First of all, how did you become a member of that church? Did that way conform to the manner of entry by which the first persons became Christians?

In many modern churches, and among TV messages, the minister will present a sermon emphasizing the need of Christ in one's personal life, and then he will extend an invitation such as the following: "If you have never received the blessings available through Christ, determine at this very moment to give your life over to Christ's control, put your trust in Him and pray with me this prayer, 'Lord, I confess I am a sinner and in need of the salvation you can supply. I put my trust and life in your hands. I want to live for Thee. I accept your offer of the free gift of your grace whereby Christ died for me. Come into my heart, Lord Jesus. Fill me with your Holy Spirit and direct my life from henceforth. In Jesus' name I pray'."

Then the minister will say something like this, "If you truly believe that Jesus was the divine Son of God and if you sincerely confessed your sins and prayed that prayer with me, you have made a big change in your life. You are now a Christian. You have begun a new life. You have been born again."

Did you ever hear this kind of invitation? Did you respond to such an invitation and then consider yourself to have become a Christian? You will not find this kind of invitation in the New Testament in connection with any conversion of sinners to Christianity. It is true that the first step in becoming a Christian is accepting Jesus as divine, as being the Son of God. After that, the believer must repent of and acknowledge his sinful state, but never in a New Testament-recorded conversion does the process stop there. These two actions are always followed by baptism — immersion in water in the name of the Holy Trinity. It is only when the process reaches its completion in baptism that the sinner receives forgiveness for past sins and the gift of the Holy Spirit, His divine presence in directing one's life. To stop before baptism is like starting to enter a building with a three step entry. If one stops on the second step, he never enters the building.

Jesus said, as quoted by Mark:

"He that believeth and is baptized shall be saved; but he that disbelieveth shall be condemned" (Mark 16:16).

Jesus coupled belief and baptism as two equal conditions of salvation. Suppose someone should tell you, "If you will come to my house, stay there a couple of hours bringing me a basket of apples, I will make you an apple pie." You would not expect the pie just because you went to the house and stayed two hours if you did not take the apples.

Recall that Peter told sinners who already believed in Jesus' divinity to:

"... repent ... and be baptized every one of you in the name of Jesus Christ unto the remission of your sins, and ye shall receive the gift of the Holy Spirit" (Acts 2:38).

Again both repentance and baptism are coupled as equal prerequisites of forgiveness and receipt of the Holy Spirit.

In telling sinners to be baptized "in the name of Jesus Christ," Peter was saying that this baptism was by the authority of Jesus Christ. Recall what Jesus, after His resurrection, told His disciples:

"And Jesus came to them and spake unto them, saying, All authority hath been given unto me in heaven and on earth. Go ye therefore, and make disciples of all the nations, baptizing them into the name of the Father and of the Son and of the Holy Spirit" (Matt. 28:18,19).

Note that making disciples or followers of Christ must involve the baptism of the convert by human agency, not by some direct and mysterious experience mistakenly viewed as personal baptism of the Holy Spirit.

Throughout the New Testament the symbol of the church as the bride of Christ is set forth. When John's disciples were concerned because John seemed to be losing ground because Jesus was baptizing so many people, John, the Baptist, explained that was as it should be. Referring to Jesus as the bridegroom and himself as the bridegroom's friend, John said:

> "He that hath the bride is the bridegroom: but the friend of the bridegroom, that standeth and heareth him, rejoiceth greatly because of the bridegroom's voice: this my joy therefore is made full" (John 3:29).

John's disciples went to Jesus and asked Him why, when John's disciples and the Pharisees observed a fast, Jesus' disciples did not do so.

> "And Jesus said unto them, Can the sons of the bridechamber mourn, as long as the bridegroom is with them? but the days will come, when the bridegroom shall be taken away from them, and then will they fast" (Matt. 9:15).

While on earth, Jesus told a parable about the kingdom of heaven and a wedding feast, symbolic of the celebration of the eventual joining of His followers, the church or His bride, with the Lord Jesus, which will take place when He returns to separate the saved from the condemned. Read Matt. 25:1-13. Those attending the feast are those who compose the church, the saved, the bride of Christ. Of those who became the first Christian converts, Luke wrote:

> "And all that believed were together, ... praising God, and having favor with all the people. And the Lord added to them day by day those that were saved" (Acts 2:44-47).

It is evident then that it is only after baptism that individuals become a part of the kingdom or church of Christ. Thus, baptism might be compared to the marriage ceremony. Two people may claim to be married, even act as though married, but they are not legally married until a wedding ceremony has been performed. Baptism is the final rite of passage from worldly allegiance to becoming citizens of Christ's kingdom. Although baptism is a ceremony, it is far from a mere ritual, as some consider it.

Why so many people argue and dispute about whether or not baptism is a part of becoming a Christian, when it is so plainly commanded and involves an act so easily accomplished, would seem to be a mystery, except that we know that Satan always stands ready to put a snare, if possible, between the sinner and his obedience to God.

Those who argue that their sins are forgiven before baptism rest their convictions on a few selected passages of scripture without consideration of all scripture bearing on the subject. Only by such careful consideration of every biblical passage concerning a given subject can one arrive at the true teaching on that subject. Every scripture on a given subject will be in harmony with each other when all are correctly understood. A sad example of this fallacious reasoning to uphold a claim that one is saved merely by faith is seen when the answer is supposedly decided by the words spoken by Paul and Silas when they answered the Philippian jailor's question, "Sirs, what must I do to be saved?" Read about the incident in Acts 16:16-34.

In answer to the jailor's question, he was told:

"'Believe on the Lord Jesus, and thou shalt be saved, thou and thy house" (Acts 16:31).

If those refusing to see the necessity of baptism in connection with forgiveness would only read a little further, in the very next verse of scripture, they would read:

"And they spake the word of the Lord unto him, with all that were in his house. And he took them the same hour of the night, and washed their stripes; and was baptized, he and all his, immediately" (Acts 16:32,33).

Before this whole incident, the jailor and his household likely knew nothing about Jesus, but the miraculous way in which Paul and Silas had been freed from prison caused the jailor to realize that he was in opposition to some superhuman force which favored Paul and Silas. The jailor and his household needed to know about Jesus before they could believe on Him. The words spoken in Acts 16:31 were just the introduction to the instructions Paul and Silas gave the jailor.

Evidently when Paul and Silas "spoke the word of the Lord" to the jailor and his household, the entire gospel message of Jesus' divinity, His crucifixion and resurrection, the necessity of accepting the truth, repenting and being baptized were explained. If not, why would the jailor and his household have been baptized? The importance of baptism is shown by the urgency of its being done immediately that night.

In this account of a sinner becoming a Christian, is seen a beautiful example and explanation of Paul's words.

"How then shall they call on him in whom they have not believed? and how shall they believe in him whom they have not heard? and how shall they hear without a preacher?" (Rom. 10:14).

The Ways

To every man there openeth
    A way, and ways and a Way.
And the high soul climbs the high way,
    and the low soul gropes the low,
And in between on the misty flats
    The rest drift to and fro
But to every man there openeth
    A Highway and a low,
And every man decideth
    The way his soul shall go.

— John Oren

The Hill

As I stood in the morn, at the foot of the hill,
    With my spirit forlorn, unresigned to His will —
"Oh, dear Lord," I did cry, "I'm so weary today,
    And the hill is so high — Is there no other way?"
Then my Shepherd replied, "Though the pathway be steep,
    I'll be close by your side, and your feet I will keep."

— Author Unknown

CHAPTER FOUR

IDENTIFYING CHARACTERISTICS OF JESUS' CHURCH

> Jesus' words: "... and broad is the way, that leadeth to destruction, and many are they that enter in thereby. For **narrow** is the gate, and **straitened the way**, that leadeth unto life, and few are they that find it" (Matt. 7:13,14)

Although many in today's society equate the word "narrow" with bigotry, ignorance and prejudice, since Jesus Himself described both the entry into the way of salvation and the way, itself, as being narrow, those who give this word the bad connotation show themselves to be the ones without true knowledge and understanding.

Since Jesus bought His church at the price of His sacrificial service and cruel death on the cross, it is His church. Ownership gives Him the sole right to determine not only the way of entry into His church, but to specify as to the worship pleasing to Him, each of its requirements as well as its exclusions. He exercised this right when He sent the Holy Spirit to inform and direct His twelve apostles in establishing His church, in setting into place its guidelines, requirements and proper examples. These pertain to its name, its organization, its purpose, its ministries, its worship and the character of its participants. Since there exist many organizations claiming to provide salvation through Christ, it should be evident that all who truly desire to attain to that eternal salvation which He promises should investigate thoroughly the means by which they hope to experience it.

A teaching or practice is said to be "scriptural" when it conforms to the teachings and examples set forth in God's word as being acceptable to Him. Therefore any such teaching or practice of the church is scriptural only when authorized by the Holy Spirit in the "Last Will and Testament" of Jesus, as recorded in what is commonly called the New Testament. It is necessary, then, to establish whether an organization which professes to be the church of the New Testament teaches and practices all of the items authorized by divine revelation. It is also necessary to note whether that particular church teaches or practices anything that is not authorized in the New Testament. Let us then note the identifying characteristics of the New Testament church.

SCRIPTURAL NAMES OR DESIGNATIONS OF THE NEW TESTAMENT CHURCH.

Throughout God's word, reference is made to the church by several designations. Any other name given by man to the church, which Jesus built, is unscriptural and therefore displeasing to God. The apostles referred to the church at various times in various ways.

Looking to the establishment of the church in the near future, Jesus called it:

"My church" — Matt. 16:18
"My kingdom" — Luke 22:30; John 18:36
"The kingdom of heaven" — Matt. 16:19
"The kingdom of God" — John 3:5; Luke 22:16

After the church was established, the apostles called it:

"the church" — Col. 1:18; Eph. 1:22; 3:10, 5:23
"the church of God" — I Cor. 1:2; Gal. 1:13
"The church of the Lord" — Acts 20:28
"churches of Christ" — Rom. 16:16 speaking
    of different congregations of the church
"the household of God" — I Tim. 3:15; Eph. 2:19
"the household of faith" — Gal. 6:10
"the kingdom of God" — Acts 28:23,31
"the kingdom of His beloved Son" — Col. 1:13
"a kingdom which cannot be shaken" — Heb. 12:28
    (reference in Old Testament prophecy — Dan. 2:44)
"Christ's body" — Eph. 1:22,23

Note that every designation has reference to Jesus' or to divine ownership of the church. Organizations which profess to be followers of Christ wear many names other than one of the above, but even if a church is called by a scriptural name, that alone does not mark it as the church which Jesus built. A church pleasing to Him must conform in all its doctrines and practices to the divine pattern set forth in the New Testament. There are churches, however, scattered all over the world who call themselves churches of Christ, who do teach the same things and worship in the same manner as did the apostles and first believers in Christ. This name, church of Christ, is not used by these congregations of Christians in a denominational sense, but simply to identify the members as followers of the Christian religion revealed in the New Testament. They believe that division of believers in Christ into denominations, each having its man-written creed and name, is unscriptural and very displeasing to God.

SCRIPTURAL PATTERN OF NEW TESTAMENT CHURCH ORGANIZATION

The New Testament church has no human head, such as the Catholic's pope. The supreme and only head of the church is Christ.

> "and what the exceeding greatness of his power to usward who believe, according to that working of the strength of his might which he wrought in Christ, when he raised him from the dead, and made him to sit at his right hand in the heavenly places, far above all rule, and authority, and power, and dominion, and every name that is named, not only in this world, but also in that which is to come: and he put all things in subjection under his feet, and gave him to be head over all things to the church, which is his body, the fulness of him that filleth all in all" (Eph. 1:19-23).

The New Testament church does not have any organized body of persons to direct or in any way affect all congregations. Every congregation is independent, though each shares a common bond of brotherly relationship extending to fellow Christians worldwide.

Paul wrote to the Christians in Ephesus:

"And He gave some to be apostles; and some, prophets; and some, evangelists; and some, pastors and teachers; for the perfecting of the saints, unto the work of ministering, unto the building up of the body of Christ: till we all attain unto the unity of the faith, and of the knowledge of the Son of God, unto a fullgrown man, unto the measure of the stature of the fulness of Christ" (Eph. 4:11-13).

Prophets (those foretelling future events unforseeable by human wisdom). Like the apostles, these prophets ceased to exist after the end of the apostolic age, as explained under the next paragraph. Certain prophecies of events still to come were recorded in the New Testament for our learning.

Apostles (those who had seen Jesus during His ministry and were specifically appointed by Him) ceased to exist on earth after John, the last individual who had seen Christ in person, died. The apostolic period was the time when direct revelation from the Holy Spirit to man was miraculously bestowed. This was necessary until those revelations were recorded in the Bible for all future generations. Since then, miraculous revelations are no longer needed and therefore they no longer occur.

"Love never faileth: but whether there be prophecies, they shall be done away; whether there be tongues, they shall cease; whether there be knowledge, it shall be done away. For we know in part, and we prophesy in part; but when that which is perfect is come, that which is in part shall be done away" (I Cor. 13:8-10).

In speaking of "that which is perfect," Paul was referring to the system of Christianity as inaugurated by the sacrifice of Christ and the establishment of His church. Dealing with the same subject James spoke of it as "the perfect law, the law of liberty" (Jas. 1:25). After the church had been established and overseen by the apostles during their lifetimes, the system of Christianity had reached that state of perfection in which the miraculous elements of the apostolic age were no longer necessary. Therefore, they ceased.

Evangelists were not specifically and formally ordained, as were prophets and teachers during New Testament times. Neither are they formally ordained today in the church which seeks to follow the New Testament pattern. All Christians should be teachers to the extent possible, but some have greater natural abilities and, through studious application and personal zeal, prepare themselves more thoroughly to make preaching or evangelism their main purpose and work in life. These are entitled to be supported by the church as long as they devote their time entirely to preaching and practicing only scriptural truth in its entirety. (I Tim. 5:18).

Pastors. In the New Testament this term did not denote an evangelist as it is commonly used and accepted by the denominational world today. According to Jesus' instruction, conferring any special title upon a religious teacher, setting him apart from other Christians, was forbidden.

> "But be not ye called Rabbi: for one is your teacher, and all ye are brethren. And call no man your father on the earth: for one is your Father, even he who is in heaven. Neither be ye called masters: for one is your master, even the Christ" (Matt. 23:8-10).

Pastor was one of several names used in the New Testament denoting appointed officials in each congregation. These were to have the spiritual oversight of the congregation. Other names referring to the same office were **elder, bishop, presbyter, overseer** or **shepherd**. This office carried the heavy responsibility of teaching the scriptures and guarding against false teachers or teachings among the congregation.

An elder was to have certain attainments and characteristics before being appointed. Those qualifications divinely specified were:

1. He must be above reproach, having a good reputation outside the church.

2. He must be the husband of one wife.

3. He must be temperate, hospitable, prudent, respectable, able to teach, not addicted to wine, gentle, uncontentious, free from the love of money, loving what is sensible, devout, self-controlled.

4. He must "hold fast the faithful word which is in accordance with the teaching, that he may be both able to exhort in sound doctrine and to refute those who contradict" (Titus 1:9).

5. He must manage his own household well, have believing children whom he controls with dignity.

6. He must not be a new convert.

7. He must be one who is not appointed unless he is willing and glad to assume the heavy responsibility.

8. His office does not permit him to act in such a way as to be "lording it over the flock" or dictatorial. Rather, he is to set a good example and guard his charge as a loving shepherd cares for and guards his flock.

See I Tim. 3:1-7; I Pet. 5:1-4; Titus 1:6-9.

Deacons. Deacons were not named in the list of those whom Paul told the Ephesians that Christ had given "for the work of service, to the building up of the body of Christ" (Eph. 4:12). Those Paul named were persons who were involved in the teaching ministry of the church, presenting spiritual truths and guarding against false teachings.

The first record of deacons being appointed in the New Testament church is recorded in Acts 6:1-6. These men were appointed to oversee a benevolent work of the church in distributing food to Christians needing it. Their service was of a temporal and physical nature rather than spiritual instruction. Nevertheless, deacons also should meet certain qualifications as noted in Paul's letter to Timothy (I Tim. 3:8-13).

SCRIPTURAL ITEMS OF WORSHIP

PREACHING — Paul instructed the young preacher, Timothy:

"I charge thee in the sight of God, and of Christ Jesus, who shall judge the living and the dead, and by his appearing and his kingdom: preach the word; be urgent in season, out of season; reprove, rebuke, exhort, with all longsuffering and teaching. For the time will come when they will not endure the sound doctrine; but, having itching ears, will heap to themselves teachers after their own lusts; and will turn away their ears from the truth, and turn aside unto fables" (II Tim. 4:1-4).

PRAYING —

"pray without ceasing; in everything give thanks: for this is the will of God in Christ Jesus to youward"
(I Thess. 5:17-18).

"giving thanks always for all things in the name of our Lord Jesus Christ to God, even the Father" (Eph. 5:20).

In these verses we learn the need for continued prayer, that prayer is to be addressed to God, and that prayer is through, or in the name of, Christ. He is mediator between God and man. Prayer is not to be made to any other than God, the Father - not even directly to Jesus, but to God through Jesus, our Mediator. These instructions apply to any prayer, whether in public or in private.

SINGING — Under the Mosaic Dispensation, God authorized the use of cymbals, harps, lyres and trumpets to be used in the house of the Lord (II Chron. 29:25), but this is not authorized in the New Testament. With the inauguration of the Christian Dispensation, all portions of the Old Testament dispensations were no longer valid or applicable to Christian worship. Not only does the New Testament not authorize the use of musical instruments in the worship, but secular history attests to the fact that it was not used in Christian worship until it was introduced by Pope Vitalianus in 568 A.D. with the use of the organ in the Roman church to accompany the singing.

The use of instruments in the worship is comparable to the burning of incense, burning of candles or lamps, offering blood sacrifices, or any other religious action authorized as worship under the Mosaic Dispensation.

Singing is authorized and commanded in the following New Testament passages:

"And be not drunken with wine, wherein is riot, but be filled with the Spirit; speaking one to another in psalms and hymns and spiritual songs, singing and making melody with your heart to the Lord" (Eph. 5:18,19).

"Let the word of Christ dwell in you richly; in all wisdom teaching and admonishing one another with psalms and hymns and spiritual songs, singing with grace in your hearts unto God" (Col. 3:16).

"Through him then let us offer up a sacrifice of praise to God continually, that is, the fruit of lips which make confession to His name" (Heb. 13:15).

It has been suggested that this verse is about sacrifice and therefore not applicable to church music. Yes, the command is to offer a sacrifice, but the sacrifice is described as consisting of praise to God out of a thankful heart. This can be described as "fruit of the lips," whether it is done by speech, prayer or song, but musical instruments cannot offer praise to God.

GIVING — Under the law of Moses tithing was commanded of all worshipers and on occasion even a second or third tithe. However, the New Testament does not command the giving of a tithe. Paul directed the Corinthians thus:

"Let each man do according as he hath purposed in his heart: not grudgingly, or of necessity: for God loveth a cheerful giver. And God is able to make all grace abound unto you; that ye, having always all sufficiency in everything, may abound unto every good work: as it is written, He hath scattered abroad, he hath given to the poor; His righteousness abideth for ever "(II Cor. 9:7-9).

" Upon the first day of the week let each one of you lay by him in store, as he may prosper, that no collections be made when I come" (I Cor. 16:2).

The phrase "as he may prosper," however, does indicate percentage giving, but not naming a definite percentage.

During Jesus' earthly ministry he noted that the Pharisees and Sadducees were very meticulous in making sure to give their tithes; yet He denounced them strongly for their hypocritical lives.

"Woe unto you, scribes and Pharisees, hypocrites! for ye tithe mint and anise and cummin, and have left undone the weightier matters of the law, justice, and mercy, and faith: but these ye ought to have done, and not to have left the other undone" (Matt. 23:23).

"For I say unto you, Till heaven and earth pass away, one jot or one tittle shall in no wise pass away from the law, till all things be accomplished" (Matt. 5:20).

Since the new covenant given through the Christian Dispensation is so much better than the old covenant with the Jews during the Mosaic Dispensation (Heb. 7:19,22; 8:6; 10:34; 12:24), it would appear to me that the ratio of giving today should be greater than that of the Mosaic Dispensation. However, that is a determination which every Christian must decide for himself.

COMMUNION THROUGH THE LORD'S SUPPER — On the night of Jesus' betrayal, before going to the garden of Gethsemane, Jesus met with His apostles to eat the Jewish Passover supper.

"And as they were eating, Jesus took bread, and blessed, and brake it; and he gave to the disciples, and said, Take, eat; this is my body. And he took a cup, and gave thanks, and gave to them, saying, Drink ye all of it; for this is my blood of the covenant, which is poured out for many unto remission of sins. But I say unto you, I shall not drink henceforth of this fruit of the vine, until that day when I drink it new with you in my Father's kingdom.'" (Matt. 26:26-29).

After the church was established, Paul wrote to the Christians in Corinth:

"The cup of blessing which we bless, is it not a communion of the blood of Christ? The bread which we break, is it not a communion of the body of Christ? seeing that we, who are many, are one bread, one body: for we all partake of the one bread" (I Cor. 10:16,17).

"For as often as ye eat this bread and drink the cup, ye proclaim the Lord's death till he come. Wherefore whosoever shall eat the bread or drink the cup of the Lord in an unworthy manner, shall be guilty of the body and the blood of the Lord" (I Cor. 11:26,27).

The scriptures just quoted give the privilege, and enjoin the duty, of communing with Christ through the memorial of His death, usually called "the Lord's Supper," although this expression is not found in scripture. However, there is no direct command as to when this is to be done. To learn when we should observe this communion, we look for the example of the early Christians who were guided by the apostles' teaching. In so doing, we find that Paul, who was on a journey returning from Greece to Jerusalem, stopped at Troas and waited there in order to meet with Christians there on the Lord's day. Of that meeting, Paul specifically said it was for the purpose of communing with Christians there.

"And upon the first day of the week, when we were gathered together to break bread, Paul discoursed with them, and prolonged his speech until midnight" (Acts 20:7).

For this reason, members of the churches of Christ observe the Lord's supper every Lord's day, the first day of the week.

Various denominational churches observe the Lord's supper at different intervals rather than each week. One seeks to justify this by saying, "We don't know that the early church kept the supper every Sunday." Recall that the first disciples were Jews. They knew that when the Ten Commandments said, "Remember the Sabbath day to keep it holy," it meant every Sabbath. Likewise, they would know that if they were directed by the Holy Spirit to observe the supper on the Lord's day, they would know that every Lord's day was intended. If your employer told you that you would receive your salary on the 15th of the month, you would know he meant every month.

In some churches where the communion service is held less frequently than every week, justification is sought by arguing that it seems more of a special event if not done so often, and thus confers greater feelings of reverence. Such false reasoning is the common mistake of people who seek to be guided by human rather than divine wisdom.

No part of Christian worship holds greater meaning to the sincere dedicated Christian than the communion with Christ through the God-intended partaking in memory with Him of His painful death on the cross. He endured this that we, guilty souls, might be freed from the penalty of our transgressions and look forward, though the gift of His grace, to eternal life with Him after His return to take us to His heavenly abiding place.

WEEKLY ASSEMBLY — From two passages already quoted with reference to partaking of communion on the Lord's day (Acts 20:7) and giving financially on the Lord's day (I Cor. 16:2), it appears that this was a weekly observance of the early church. Furthermore, in the letter to the Hebrew Christians, the author gave this exhortation:

> "not forsaking our own assembling together, as the custom of some is, but exhorting one another; and so much the more, as ye see the day drawing nigh" (Heb. 10:25).

ATTITUDE OF WORSHIP — Jesus revealed the kind of attitude which one should have if he truly worships. I fear that the reason so many people today complain of boredom or failure to enjoy church attendance is their lack of or small sense of two qualities which Jesus said are necessary:

> "But the hour cometh, and now is, when the true worshippers shall worship the Father in spirit and truth: for such doth the Father seek to be his worshippers. God is a Spirit: and they that worship him must worship in sprit and truth" (John 4:23,24).

To worship "in spirit" means sincerely to feel a reverential awe toward the majestic, omnipotent, omniscient Being, to whom each one owes his very existence, both physically and spiritually. At the same time, one should feel a deep humility and gratitude toward that same loving, compassionate Being, who was willing to send His "only begotten Son," from heaven to earth to die a cruel, agonizing death on the crucifixion cross — a guiltless One bearing the guilt of the sins of all who, penitently and obediently, serve the Lord.

To worship "in truth" means that the object of worship is the one and only true God. To worship "in truth" also means that the worship consists in following exactly the divine injunctions as to the manner of worship which He has revealed that He desires it to be, adding nothing and omitting nothing. God has been very explicit in giving His directions, and He has just as explicitly forbidden all else. Note His words delivered through Moses:

> "Ye shall not add unto the word which I command you, neither shall ye diminish from it, that ye may keep the commandments of Jehovah your God which I commanded you" (Deut. 4:2).

Although we do not live under the laws given to Moses, the moral principles revealed in the Old Testament are still applicable under the Christian Dispensation. We worship the same God that Moses worshipped. That God has not changed. What he hated then He still hates, and what He loved then, He still loves. An admonition similar to that of Moses is found at the close of God's sacred book.

> "I testify unto every man that heareth the words of the prophecy of this book, If any man shall add unto them, God shall add unto him the plagues which are written in this book: and if any man shall take away from the words of the book of this prophecy, God shall take away his part from the tree of life, and out of the holy city, which are written in this book" (Rev. 22:18,19).

MINISTRY OF THE CHURCH — The primary purpose of the Christian religion is to save souls. After one becomes a Christian, he is consequently a part of Jesus' church. In giving the Great Commission, Jesus told the apostles to instruct those who believe, repent and are baptized to teach these truths to others that they, too, might be saved.

> "And Jesus came to them and spake unto them, saying, All authority hath been given unto me in heaven and on earth. Go ye, therefore, and make disciples of all the nations, baptizing them into the name of the Father and of the son and of the Holy Spirit: **teaching them to observe all things whatsoever I commanded you**: and lo, I am with you always, even unto the end of the world'" (Matt. 28:18-20).

Note that Jesus did not say, "Go and invite the lost to your church services to teach them the truth." He said, "**Go**, not "**Come**." Although the unsaved may learn by attending church services, if the church depends on this method chiefly, the world will never be converted.

Services of the church assembly are primarily for the further teaching of baptized penitent believers and for mutual encouragement and edification. Because of the attendance of children of Christian adults and those outsiders who may visit services, it is important that the manner of entering the church, as well as the identifying characteristics of the church, also be taught from the pulpit.

Another important service of the church is benevolent works.

> "Pure religion and undefiled before our God and Father is this, to visit the fatherless and widows in their affliction, and to keep oneself unspotted from the world" (James 1:27).

Although these words are directed toward the individual Christian, the New Testament contains examples of the church as a congregation serving in these capacities. The first recorded example is noted thus:

> "Now in these days, when the number of the disciples was multiplying, there arose a murmuring of the Grecian Jews against the Hebrews, because their widows were neglected in the daily ministration" (Acts 6:1).

The problem was solved in this way:

> "And the twelve called the multitude of the disciples unto them, and said, It is not fit that we should forsake the word of God, and serve tables. Look ye out therefore, brethren, from among you seven men of good report, full of the Spirit and of wisdom, whom we may appoint over this business" (Acts 6:2,3).

From instructions which Paul gave Timothy, the early church was to care for certain widows. See I Tim. 5:3-13.

Paul was sent from the church at Antioch of Syria on a long journey during which he not only preached and established churches in many areas, but he was also to collect money to take to Jerusalem

Christians because of a special need there. Reference was made to this when Paul wrote to the Corinthian church.

> "Now concerning the collection for the saints, as I gave order to the churches of Galatia, so also do ye. Upon the first day of the week let each one of you lay by him in store, as he may prosper, that no collections be made when I come. And when I arrive, whomsoever ye shall approve, them will I send with letters to carry your bounty unto Jerusalem: and if it be meet for me to go also, they shall go with me" (I Cor. 16:1-4).

God in Heaven has set before us the way which He has chosen for us to please Him. The world offers what seems to many people more exciting, more inspiring ways. But the lures of the world are empty promises goading one on to eternal destruction.

If you truly seek life with eternal happiness, consider carefully what Joshua said in the long ago:

> "And if it seem evil unto you to serve Jehovah, choose you this day whom ye will serve: whether the gods which your fathers served that were beyond the River, or the gods of the Amorites, in whose land ye dwell: but as for me and my house, **we will serve Jehovah**" (Josh. 24:15).

You and I

The world's great heart is aching, aching in the night,
    And God alone can heal it, and God alone gives light;
And the ones to bear the message and to speak the living word,
    Are you and I, my brothers, and the millions that have heard.

We grovel among mere trifles, and our spirits fret and toss,
    While above us burns the vision of the Christ upon the cross;
And the blood of God is streaming from His broken hands and side,
    And the voice of God is pleading, "Tell thy brother I have died."

— Author Unknown

CHAPTER FIVE

THE DEMAND FOR CHANGE IN CHURCH WORSHIP

Within the last few decades, there has risen within our country, among the last two generations, a growing spirit of unrest, dissatisfaction, a sense of lack of personal fulfillment, a search for some way to discover true happiness and contentment. Among many there is a yearning and thirst for some way unknown to them to find success and lasting satisfaction. It is common for some to express their search as an effort to find themselves. Choosing to reject the counsel of older generations, who have found that peace and contentment, the searchers are turning to philosophies of human origin, their own opinions and judgments or those of their peers, to atheists, humanists, or even to the occult. In none of these can be found the object of the quest.

This frustration is the result of various conditions, but perhaps the situation bearing the most compelling influence has been the changes brought about during the last few decades in public education for the nation's youth. Until then the public schools were a strong force promoting God, country and the rights of others. The principles of Judeo/Christian morals, based on the Ten Commandments, were strongly upheld. In fact, for long beyond the first century of our history, belief in God and in the Bible as His inspired word were mandated as prerequisite qualifications of every teacher in public schools. The Bible was the first textbook used. All of the early schools of higher learning were started for the very purpose of promoting faith in God and His word.

When the misnamed American Civil Liberties Union (ACLU), certain women's organizations, Planned Parenthood, the National Education Association, professing atheists, humanists, and other organized instruments of Satan succeeded in removing prayer, the Ten Commandments and every vestige of Biblical allusions and influence from the public schools, the result has been what Satan has long hoped to accomplish.

In place of moral instruction regarding absolute values of right and wrong behavior, the young have been taught that men evolved from — they aren't sure what — that the Bible is a collection of myths and that each individual must chart his own way. Teachers are not only permitted, but in many instances compelled, if they wish to continue teaching, to promote ideas originating in humanistic philosophy and the occult. Sexual permissiveness and immoral, as well as actually illegal, lifestyles are presented not only as acceptable but desirable in today's society because "Times have changed," we are told.

As a result, many have been led astray from the old paths which formerly characterized our nation's citizenship and political leadership. This nation's beginnings and national heritage have been rooted in trust in God as the provider and maintainer of our well-being. George Washington was seen fallen on his knees before God as he faced the conflict of Valley Forge. History records Benjamin Franklin's calling the Constitutional Assembly to prayer, and out of that meeting emerged the Constitution of the United States. Repeatedly Abraham Lincoln, in the presence of his cabinet, prayed, begging that God's will prevail during the Civil War. Such leaders as these gave America its spiritual heritage. They adhered with strong belief to the divine assertion, "Blessed is the nation whose God is the Lord" (Ps. 33:12).

Our nation became great because, although like all human institutions it has had its imperfections, it has in the past and until very recently advocated and sought to maintain God's moral laws among its civil laws and in the hearts of its citizens.

But with the advent of the so-called "baby-boomers," a considerable and growing segment of society began to question the moral traditions of our nation, even advancing further toward questioning and denying the absolute values and teachings set forth in God's word. Furthermore, the administration of our laws, through our court system has not been in keeping with the former prevalent moral sense of justice and responsibility. Even some of the signals coming from the highest seat of government in the land are in conflict with the common ideals of our former society. The moral conscience of our nation has become dull and impotent, thus inviting national disaster, which historically has always resulted when a nation is consumed with moral decay.

An old legend of Greek mythology tells of an island in the Mediterranean Sea inhabited by so-called fascinating creatures who were half woman and half fish. When these mermaids observed ships nearing the shores of the islands, these enchanting sirens appeared singing beautiful songs accompanied by their harps. Thus the sailors were lured on toward the rough rocky shores where the vessels were battered and destroyed.

Satan likewise has set forth before recent generations his time-worn sirens of the urge for individual choice beyond imposed restrictions, for the satisfaction of personal desire above regard for law and the welfare of other people, for the supremacy of human reasoning and judgment in dictating one's conduct according to one's personal situation, and for the concept that through the attainment of personal achievement — whether by satisfying fleshly passions and attainment of prestige, power, or wealth — the quest for peace, happiness and well-being can be achieved.

These Satanic lures are not new. Every generation has experienced contact with them but, because of the development of character through consistent teaching of proper moral values in the homes and schools, the vast majority of this country's citizens, until two or three decades ago, lived with reverence toward God and respect for law and the rights of others. In America, all Christians within the church patterned after the New Testament have been noted for having great familiarity with the scriptures and, in the main, until recently they have had a deep-rooted faith in God strong enough to resist these siren calls and answer each with a "Thus saith the Lord," just as Jesus did when He refused to yield to the temptations of Satan on the mountain top immediately following His baptism. Having resisted Satan's sirens, Jesus was now ready to begin His public ministry (Matt. 4:1-11).

It is not only within the New Testament church today that some have felt the pressure of the younger generations for change in the time-honored and divinely enjoined manner of worship, but the secular world as well has taken note of it. Giving attention to this fact, the following article appeared in the weekly bulletin of the church of Christ in Little Rock, Arkansas.

The Church Will Never Be The Same

According to the April 5, 1993 issue of *Time* magazine the church will never be the same because the baby boomers, the generation that forgot God, is going back to church.

But it's not going to be business as usual. These returnees are described as "traveling from church to church or faith to faith, sampling creeds, shopping for a custom-made God." While most say that they believe in God, "One-third also believe in reincarnation, ghosts and astrology. The God of their understanding is not necessarily the personal, all-powerful and all-knowing deity of orthodoxy. Nor is the Jesus affirmed by boomers necessarily the Son of God and unique Saviour of humanity."

In an effort to attract, more and more churches are becoming "customer oriented." As an example of this, one church was cited as having songs one Sunday morning ranging from *Oh, What a Beautiful Mornin'* to *Danny Boy.* The meeting climaxed in hugging with the preacher raising his arms high and booming, "Hey, God, make my day! Go for it!"

In the *Time* article mention is made of the book, *The Churching of America 1776-1990,* by sociologists Roger Finke and Rodney Stark. Martin E. Marty, the historian, summarized their interpretation: "No God or religion or spirituality, no issue of truth or beauty or goodness, no faith or hope or love, no justice or mercy; only winning and losing in the churching game matters." Marty remarked that it is "lethal" to reshape churches around the claims of these returnees.

— John Gipson

Your reaction? Is it anything like the response in *Time*, April 26, 1993?

As a baby boomer, I am fascinated by my generation's apparent return to religion. Unfortunately, it seems that the philosophy of the Me generation has not carried over to the quest for spiritual wealth. We appear to be searching not for a moral code, but for a justification of our lifestyle. While it is true that Jesus never turned people away for asking too many questions, there is no mention in the New Testament of packaging the answers to meet the wishes of the audiences or to fill pews, and no one said the way to heaven was easy.

Forgive me if I can't get too excited about baby boomers returning to religion. Until we learn submission to the will of God we may be something, but Christian we are not.

— John Gipson

In some congregations of churches which have in the past sought to preserve the purity of doctrine and practices which conform to the God-given pattern followed since the climax of the restoration period, there is now a rising sentiment and clamor for change. Some go so far in the demands for change as to affirm that if the church does not change, it will not survive during the next century. Some types of change advanced are not necessarily bad because they are related to matters which do not affect the principles or practices of the New Testament church. Such changes are inevitable and have been made from time to time in the manner of conducting church worship. The gravity of the great demand for change now is in the fact that many, even within the church, have the erroneous concept of the Lord's church as one among many acceptable denominations. These advocates of change speak in terms of inducing the "unchurched" into the Lord's church by offering them that which caters to their desire for entertaining, contemporary presentations that extort from the viewers mystical inspirational fervor which they have not experienced in listening to simple preaching of biblical truths, or in participating in prayer, or by returning to the Lord a part of the financial blessings received of Him, or from communing with the crucified Savior through the memorial which He established to commemorate that sacrifice.

These advocates of change in the church are voicing the sentiments of the denominational world, often even participating in interdenominational meetings and religious campaigns. In so doing they are virtually rejecting the particular characteristics which distinguish the church which Jesus built, including the essential final rite of baptism for the remission of sins necessary to church entrance. Those who thus depart from biblically established principles because of a lack of understanding of those principles and a sincere dedication to their promotion are easily led by peer pressure and worldly opinions. They do not seem to understand that the primary purpose for which Jesus died was to save souls, not simply to get persons involved in attending some church. Those who advocate drastic changes are simply "going with the flow" without consideration of the fact that the flow naturally gravitates to the lowest possible level and eventually becomes stagnant.

In seeking to change some of the worship designed by the divinely directed pattern of the early church, those promoters of change are assuming the presumptuous attitude that their way is better than God's way. They seek innovative ways to lure people into investigating the church. They promote the idea that the most effective power in drawing men to follow the Lord is to entice them by entertaining with dramatic productions, with artistic presentation of intricate choral displays of beauty, rhythm of the modern band, solos by gifted singers, orchestral presentations and such like. In other words, don't expect to draw men to Christ by inviting their attention, merely to listen attentively and thoughtfully to God's word as proclaimed by the plain preaching of the gospel. Directed by the Holy Spirit, Paul's writing conveys an entirely different attitude:

> "For I am not ashamed of the gospel: for it is the power of God unto salvation to every one that believeth; to the Jew first, and also to the Greek" (Romans 1:16).

Man has experienced the truth of this statement throughout the history of the church. It is the **power of the gospel**, not the appeal to the fleshly appetites, through which God calls the sinner to repentance unto salvation.

God's servants are to be the light of the world and the salt of the earth (Matt. 5:13). People of the world walk in spiritual darkness. The light of the gospel, when reflected in the lives of Christians can expel the darkness and reveal the way of safety. Salt has a preserving quality. If the church, which professes to follow Christ, goes with the flow of worldly attractions, how can the purity of the church be maintained? Another characteristic of salt is that when applied to a wound, it is irritating. Likewise, when the salt of Christian teaching is applied to worldly practices, those guilty of such may become irritated and rebellious. Nevertheless, the healing of guilt can be attained **only** through strict compliance with divine instruction.

The sentiments of the majority of dedicated Christians are reflected in these further comments written by a Christian minister. They concern the methods of many of those who cry out for change and are willing to depart from revealed truth to get it.

> Maybe I have read too many books on "church growth." Instead of being "turned on," I'm more and more "turned off." The emphasis seems to be on pleasing the customer. Meeting their "felt-needs." Giving them what they want.
>
> Over and over we are told that churches must be "seeker-friendly." Does that mean that we let people "hold the truth in unrighteousness"? Does it mean that we abandon the realities of truth for the sake of a comfort zone? Does it mean we cry, "Peace, peace" when there is no peace?
>
> Wasn't the sale of papal indulgences by Johann Tetzel "seeker-friendly"? Finding out what people want and giving it to them can be both popular and profitable in the short run. But it may also be a sell-out of the Gospel.
>
> Just because we please ourselves doesn't mean that we please God. "Come to Bethel, and transgress; to Gilgal, and multiply transgression; bring your sacrifices every morning, your tithes every three days; offer a sacrifice of thanksgiving of that which is leavened, and proclaim freewill offerings, publish them; for so you love to do, O people of Israel! says the Lord GOD" (Amos 4:4-5). Being "user-friendly" doesn't always translate into being "God-friendly" as Amos was quick to point out.
>
> Richard Niebuhr criticized liberalism as "God without wrath [bringing] men without sin into a Kingdom without judgment through the ministrations of a Christ without a

Cross." Some, it seems, are almost willing to go that far to attract a crowd.

— John Gipson

Let us note some examples of how some within the church seek to assuage the waves of demand for changes in the long-time honored practices of worship guided and restricted by divine regulations.

In the September 12, 1992 issue of the Dallas Morning News, there appeared the following article written by a news reporter.

Preacher Follows Own Conscience and Starts Church

Can a guy who likes professional wrestling be worth your time on Sunday morning?

So asks a brochure announcing the start of a new North Dallas church.

Randy Mayeux, 41, pastor of the nondenominational Christ Church North, is shown holding a box of popcorn while standing in the ring at the Sportatorium and cheering on two wrestlers.

Compared with other questions — Does God exist? What is the nature of evil? When will the Red Sox win the World Series? — the question on the brochure has more to do with Mr. Mayeux than theology.

Born in Jacksonville, Fla. Mr. Mayeux was 1 year old when his mother was divorced. He grew up without a father and had virtually no contact with the church.

But one of his most pleasant childhood memories was going to pro wrestling matches every Thursday night with his maternal grandfather, Francis Lowery, a carpenter.

Mr. Mayeux became a Christian in the summer of 1968 after graduating from high school in Harlingen, Texas. After attending a revival by Baptist evangelist James Robinson, "I felt the call of God to preach," he said.

A member of the Church of Christ who was attending Abilene Christian College (now a university) convinced Mr. Mayeux that becoming a Baptist might lead to his eternal damnation.

That's when he switched to the Church of Christ, going to Abilene Christian on a tennis scholarship.

After serving as a youth minister at two congregations, Mr. Mayeux took a preaching post — the equivalent of pastor — at Atlantic Church of Christ in Long Beach, Calif. The church attendance grew from about 90 when he came to the church in 1976 to 600 when he left in 1987 for Preston Road Church of Christ in University Park.

"After years of declining membership, attendance at Preston Road grew from 230 to 530," said Mr. Mayeux. The church attracted more singles and young couples, but Mr. Mayeux was frustrated by the congregation's traditional approach.

In the Church of Christ — which has produced such singers as Amy Grant — singing is without musical accompaniment. Mr. Mayeux tried to bring in an a capella singing group for worship services and proposed that women participate in worship services.

He also differed publicly with a key doctrine of the Church of Christ — that it is only through a believer's baptism by immersion that sins are forgiven. In this traditional view, a belief is prerequisite for baptism, but it is not sufficient for salvation.

In 1989, a youth ministers' conference hosted by Lubbock Christian College, Mr. Mayeux said he believed that Mother Teresa and Billy Graham are Christians and that they will go to heaven.[9]

Contending for the Faith, a fundamentalist publication in Pensacola, Fla., got hold of the tapes from the conference and published the remarks. The publication called him a "dyed-in-the-wool liberal of the deepest dye."

---

[9]In quoting Mr. Mayeux' statement regarding the two well-known persons, the writer is not passing judgment on the final destiny of the two persons mentioned. Only Jesus, when He returns in His role as Supreme Judge of the living and dead, can make that determination.

At least one elder tried to get him fired. He then started thinking about leaving.

"I felt I had a real calling to reach unchurched people and felt I could not do that in a Church of Christ setting," said Mr. Mayeux. He resigned in June 1991 and worked on his doctoral dissertation in rhetoric from the University of Southern California. His main aim was to start a new church.

"I didn't want to split the church. It would have served no purpose," he said of the somewhat amicable parting.

With the new church — the first service is Sunday at 10:45 a.m. at the Jesuit College Preparatory School auditorium at 12345 Inwood Road — services will be modeled after Bill Hybels' Willow Creek Community Church in South Barrington, Ill., which is considered the model for mega-churches.

The new church will use a "seeker-targeted" Sunday morning service, with a band and the use of contemporary music; Wednesday night services are designed for believers.

It was reported to me, the author, by some who attended more than one of Mr. Mayeux' services that he also made use of other innovations generally held unacceptable to the New Testament church of Christ.

In a personal conversation between Mr. Mayeux and this writer, an attempt was made to appeal to him to consider some scriptural applications to his actions. He refused to discuss them, choosing rather to introduce other subjects where he wanted to inject controversy, bringing the discussion to a close with the statement that he was tired of being told what he could or could not do. His attitude appeared belligerent, far from an attitude of seeking to act upon a firm foundation of faith in biblical revelation.

It might be mentioned in passing that in establishing his new church, he carried with him from the Preston Road church members of the younger generations who had become Christians under the influence of Mr. Mayeux' dynamic personality. They may have had zeal, but it was not according to knowledge.

Of a similar situation, regarding the lack of faith among the Jews who rejected Christ, Paul wrote:

"For I bear them witness that they have a zeal for God, but not according to knowledge.

For being ignorant of God's righteousness, and seeking to establish their own, they did not subject themselves to the righteousness of God" (Rom. 10:2,3).

In an issue of The Dallas Morning News of December 1992, under the picture of a wrestler in a ring, a columnist wrote the following article:

Seekers Anonymous

Last September, after four uneasy years of preaching—and serving as house liberal—at a mainstream Church of Christ, pastor Randy Mayeux founded Christ Church North using an unorthodox direct-mail campaign. One of the fliers (above) plays off Mayeux' "secret vice," a love of professional wrestling. And that's not the only unusual thing about the new church.

On a recent Sunday, members and visitors entered to the theme from "Bonanza." Next they watched a clip from *City Slickers*, in which actor Jack Palance gets philosophical. Services usually include a popular song (like the Beatles' *Nowhere Man*) that poses a dilemma. Then comes a contemporary Christian song with lyrics that "answer the human needs raised by the pop song," says Mayeux.

Mayeux insists that his approach is not watering down the message of Christianity. "We're just designing an environment for the person who is not churched," says Mayeux, who follows "seeker-targeted" methods. There's no pressure, no hard sell. A "seeker," Mayeux says, "does not want to say anything, sing anything, sign anything, or give anything" until he or she has decided.

"I believe Scripture is a way to find God," says Mayeux, "But I'm uncomfortable with churches that draw lines the Bible doesn't draw."

— Chris Tucker

In the February 1993 issue of the "Christian Chronicle," there appeared an article describing another experiment to reach the "unchurched" by means of a departure from the divinely-prescribed methods:

> A new congregation recently begun in Abilene, Texas, is built on a perceived need for the church everywhere in the United States.
>
> "If we were reaching our children," says Kent Smith, a specialist in domestic missions at Abilene Christian University and one of the leaders of the Abilene Mission church, "we would have grown 15 or 20 percent over this past decade, but the growth has been flat."
>
> Smith is eager to use this congregation to experiment with ways of strengthening the church, which he sees as having an identity crisis. He also wants to give students a chance to try out evangelistic techniques, so that they, themselves, may go out and plant new churches.
>
> The Abilene Mission church meets Sunday mornings in a room of the Abilene Civic Center. Upon walking in from the parking lot, one is greeted by several people who introduce themselves and provide an informational brochure about the church. Inside there is more greeting and people are encouraged to have refreshments.
>
> The service begins when five song leaders invite everyone to join in praise. The words of the devotional-type songs are flashed on a screen by an overhead projector. Reg Cox, graduate student and part-time counselor at ACU, gives the announcements, and there is loud applause at the news of the birth of a baby whose mother has had complications over the past few weeks. Cox encourages people to join in the worship at their own comfort level. Most of the nearly 250 people remain standing during the half-hour or so of singing and dramatic Scripture reading.
>
> The 30 or so children present are then assembled for a lesson on the "seed" and the "word," and each child is given a seed. The high point of the lesson comes after the seeds have been planted and a seven-foot canvas is raised on which a tree and fruit have been painted. The children then go to a Bible class.

A Nigerian family tells about how the mother was cured of cancer following a prayer and fasting. She was provided money by the President of Nigeria for a trip to a London hospital where prayer turned her near-death condition into one of health.

Then Smith brings a lesson from Mark 1-3 in which Jesus is shown acting in the lives of people who acknowledge that they are helpless before him. (Passages of Scripture and this message will be discussed during small-group sessions on Sunday evening where communion also will be served.) No invitation concludes the sermon, but families are stationed in all corners of the building, so that people may go there for prayer after services. If anyone is interested in knowing more, he or she is invited to Sunday evening sessions at someone's home.

"Seeker-sensitive," is how Cox describes the congregation. He believes that the unchurched in Abilene do not feel comfortable in a traditional church setting or even with a traditional church name. He wants this Sunday service to be a bridge to the unchurched, so that a deeper relationship with God can follow. "I'm excited that we can do real live evangelism in Abilene, Texas," says Cox. The church has met since May and has had several baptisms.

Noting, too, that people had been praying for a year concerning this work, Cox says, "This church is about prayer. Every day from 5 to 7 a.m. a group prays. This is the missing link in most church work."

A seventh-generation of the Restoration Movement and the son of a preacher in the Middle West, Smith emphasizes that he is working "to restore wholeness to a broken world by the power of Jesus Christ." He believes that in North America, authentic community is almost unknown.

One of the innovations in the church concerns the use of women. The five-member group song leaders is made up of three men and two women. The teacher of the children's class before the congregation is a woman, and the reader of the Scriptures over the public address system is a woman. Smith believes that in North America in the 20th century for women to read Scriptures or help with the singing is not usurping authority.

The Minter Lane church, Abilene, planted the Mission church. Its leaders meet once a month with the Minter Lane elders to discuss the work and pray together.

The Abilene Mission church tries different strategies and abandons those which do not work. At the heart of this effort is an attempt to provide some ideas for congregations wanting something more than they presently have, but without violating Scripture.

— Editor, Jack Welch

The present writer does not question the motives of those initiating and conducting the services of this church. Without mention of other highly questionable acts performed at this service, I would point only to the most glaring and evident way in which certain actions were totally and unmistakenly out of line with scriptural admonition and precedence. It was stated, in explanation and in an evident attempt at justification, that "Mr. Smith believes that in North America in the 20th century for women to read scriptures or help with the singing is not usurping authority." This is said in spite of God's explicit message otherwise.

> "let the women keep silence in the churches: for it is not permitted unto them to speak; but let them be in subjection, as also saith the law" (I Cor. 14:34).

Mr. Smith should know, as all who stand firmly for biblical principles, that from time immemorial people have used that same excuse for avoiding obedience to God: **but I believe.** " He should know that one's personal belief does not change even slightly what God approves. His directions for man's actions and consequent spiritual welfare were written **for all people of all subsequent generations** from the time they were first penned until the end of time, including the 20th century. If something was wrong in the church which the apostles directed under the supervision of the Holy Spirit, that same thing is wrong today.

Just as the Constitution of the United States applied to the generation living when the law was written, it applies equally today. It cannot be changed except through amendments by consent of the nation's people. In many instances today, the courts are twisting the construction words of the Constitution trying to make it say something contrary to its original intent. Because of this our courts are overrun, the streets are crime-ridden and general unrest prevails within our country.

God's laws are even more binding than the Constitution and cannot be amended to suit men's ideas. Nevertheless, many would-be Christians seek to justify their actions by what they believe, thus wresting the scriptures to the destruction of themselves and also taking others with them. Of such, the apostle Peter warned:

> "knowing this first, that in the last days mockers shall come with mockery, walking after their own lusts" (II Peter. 3:3).

> "... Paul also, according to the wisdom given to him, wrote unto you, as also in all his epistles, speaking in them of these things; wherein are some things hard to be understood, which the ignorant and unstedfast wrest, as they do also the other scriptures, unto their own destruction" (II Peter 3:15,16).

To maintain its purity, the church must not allow these innovators, who seek to worship according to their own beliefs rather than by the plainly revealed desires of Him whom they seek to worship, to prevail.

Some may seek to justify their actions in giving way to those who insist on change by saying they are following Paul's example, of which he made this statement:

> "And to the Jews I became as a Jew ... not being without law to God ... To the weak I became weak, that I might gain the weak: I am become all things to all men, that I may by all means save some" (I Cor. 9:20-22).

However, Paul's actions were not parallel to the kinds of activities done by those who actually disobey plainly spoken divine injunctions. Paul did things he was not obligated to do, but things that were not wrong for him to do. He did them to prevent his critics from feeling that he should do those particular things and that by his not doing so, they would thus be hindered in accepting the gospel which he preached.

The two cases cited in Dallas and Abilene, Texas, are examples of extreme and evident unscriptural methods of trying to appease those who consider the longtime manner of worship practiced in churches of Christ as old-fashioned, outmoded, boring and unacceptable today.

There are a few churches of Christ where pacifists are trying in another way to please the demands of those who cry out for change and at the same time not upset those who believe in strict adherence to divine instruction. This is being done by having two worship services on Sunday mornings, one for the so-called "traditionalists" and one for those who want things done in a manner conforming to "contemporary" ideas. This action fosters and encourages a false conception of what it means to please God. Throughout the Bible, both in the Old Testament and the New Testament, God has been exact in His requirements of man. Noah was given exact dimensions and details for building the ark, which provided the means of his salvation from the flood waters. Moses was given exact measurements, materials and minute details of the tabernacle structure, even visibly shown its pattern. Every detail of priestly garments and services was carefully explained. God expected exact obedience. When the tabernacle worship was first begun, He provided a visible and terrifying example of the exactness He demanded when He struck dead instantly Nadab and Abihu. Their sin? They were offering incense made according to God's direction in the place where He prescribed, at the time He directed. What was wrong? They **presumed** to use ordinary fire, "strange" fire rather than the sacred fire sent of God for the use in sacrificial worship. They wanted to do it their way, just as the contemporary worshippers do today.

Concerning God's punishment of Nadab and Abihu, the Lord explained to Moses:

"...I will be sanctified in them that come nigh me, and before
all the people I will be glorified" (Lev. 10:3).

On another occasion many years later, the same lesson again needed to be impressed on the Lord's people. The sacred Ark of the Covenant was being taken to Jerusalem on a cart. Passing over a rough spot, the oxen stumbled and it appeared to Uzzah that the ark was about to topple off the cart. Obeying the natural impulse to prevent this, Uzzah reached up to steady the ark. Immediately, he was stricken dead by God, who from the beginning warned that no one but the high priest was to touch the ark. (See II Sam. 6:7). Uzzah was doing what seemed right to himself, but not what was in accord with God's instructions.

During the period described in the book of "Judges," there was a time when after Samson's death there was no ruler in Israel (Judges 21:25). Every man did that which was right in his own eyes. God was displeased because His commands, made for man's good, were disregarded. The natural result was a pervading atmosphere throughout the land of unrest, moral decay, and extreme chaos.

It is a sad fact that today in our own once predominantly Christian nation, large segments of society are doing exactly what Israel was doing, regulating (rather justifying) its own conduct by seeking to determine what is right in its own eyes. It is this attitude, spawned in part, by the feminists' successful efforts in persuading many women that they should in all things be equal to men, that some women in the church, as well as men, fail to understand the God-given role of women in the furtherance of Christianity. Although the souls of men and women are of equal value in God's sight, He has prescribed separate spheres of activity for each within the church. For women to disregard this fact and insist on being allowed to participate within the realm of worship God planned for men only, or for the elders whose responsibility is to guard the purity of the church, to allow women to do so, amounts to a sin of presumption, which like all sins, is cause for divine disapproval and eventual punishment.

A discussion of women's work in the church as prescribed by divine revelation will be discussed in a later chapter.

An article was published in "Image" (Sept/Oct '93), a religious publication. The article was entitled "Worship in Transition." The article was a brief adaptation of a speech delivered by Jack R. Reese during a conference at Harding University in Searcy, Arkansas.

The discussion was about the "emotionally-laden and potentially divisive" nature of the current issue of demands for change put forth by some in the Christian brotherhood. The speaker related various types of attitudes which were demonstrated through his conversations with many different individuals in the church. One such person held membership in a congregation which had two morning assemblies — one a "traditional type of worship," the other catering to those desiring a "contemporary type of worship."

Saddened to the point of weeping, this person being interviewed tried to verbalize his frustration. Among other things, he expressed his feeling by saying that with each passing Sunday, he felt to a greater and greater extent that he was an outsider, a visitor in his own home church. He said, "I'm not a far right-winger. I am open to change and can live with different expressions of worship as long as they are biblical. I'm not sure that any single thing we are doing is wrong, but I don't understand why we are doing them, why the assembly seems more a time for entertainment than worship." Although he and his wife continue to attend the "traditional" service, he said he felt punished for having gone. "It's like the worship committee tries to make our services as boring as possible. It's clear around here that 'traditional' is not acceptable, not as spiritual as contemporary."

He said that many of his friends had been long-time members of that congregation but had started attending elsewhere, and that the wife of one of the staff-members of that congregation had remarked, "It's probably best that they are gone."

By contrast, Mr. Reese told of another conversation with a preacher who represents the attitude of many of those pushing for a change from the "traditional" way of worship to a "contemporary kind of worship." Here is a portion of this preacher's response. "Our assemblies no longer connect with the outside world—if they ever did. Worship services are thoughtlessly thrown together. Most of the songs reflect the rural 1930s—or, in some instances, 18th century England—but not the 1990s in urban America. The preachers use Church-of-Christ jargon, which outsiders can't relate to. It's not surprising that so many people—especially Baby Boomers—are leaving. They used to live with it patiently. But they're not going to tolerate it any longer."

Note that this preacher himself used a denominationally-slanted expression "Church-of-Christ jargon," seemingly not understanding that the terms used in the biblical preaching of the gospel in the church today are the same terms used by the Holy Spirit in conveying God's message to His people. "Church-of-Christ jargon" casts dispersion on God's terms. Terms commonly used in the church have been understood by people through centuries among all classes and people of all cultures. They may not have been appreciated, but they were understood. Those would-be Christians of the baby-boomer generation are unable to understand because they look through worldly eye-glassses and are thus spiritually blinded. Their efforts seem not to be seeking the truth but hoping to fulfill their responsibility to God in a way pleasing to themselves. These are like the people of old who insisted on continuing their lives as they pleased, scorning the warnings sent from God.

The nation of Israel had turned away from God and the people worshipped as they pleased. God sent His prophet who condemned the heedless nation:

> "Hear now this, O foolish people and without understanding, that have eyes, and see not; that have ears, and hear not: Fear ye not me? saith Jehovah: will ye not tremble at my presence ...?" (Jer. 5:21,22).

The people remained unmoved by Jeremiah's warnings, but God continued to send other prophets to proclaim His message:

> "Son of man, thou dwellest in the midst of the rebellious house, that have eyes to see, and see not, that have ears to hear, and hear not; for they are a rebellious house" (Ezek. 12:2)

The people still refused to heed and, therefore as promised, the whole nation was carried away on a long difficult journey far from their homeland away from the temple where God had commanded them to worship. They were now exiles among a people, the masses of whom despised the Jews, God's chosen people. It was 70 long years before any of them could return home. All of this happened, just as the prophets had warned so many times.

Mr. Reese says that the preacher, who was being interviewed and whose words of criticism for the "traditional" type of worship quoted earlier in this writing, was asked what he considered to be the problem today. His response was:

> "The emphasis has been more in doing the right acts of worship in the right manner than on actually experiencing

devotion to God. We have followed certain prescribed patterns but have missed the heart of worship."

If this statement is true, and in many cases it may be, it is a sad commentary on the status of the Lord's church because Jesus said that to please Him, one must "**worship in spirit and in truth**." (See John 4:24). If this preacher's conclusion is correct, then those engaging in such worship are worshipping in truth, but not in spirit. However, this preacher's conclusion involves the matter of his judging his fellow-Christians, which is an act of which man is not truly capable because he cannot judge the motives or inner emotions of others. It may be that the reason that kind of traditional worship in which Christians engage is seen as empty ritual is because the one making the accusation is judging others by his own feelings and lack of spiritual dedication as he, himself, performed what he considered mere ritual. If the accusation is true, it is not because the so-called ritual is wrong but rather because the attitude of the participant is insincere.

When further asked by Mr. Reese what this preacher thought needed to be done to solve the problem, he answered:

"We need to reconsider everything, including women's public role and the use of instrumental music. Of course I want to be biblical...I have no intention of selling out the authority of the Bible to the latest fads of contemporary culture. But I'm not convinced that our traditional views have themselves adequately reflected the meaning of Scripture."

I would like to know how this gentleman can keep from being "unbiblical," as he says he doesn't want to be, when he advocates a course of action in absolute opposition to a precise simple divine announcement:

"let the women keep silence in the churches: for it is not permitted unto them to speak..." (I Cor. 14:34).

It is evident that Paul was speaking of the public assembly. Priscilla, with her husband Aquilla, taught Apollos, an eloquent preacher and a man versed in the scriptures, but they did the teaching privately. They "took him unto them and taught him the way of the Lord more accurately." However, Priscilla, who was a Christian, was "in the church" because a Christian is always in the body of Christ, which is the church. See Acts 18:24-26. This is proof that Paul used the term "in the church," meaning in the public assembly.

Furthermore, this preacher said, "I have no intention of selling out the authority of the Bible." Yet, where does he find authority in the Bible for instrumental music in the worship? Jesus said all authority had been given to Him. In the New Testament He revealed the kind of music He desires. For something to be done by one's authority, it must be dictated by that person. Jesus did not give any authority for the use of instrumental music in the worship.

Regarding the man just quoted, Mr. Reese commented in his writing:

> "He is kind and gracious but obviously impatient with the current state of affairs. He expresses some frustrations that our Christian universities are not supportive enough of worship renewal. He doesn't plan to leave the Restoration Tradition; but increasingly, he is drawn to resources among large evangelical churches."

The dissatisfied preacher went on in his discussion to search for words with which to describe what he wants to experience during worship. He said:

> "The word 'mystical' might be too strong, but it moves in the right direction. I want worship that is sacramental — that believes God actually encounters his people in worship. I have no interest in gimmicks, flash, or entertainment. I love most of the contemporary songs, but I also desire hymns that exhibit more than emotive simplicity, hymns with a rich theology that roots the church not only in the Bible but in the heritage of Christians in the past."

> "I desire worship that encourages silence as well as singing, confession and lament as well as praise, that does not partake of the shallowness of popculture but at the same time is not stilted, 'high church,' or irrelevant."

Evidently this man has not enjoyed and been blessed with the kind of experiences that many so-called "traditionalists" feel when they engage in the manner of worship exemplified by the worship of early Christians as they were led by the Holy Spirit through the apostles.

Jesus promised that when two or three of His followers meet in worship, He will be in their midst (Matt. 18:20). When a worshipper worships "in spirit," recognizing that He is in the very presence of Jesus in a special way, what more does one need in order to feel the awesome atmosphere of the occasion? A partaker of the communion bread and fruit of the vine—does not he have a "personal encounter" spiritually with Christ, who told His apostles at the Last Passover Supper before His crucifixion that He would not again drink the fruit of the vine with them "until that day when I drink it with you in My father's kingdom"? If this preacher is hoping for some miraculous exhibition of Jesus' presence, some strange spiritual experience, some kind of direct personal recognition or revelation, that hope will never come to fruition until Jesus returns to judge all mankind of all the ages. (I Cor. 13:8-13; Jude 3).

I would ask, "How can we find hymns 'with a rich theology' that are rooted in the Bible and our Christian heritage, as the preacher desires, more so than such hymns as 'What Can Wash Away My Sins?,' 'Amazing Grace,' 'Whiter Than Snow,' 'What A Friend We Have In Jesus' and so on and on?" These and many other similar songs have been sung and enjoyed by generations and are just as relevant today as when first written. However, the use of such songs does not prevent using other "psalms, hymns and spiritual" songs of more recent vintage. In fact, many other songs written in language commonly used today are used and have been for some time, by the so-called "traditionalists." One such song that has gained wide use is "Our God — He is Alive." There are many others. Just examine new song books used in many congregations.

Still another preacher whom Mr. Reese quoted seems to have made a pertinent statement in summation of the matters that had been discussed. He said:

> "The fundamental problem is that a group of young leaders has arisen more influenced by culture than the Bible. A **generation of untaught, unprepared, and unconcerned**

> **brethren** are influencing our people **from the pulpit and the classroom.** Their concern for social acceptance has helped to erode the very foundation of our faith — biblical authority."

We cited earlier in this chapter two explicit examples of such cases.

Mr. Reese commented on some kinds of activities that have been employed in some congregations that are trying to satisfy those who are vociferously demanding change.

> "Some churches have choirs and dramatic skits on a regular basis. Many members clap their hands with the music or at the end of a song. Some members raise their hands during singing and prayers, giving the whole service a Pentecostal flavor. More and more churches allow singing during the taking of communion. Preachers invite members - men and women - to the front to give testimonials... All of these are a departure from biblical authority."

Not only are these actions a departure from biblical authority, but they exhibit rebellion against that authority — in most cases perhaps not a conscious rebellion, but due to insufficient knowledge and understanding of His word, these efforts are made to further God's cause by catering to those who are under the false impression that women must be liberated to fill places formerly occupied by men. These are efforts to add to the church through the ingenuity of man, rather than of converting sinners through the God-given process of conviction of guilt and acceptance of God's plan of salvation. Any attempt to sidestep following God's directions is sadly and disastrously misguided.

Concerning those few congregations which hold two morning services, one "traditional" and one "contemporary" in an effort to please both, I would ask that serious consideration be given to Paul's warning to Christians in Rome:

> "Now I beseech you, brethren, mark them that are causing the divisions and occasions of stumbling, contrary to the doctrine which ye learned: and turn away from them. For they that are such serve not our Lord Christ, but their own belly..." (Rom. 16:17,18).

The conflicting nature of the two services sends forth the message that both types of worship are acceptable to God. This is not true in the light of scripture. The result has been division in the church and feelings of dissatisfaction and criticism of one group toward the other. It may even divide families. Observation will make it evident that among the "traditional" worshippers are found mostly more elderly people who have been church members over a long period of time and are much more familiar with the scriptures than those of the younger generation. The "conventional" worshippers will be chiefly the younger generations and new converts. Eventually, if the same procedures continue, the "traditional" worshippers will die and with them the "traditional" or scripturally-guided church will also die and the church will go deeper and deeper into apostasy unless leaders assume more seriously their awesome responsibility of feeding and guarding their flocks.

Also regarding the recent experiments to please both "traditionalists" and those advocating "contemporary" styles of worship, may I inject some comments relative to the terms "traditional" and "contemporary?" The terms are not biblical as relative to Christianity. In the New Testament, the term "tradition" is used only with respect to the Jewish leaders, the Pharisees. Jesus said of them,

> "Ye leave the commandment of God, and hold fast the tradition of men... Full well do ye reject the commandment of God, that ye may keep your tradition" (Mark 7: 8,9).

The tradition of which Jesus spoke is explained in Isaiah's words long before spoken to Israel, and repeated by Jesus to the Pharisees:

> "...This people honoreth me with their lips,
> But their heart is far from me,
> Teaching as their doctrines the precepts of men"
> (Mark 7:6,7).

The Pharisees' tradition was of their own making, "the doctrines of men," not the actual commands of God.

Referring then to those Christians today, who are carefully trying to confine their acts of formal worship to the exact divine commands given by the Holy Spirit and by the examples of New Testament worship as guided by the inspired apostles, the worship of the first Christians cannot biblically be defined as "traditional." The proper designation is "scriptural."

On the other hand to refer to those who seek changes in the manner of church worship as "contemporary," as opposed in essence to "scriptural" is truly nothing new, for there have always been those who advocated change and actually introduced changes, which as was explained in a previous chapter of this book resulted in the great apostasy and almost complete corruption of the church from which it has required centuries, countless suffering and much martyrdom of those who sought to rescue it and restore the purity of doctrine existing in the beginning of the church.

There are those in the church who whould seek to justify introducing innovations such as dramatic skits, special choral groups, and other changes into the worship of the service by the time-worn excuse, "The Bible does not say, 'you must not do these things.'" This is a sad rejection of a reasonable deterrant, the recognition that God's words deal more with establishing principles than with minute specified actions. For instance, He did not say, "Thou shall not waste your time and corrupt your sensitivity to evil by attending trashy movies or watching soap operas or T.V. talk shows which depict every kind of sensual and worldly behavior known to man." Instead, God simply announced a principle by which such conduct is condemned.

> "Finally, brethren, whatsoever things are true, whatsoever things are honorable, whatsoever things are just, whatsoever things are **pure**, whatsoever things are lovely, whatsoever things are of good report; if there be any virtue, and if there be any praise, think on these things" (Phil. 4:8).

God did not say, "If you can fare better by depending on what the civil government doles out than by working to earn your living, then accept the welfare money. After all, you have a right to it." No, instead God announced a principle:

> "For even when we were with you, this we commanded you,
> If any will not work, neither let him eat" (II Thess. 3:10).

Jesus exhorted the faithful to trust in God and serve Him, realizing that He who provides for the birds and lilies of the field tells mankind to be not anxious regarding their concern for the necessities of life, because of His promise to those who would please Him:

> "But seek ye first his kingdom, and his righteousness; and all these things shall be added unto you" (Matt. 6:33).

God did not say "You may not be able to get people interested in coming to church by following the plan of worship given to you by My instructions through the apostles and their example. Nevertheless, I forbid you to use skits, choirs and other schemes of Satan to lure them." No! Instead God gave us an example of the kind of worship He desires. He gave us a pattern of that worship just as He gave Moses on Mt. Sinai, not only verbal detailed descriptions of the tabernacle and proper items for worship therein, but He showed Moses a visual image of the tabernacle as it should appear when completed. Then Moses was told:

> "And see that thou make them after their pattern, which hath been showed thee in the mount" (Exodus 25:40).

The writer to the Hebrews referred to this scripture when he was comparing the covenant of the Old Testament and the new covenant of the Christian Dispensation. Every detail of the tabernacle and related worship therein was a type of the church and Christian worship. As God's people were given the details of the worship they were to render to God under the Mosaic covenant, so in the Christian Dispensation God's people have been given the specific items of worship which He desires. These consist of regular assembly, preaching, prayer, singing, monetary contributions, observance of communion with Christ through the memorial which He instructed, that is, partaking of the bread and fruit of the vine, all of which activities are to be done by the worshipper in a spirit of awe, thanksgiving and reverence in recognition of the majesty, power and compassion of the supreme Being who made possible man's redemption from sin and eternal condemnation.

Real worshippers come together to manifest the joy of fellowship with each other and their desire to proclaim the marvelous magnificence of a supreme Being who manifested His love and concern for mankind by the unthinkable ordeal of an innocent Jesus suffering and dying on the cross. True worshippers gather to express heart-felt emotions, not to be entertained. True worship must involve personal activity. It is not a passive spectacular activity.

> "The 'user-friendly' religion of today seems a far cry from the demands of the Man of Galilee. Something has gone haywire when 'serving God' has been twisted to 'servicing the self.' But that's where the emphasis often lies— even within the walls of the church house. The challenge to grow calls forth entertainment in lieu of worship, and recreation in place of character development and service. Sermons take on the flavor of Dale Carnegie rather than the apostle Paul, and singing psalms, hymns and spiritual songs gives way to Broadway show stoppers with featured stars, bands and special lighting effects. Time was when belief changed behavior, and Christians changed the culture. I wonder if that time will ever come back?"
>
> — John Gipson

We seem to have lost sight of the fact that the worship service is primarily an occasion for those who already are Christians, not for the purpose of converting sinners. It is an occasion where Christians are to encourage and strengthen each other through discussion of Biblical truths. Conversion of sinners requires going to them, making contact with them wherever there is opportunity.

If God had placed in the Bible a distinct "Thou shall not—" for every act possible in man's conduct, His book would be so big and cumbersome that one would never be able to read its contents or even handle the book. The wiser course was to instruct by principles which could be applied to every situation that might occur.

In summation of refutation that anything not specifically prohibited is acceptable, note should be taken of these warnings:

> "Ye shall not add unto the word which I command you, neither shall ye diminish from it, that ye may keep the commandments of Jehovah your God which I command you" (Deut. 4:2).

> "What thing soever I command you, that shall ye observe to do: thou shalt not add thereto, nor diminish from it" (Deut. 12:32).

Since the time when Adam and Eve introduced sin into the world, fleshly man has fought a constant battle to remain independent, free from authority. Christian life is basically learning to submit to an authority higher than one's own. In all matters, whether in the manner of worship or in the decisions of one's personal life, lasting success and moral victory lie in the development of complete and humble humility to do the will of God. All who desire to serve God acceptably must respond to the same call made to Israel by the prophet long ago:

> "Thus saith Jehovah, Stand ye in the ways and see and ask for the old paths, where is the good way; and walk therein, and ye shall find rest for your souls..." (Jer. 6:16).

Let us not be like Israel who said, "We will not walk in it."

It becomes evident, then, that the conflict between those who seek to be directed strictly by the scriptures and those who seek to add innovations of various kinds is a conflict older than the church itself. It has been rightly said that the apostasy of the church is only a generation away. Unless Christians of today preserve the purity of the church regarding both doctrine and practice, the purity of the church in doctrine and practice of future generations is in jeopardy. The church has always been, and always will be at crisis, as long as this world stands because Satan never ceases from his dastardly purpose of destroying the church.

Most people recognize from the media, that those who stand for morality in the public arena, are implied to be, if not openly accused, of being narrow-minded, unreasonable bigots trying to bind their personal beliefs upon society. There are some who have been wise enough to enter the "narrow gate" of which Jesus spoke and are therefore within the church, but sad to say, they advocate changes in the teachings and practices of the church that are not according to admonitions and instructions of the scriptures. These persons consider others, who insist on staying in the "old paths" established by the apostles through guidance of the Holy Spirit, as being unreasonable and merely adhering to tradition. This attitude is based on the assumption that the Bible's meaning for us today is different that what it meant for those in days of old, and that the dynamics of one's relationship with God depend on the interplay of emotions involved. Therefore worship must involve the element of entertainment, excitement and attention-getting so that the worshipper is not bored with repetitions week after week of similar experiences.

Those advocating change seem to consider worship to be a spectator activity, but in God's plans worship is to be a participating experience. It appears that those persons have never felt the overpowering emotions of deep appreciation for deliverance from a disastrous fate and the gratitude due God for that deliverance. They evidently have not experienced the restraint needed to withhold the tears of emotion when singing about the suffering of Christ on our behalf that we might be saved. They evidently have not felt the awesome presence of God as they lifted their thoughts in prayer to an everpresent loving God. They evidently have not known the joy of being able to return for God's purposes a portion of the material gain conveyed on them through the kindness of God. They evidently have not felt the deep reverence, awe, and appreciation of God's presence and His mercies when communing with our Savior during the commemoration services of communion at the Lord's table. How sad!

Cannot those who demand such changes, as those previously mentioned and others, realize that it matters not how dramatic is the production of the actors who play the parts of a historical scene? It matters not how perfectly an orchestra performs. It matters not how beautiful are the strains of the organ accompanying songs or solo presentations. It matters not how well the singers harmonize or the soloist sings. It matters not how ornate or distinguishing are the robes of the choir or so-called clergy. It matters not how appealing to the body rhythms are the sounds of the bands. All of these things may appeal to the fleshly appetite, but they do not influence the spiritual emotions as God intended His worship to be. They are not authorized by His word. They are intrusions and obstructions to the pure worship God desires. They are displeasing and unacceptable to Him.

I Don't Get Anything Out Of The Services

Has worship become a lost art? I'm afraid that many of us go through the motions without ever really reaching out to God. Consequently, we tend to leave a service much as we came in. Before long there is the tendency to dismiss the whole concept of assembling for worship. At its best it is boring. At its worst it is almost unbearable. So we throw up our hands, discard church attendance, and find something to do that we really enjoy.

We see others that truly look forward to the experience, but for the life of us we can't figure out why. Yet deep down we suspect that maybe we are the losers. Why is it that for so many folks worship services are the high points of their week? Are we made of different clay? Or is it that we don't know the first thing about what they are doing?

I have discovered that true worship demands preparation. How can anyone be in the right frame of mind if he has stayed up late Saturday night, forced himself out of bed with the sound of the alarm, argued with his wife, and threatened his children with death if they don't get a move on? This is followed by piling into the car, driving faster than we should, arriving late, and having to stumble over people sitting on the ends of the pews to find a seat in the middle. And to add insult to injury, the preacher stands up and delivers a sermon on giving. I'm angry when I come in, and mad when I leave. It would take a miracle for me to get anything worthwhile out of a situation like that.

On the other hand, let's suppose that I get a good night's sleep on Saturday. I awake feeling refreshed. I have time to get ready without rushing. I arrive early (If I had my way one would have to park the car and walk about a block on a winding sidewalk through the trees to reach the front door of the church house) and greet the other worshipers. I take my seat with several minutes to spare. During this time I read the scriptures, meditate and pray. When the service does start I am in the spirit. I receive a blessing because I have prepared myself to receive a blessing.

The fault, dear Brutus, is not in their service. It's in ourselves.

— John Gipson

Divine history records the story of King Saul, who failed to obey exactly what God had commanded him to do. God told him through Samuel to completely destroy the Amalekite nation and even all of its livestock because the nation had acted in opposition to the nation of Israel, God's people. Saul followed God's instructions except that he brought back to Israel the Amalekite king and the best of their sheep and oxen. Upon his return, Saul said to Samuel, "I have carried out the command of the Lord."

But Samuel replied, "What then is this bleating of the sheep in my ears, and the lowing of the oxen?"

Saul tried to shirk his responsibility by blaming what was done on others, just as many often do today, when they do wrong. He said, "The people spared the best of the sheep and oxen to sacrifice to God."

Samuel spoke God's condemnation on Saul, telling him that because of his lack of complete obedience, God had rejected Saul as the king of Israel in that his descendants would not continue on the throne after Saul's death. Samuel's reprimand of Saul is one that every generation, if it is to please God, must understand and by it be guided in serving God. The sin of Saul was so heinous in Samuel's sight that he refused any further communication with Saul for the remainder of Samuel's life. Let us hear and heed the message given to Saul.

> "And Samuel said, Hath Jehovah as great delight in burnt-offerings and sacrifices, as in obeying the voice of Jehovah? Behold, to obey is better than sacrifice, and to hearken than the fat of rams. For rebellion is as the sin of witchcraft, and stubbornness is as idolatry'..." (I Sam. 15:22,23).

From this incident and Samuel's statement, it is evident that God intended that we be impressed with the need for strict obedience in all things as well as when the question of making changes in the manner of church worship is considered. Change cannot have God's approval if, even in one detail, it conflicts with God-given instructions for worship or any other matter.

Prejudicing the Issue

Recently a man who advocates radical changes in the teaching and practice of the Church said: "I used to think 'Come now, let us reason together' meant something to our brethren." He then commented on his difficulties in convincing conservative brethren of his position -- they were narrow-minded and unreasonable.

We increasingly are hearing such prejudicial statements against those who advocate conservative positions. The usual tact used by those who cry for change assumes that the Bible does not mean for us today what it said for the people in antiquity, that it was only a socially molded revelation and that the dynamics of one's relationship with the Lord depend upon the emotions or the entertainment factor involved.

Admittedly, some conservative people are uncritical in their thinking and seem to retain certain beliefs and practices simply because these have "always" been. But uncritical thinking occurs in every spectrum of belief. God expects people to think, to reason, to discern what His word says. Paul blasted the Corinthians for their arrogance (I Cor. 5-6). The character of that arrogance is not revealed, but a fair inference is that some Corinthians believed that they were so liberated and open-minded that they could tolerate even an incestuous relationship in their midst and remain unscathed (I Cor. 5:1-8). Paul demanded a drastic disciplinary approach to deal with this aberrant behavior. He further emphasized the need for restraint and self-control and decreed that those who behave contrary to God's will would fail to inherit the kingdom of God (I Cor. 6:9-10).

In these statements, Paul implies that boundaries exist beyond which people may not pass and still remain faithful to God. Somewhere along the line there must be conservatism

—a resistance to change—if that change ignores the boundaries of what God has established. But many people prejudice the issue by implying that people who are not in favor of change are unreasonable.

Jesus once declared "Enter by the narrow gate..." (Matt. 7:13). Our desire should be to be as narrow as he demands and as broad-minded as he allows. When the Lord pleads: "Come now, let us reason together" (Isa. 1:18), we must remember that he sets the terms of reason, not we.

— Dale W. Manor

As for changes, yes, I freely admit we can have changes, but only regarding matters with which absolute guidelines have not been revealed in the scriptures. In matters of judgment and opinion, there is freedom for changes, but in matters of divine authority, we must not waver. We can vary the order in which various items of worship are done. We can vary the places and times of worship services as long as they are on the Lord's day. We can vary the songs we sing as long as they are of a spiritual and reverent nature. The divine injunctions require psalms, hymns and spiritual melodies. They are to reverberate from human heart strings and voice the praise and glory of God, gratitude for His love and blessings, the joy of forgiveness through Christ, or many other sentiments experienced by the servants of God. There are a multitude of matters in which God has left us the freedom to choose our way of worship, but in the public assembly we must abide by His immutable laws if we hope for His approval.

I would suggest that the really big change that may be needed is a strong change in attitude in the hearts of some of the church members rather than a change in the manner of worship. Christians, and the church as a whole, must realize that the sole purpose for which Christ died was that humanity might be delivered from the clutches of Satan and from the same damnation that Satan and his followers will suffer throughout eternity.

Since God, Himself, provided that means of salvation and since He revealed to us the nature of that means as well as the way to achieve access to that means, those who expect His promised reward must be willing to accept both in faith and practice His instructions for accomplishing His purpose.

Jesus' command given to His apostles, and passed from them to us, was to

"Go... make disciples of all the nations, baptizing them into the name of the Father and of the Son and of the Holy Spirit: teaching them to observe all things whatsoever I commanded you..." (Matt. 28:19,20).

By divine guidance Paul told Timothy how to carry out this command:

"preach the word; be urgent in season, out of season; reprove, rebuke, exhort, with all longsuffering and teaching. ... be thou sober in all things, suffer hardship, do the work of an evangelist, fulfill thy ministry" (II Tim. 4:2-5).

Too often in congregations today, the chief efforts seem to be publicizing the places and times of assembly of the church and inviting others to attend. Sad to say, much effort often is needed just to persuade **all members** to be present at all services. This should not be necessary. The divine purpose of the church assembly was for the further teaching and encouragement of those who have accepted the call of the gospel and to help them unite in their efforts to go out among the world and make this gospel message known.

Jesus said, "Go." Too often, the church only says, "Come."

The purpose of Christ's death and the gospel message was not to make "church attenders." The purpose was to reveal the fact that, without access to acceptance and dependence on Christ, every individual who grows to reach the age of accountability is destined to eternal destruction. The church is the **result** of obedience to the gospel - **not the drawing power** by which souls are saved. Jesus is the drawing power.

Jesus said, "And I, if I be lifted up from the earth, will draw all men unto myself" (John 12:32).

The divine directions for worship were for activities of those who were already Christians by reason of having obeyed the gospel invitation. Since visitors and children of adult Christians are usually present at worship services, it is proper that the gospel message inviting sinners to become Christians should be given regularly and from time to time be more minutely explained, but the church cannot depend on worship services as the chief means of carrying out the great commission.

Many congregations recognize this truth and are using various ways to carry out the divine command. New Testament examples mention public preaching in places other than the private meetings held among Christians for worship. Missionaries Paul, Barnabas and Silas went to the synagogues where Jews met on the Sabbath and preached. When the great persecution arose in Jerusalem, Christians fled to other areas "preaching the word" wherever they found opportunity (Acts 8:1-4). Peter preached to a household and others in the house of Cornelius (Acts 10). Philip taught one man the gospel (Acts 8:26-39). Note that Paul even taught the word of God in a secular school:

> "... he withdrew from them [those that became hardened and disobedient] and took away the disciples, reasoning daily in the school of Tyrannus. And this took place for two years..." (Acts 19:9,10).

Jesus left the avenues of teaching the gospel message open to men's judgment and ingenuity. Therefore, different means, in addition to the scriptural examples of New Testament means of public speaking and individual teaching are often now employed. Churches use T.V. ministries, radio ministries, home studies, printed literature, hospital and person-to-person ministries and other means of instruction. However, these do not change the God-given pattern of worship. With that, we dare not tamper.

After individuals have accepted the gospel, there is need that they be instructed as to the differences between the church that Jesus built and the various sects, denominations, even cults, all of which claim to be Christian but which, although holding some truths, reject other truths and make additions to scriptural teaching. These varieties of religion exist because of the great apostasy of past ages and the slow recognition of different departures from the truth. Some denominations who claim to follow Christ have yet to recognize some of the errors promulgated by the apostate church, and while in these churches some of these errors have been corrected, many churches still practice digressions from scriptural teaching such as non-autonomous congregations, distinction between clergy and laity, instrumental music and various doctrines directly opposed to biblical teachings and practices.

Congregations calling themselves simply churches of Christ believe that by leaving the idea of reforming the apostate church and being guided by the Bible alone, casting aside all man-made creeds, organizations and persons exerting power over the Lord's church except each congregation's self-appointed elders, the purity of the New Testament church in faith and practice has been restored. This guiding principle has resulted in the present manner of worship conducted in churches of Christ, as well as determining also the necessary characteristics of one who seeks to please God in attitudes and activities of each one's own personal private life and conduct.

In order that all who enter the Lord's church should understand and appreciate these truths, we must have bolder, more inclusive teaching and preaching of the complete will of the Master, not just select bits and pieces of it. We **must** have more decisive and authoritative recognition and refutation in Bible classes and the pulpit of false teachings being circulated throughout the brotherhood. We **must** have more preachers who are willing to speak out with the truth on controversial subjects that are dividing the church. We **must** have willingness to proclaim with firmness the truth with no evasions seeking to appease those who introduce or perpetrate ideas which lead to error. We **must** have **teachers** and **preachers** who are willing to proclaim the God-given truth even knowing that some listeners will be antagonistic. This must be done in a spirit of love and genuine concern for others, not with an acrimonious, pious spirit of egotism or self-emulation, yet with decisiveness, firmness and divinely given authority.

Likewise, we must have more biblical literacy among all church members, more serious dedication and more time spent in personal, private study, meditation and accumulating knowledge and understanding of God's word accompanied by an attitude of humility and submissiveness. We need a quiet and more reverent atmosphere among worshippers before formal services begin, thus fostering a readiness to engage in the privileged period of real communion with God and a renewal of personal dedication. We need people willing to yield to God.

Broken Dreams

As children brought their broken toys
    With tears for me to mend,
I brought my broken dreams to God
    Because he was my friend.

But then, instead of leaving him
    In peace to work alone,
I hung around and tried to help
    With thoughts that were my own.

Soon I snatched them back and sobbed,
    "Why are you so slow?"
"My precious child," he gently sighed,
    "What could I do? You never did let go."

— Margaret Fishback Powers

Allegory

On a dangerous seacoast where shipwrecks often occur, there was once a crude little life-saving station. The building was just a hut and there was only one boat, but the few devoted members kept a constant watch over the sea, and with no thought for themselves went out day and night tirelessly searching for the lost. Many lives were saved by this wonderful little station, so that it became famous. Some of those who were saved, and various others in the surrounding area, wanted to become associated with the station and gave of their time and money and effort for the support of the work. New boats were bought and new crews trained. The little life-saving station grew. Some of the members were unhappy that the building was so crude and poorly equipped. They felt that a more comfortable place should be provided as the first refuge of those saved from the sea. So they replaced the emergency cots with beds and put better furniture in the enlarged building.

Now the life-saving station became a popular gathering place for its members, and they decorated it beautifully and furnished it exquisitely because they used it as a sort of club. Fewer members were now interested in going to sea on life-saving missions, so they hired lifeboat crews to do this work. The life-saving motif still prevailed in this club's decoration and there was a lifeboat in the room where the club initiations were held.

About this time a large ship was wrecked off the coast, and the hired crews brought in boat loads of cold, wet and half-drowned people. They were dirty and sick and represented every skin color under the sun. The beautiful new club was considerably messed up. So the property committee immediately had a shower built outside the club where victims of shipwrecks could be cleaned up before coming inside. At the next meeting there was a split in the club membership. Most of the members wanted to stop the club's life-saving activities as being unpleasant and a hindrance to the normal social life of the club. Some members insisted upon life-saving as their primary purpose and pointed out that they were still called a life-saving station. But they were finally voted down and told that if they wanted to save the lives of all the various kinds of people who were shipwrecked, they could begin their own life-saving station down the coast. They did. As the years went by, the new station experienced the same changes that had occurred in the old. It evolved into a club, and yet another life-saving station was founded.

Today, you will find a number of exclusive clubs along that shore. Shipwrecks are frequent in those waters—but most of the people drown!

Parable taken from the following source: Story of Theodore Wedel of Washington Cathedral College of Preachers, **The Christian**, Vol. 103 (October 17, 1965), p. 6-7,13.

Throw Out the Life-Line

Throw out the Life-Line across the dark wave;
  There is a brother whom someone should save;
Somebody's brother! O who then will dare
  To throw out the Life-Line, his peril to share?

Throw out the Life-Line to danger-fraught men,
  Sinking in anguish where you've never been;
Winds of temptation and billows of woe
  Will soon hurl them out where the dark waters flow.

Soon will the season of rescue be o'er,
  Soon will they drift to eternity's shore;
Haste then, my brother, no time for delay,
  But throw out the Life-Line and save them today.

— E.S. Ufford

Let the Lower Lights Be Burning

Brightly beams our Father's mercy
  From the lighthouse ever-more,
But to us He gives the keeping
  Of the lights along the shore.

Dark the night of sin has settled,
  Loud the angry billows roar;
Eager eyes are watching, longing
  For the lights along the shore.

Trim your feeble lamp, my brother!
  Some poor sailor, tempest-tossed,
Trying now to make the harbor,
  In the darkness may be lost.

Let the lower lights be burning,
 Send a gleam across the wave!
Some poor fainting, struggling seaman
 You may rescue, you may save.

— P.P. Bliss

CHAPTER SIX

BIBLICAL ILLITERACY

The Restoration Movement culminated in the idea that Jesus' church today must be guided **only by the concept that it must seek in every way to pattern itself both in doctrine and practice according to the church of the first century, as it is revealed in the New Testament.** Those who arrived at this decision did so through a process covering many centuries. Although this was the concept of the New Testament church taught by the apostles, after their deaths, because the recorded scriptures were not available to the masses, most individuals had no opportunity to study the writings of the apostles. Consequently, as the years passed, the doctrines and practices of the church drifted further and further from the truth until eventually over hundreds of years the church became almost totally apostate and morally corrupt. Just as it took centuries to reach this deplorable state, it took added centuries, after the masses gained access to the Bible, for men to discover, bit by bit, the many ways in which the church had strayed and actually forsaken entirely the pure and simple doctrines and practices of the New Testament church. This realization was accomplished only through continuous, concentrated and diligent study of the sacred word by many individuals. The apostasy occurred because men were not able to study God's word for themselves. Their only course seemed to be to follow their teachers, not knowing that by doing so they were following false teaching.

When recalling that the great apostasy occurred because of the lack of access to the scriptures by the masses, Christians today should be tremendously thankful that they have no problem in this respect. They should treasure this privilege of easy access to the Bible so greatly that they would avail themselves of the opportunity to be well informed as to what God desires of them, and therefore study the scriptures diligently and with frequent regularity. But, is this the case?

As we near the dawn of the 21st Century, the church of our Lord and Savior is progressing toward a very threatening and precarious situation because there is widespread and growing scriptural and spiritual illiteracy becoming more and more evident in many congregations of Jesus' church in America. Members of God's family, the church, understand that they were born into this family through the process of profession of faith in Jesus as God's divine Son, by confessing and repenting of past sins and then finally by immersion in water by the authority of the Father, the Son, and the Holy Spirit.

In too many instances, however, these newborn Christians have not made many changes in their everyday lives. Once inside the church, the ark of safety, many seem content to do as they see many others do. They attend most of the services, especially on the Lord's day; they listen quietly during public prayers (often not really hearing or entering into the prayer); they sing; they give of their means (often too little and grudgingly); they partake of the communion bread and fruit of the vine (often seeming to lack a deep truly reverent emotional response), and they listen to a sermon (often with little concentration and hence with failure to look for personal application).

What evidence is there that such a situation exists?

The evidence is seen in those who profess to find little meaning after attending services regularly, and therefore remark that the services are boring.

The evidence is seen when, in multiplied instances, members of the Lord's church admit that they would offer no objection to the introduction of musical instruments into the worship. It is evident that if they are sincere in desiring to please God, they have this attitude because they do not understand why the use of instruments in the worship would displease God.

The evidence is seen in the number of church leaders who know more about what modern psychologists say about human behavior than what is revealed in God's word.

The evidence is seen in church members who attend weekly denominational Bible studies rather than those of the Lord's church.

The evidence is seen in those who can with few qualms absent themselves from the Lord's day worship services because they consider some worldly function to be more important in their own lives.

The evidence is seen in those that fail to give generously and gladly of their means because doing so would involve a sacrifice on their part.

The evidence is seen in those church members who speak of a preacher as "pastor."

The evidence is seen in those who call "Christians" everybody that calls himself Christian, regardless of his beliefs and practices.

The evidence is seen in "Christian" women who follow, and allow their daughters to follow fashion, even when it dictates mini-skirts, skimpy, tight revealing skirts or immodest shorts.

The evidence is seen when "Christians" engage or allow their children to engage in mixed swimming parties where skimpy, lust-provoking clothing is worn.

The evidence is seen when "Christians" allow their sons and daughters to attend ballroom dances, whether high school proms or otherwise.

The evidence is seen in "Christian" parents who allow their children to participate in all the worldly activities of their associates because "everybody's doing it."

The evidence is seen in the growing number of children from "Christian" families that are lost to the church because parents did not diligently and persistently nourish them with spiritual instruction and personal consecration by example as directed in the holy book.

The evidence is seen when "Christians" spend valuable time watching soap operas, talk shows and most current movies, thus concentrating their thoughts on all kinds of moral filth and immoral conduct.

The evidence is seen in Christians who are more familiar with all the popular movie stars than with Bible truths.

The evidence is seen in "Christians" who choose to fill their minds with worldly concerns, yet know very little about or are not vitally concerned about what other Christians are doing to proclaim the gospel.

The evidence is seen in "Christians" whose chief concern is in sports, or in dedication to being seen as physically attractive, or who give extended time and effort to learn and practice strict adherence to proper nutrition and exercise for the good of the physical body, but who find little time for seeking sufficient and proper spiritual nutrition and participation in exercising spiritual activities for soul saving throughout the world.

The evidence is not only seen, but is loudly proclaimed by those professing to be Christians who have studied the Bible so little that they cannot give a real reason for the faith which they profess.

You may reply in disbelief and surprise, "What an indictment of some church members!" Nevertheless, such is sadly true.

The foregoing accusations are not a bold blanket charge or description of all church members or of all congregations — not even of a majority. But they do apply to a number large enough to merit great concern and present danger recognized by many to the continuance of purity and truth as God wants His gospel to be proclaimed and practiced by His followers.

I am happy to say that there still exists in this country and in other countries over most of the western world, and in an increasing number even among many eastern countries, multiplied thousands of Christians who read and treasure their Bibles. These people enter joyfully into singing praise and gratitude to God out of loving, appreciative hearts. These people regularly attend the worship services. They listen carefully to prayers, joining intelligently and emotionally. These people give generously, thankfully and even sacrificially of the income with which they have been blessed. They partake of the communion bread and fruit of the vine with meditation on its meaning and gratitude to God for the gift of Jesus — the atonement for man's sins; they listen attentively to the proclaiming of God's word during the sermon, expecting to glean instruction and/or encouragement by which their own lives will be enriched and enabled to serve God more abundantly. They leave the worship services with renewed enthusiasm for service in the Lord's vineyard. They are mindful throughout each day of the week until the following Lord's day of their relationship with Christ and fellow Christians. They seek avenues of serving through telling others the good news of the gospel, through helpfulness and concern for the problems of others. They look for ways to let the light of Christianity shine in their personal activities. They are more concerned with serving God than with having fun and catering to the desires of the flesh. They are regular, serious students of God's words, craving more and more knowledge of the scriptures. They convey to their children and others that the most important thing in life is serving God faithfully, and that His way leads to happiness, both now and eternally. They practice what they preach. They discipline themselves and teach their children to do likewise. They seek to do as Paul commanded:

> "And be not fashioned according to this world: but be ye transformed by the renewing of your mind, that ye may prove what is the good and acceptable and perfect will of God" (Rom. 12:2).

A humorous, but truly sad, illustration of common scriptural illiteracy is revealed in this anecdote of one who listed a series of familiar sayings, such as the following, and asked his listeners to find the scripture citation:

> "Money is the root of all evil."
> "Honesty is the best policy."
> "Honest confession is good for the soul."
> "Cleanliness is next to godliness."

Interestingly, everyone began to look diligently, each trying to be the first one to give the answers. After watching for a while the frustration of the searchers, the questioner confessed that none of these statements is found in scripture, although each is rooted in biblical truth.

On another occasion, a minister was asked by a church member, "Where is the scripture that says, 'Every tub shall sit on its own bottom?'" The minister wisely replied, "There is no such scripture but its meaning conforms to biblical teaching," for the prophet Ezekiel declared:

> "The soul that sinneth, it shall die: the son shall not bear the iniquity of the father, neither shall the father bear the iniquity of the son..." (Ezekiel 18:20)

Getting back to serious speaking, all recognize that the physical newborn infant must have adequate nourishment and exercise to survive and grow into a healthy mature adult, and even as an adult, these two things are necessary to maintain life, vigor and health.

The same principles apply to the spiritually newborn, those who are born into the church, the family of God, through the process of obedience to the gospel. The apostle Peter wrote to those who address God as their spiritual Father:

> "knowing that ye were redeemed, not with corruptible things, with silver or gold, from your vain manner of life inherited from your forefathers, but with precious blood, as of a lamb without blemish and without spot, even the blood of Christ ... who through Him are believers in God ... having been begotten again ... as newborn babes, long for the spiritual milk which is without guile, that ye may grow thereby unto salvation" (I Peter 1:18-2:2).

If you, as a Christian, "long for" spiritual nourishment, you will be seeking it at its source, the Bible. You will not confine your attention to learning that which you receive by listening to sermons, two or at the most three each week, and perhaps to Bible classes once or twice a week. Many church members do not even give this much attention to acquiring spiritual nourishment. Even an additional nightly reading of a random biblical passage, or chapter, does not suffice to meet the need of the spiritual growth God desires and expects. One needs not **just to read, but to study** a scripture in order to obtain its full meaning. There is a tremendous difference between reading and productive study.

Many people do not actually know how to study, even if they have a desire to do so. Some necessary guidelines must be utilized before one can properly understand a given scripture.

1. One needs to have a clear concept of the consecutive events in the message of the Bible as a whole, before he can understand how any one selected passage fits into the whole scheme of God's plan for man's redemption.

2. A scripture must be seen in the light of its context. It must retain the same meaning as when first written, when applied to a present situation.

3. The meaning of any selected passage can be clearly and properly understood only when it is understood as it harmonizes with every other scripture bearing on the same subject.

4. A biblical statement must always be taken in a literal sense except when it is evidently and unmistakenly figurative as in such passages when Jesus said, "I am the door" or "I am the bread of life."

5. The attitude of honest study must be "How does this scripture apply to me?" Even though the Bible was written many years ago, its spiritual truths are eternal. Its message is relevant to every individual of every generation. One must not approach a scripture with the attitude, "What do I think this passage means?" One must first determine what the meaning was for the situation when the words were penned. Only then can one search for the lesson as applied to his own situation. God had a reason for having written and preserved every word and portion of the Bible. The diligent Bible student must search for that meaning.

Many people today in a class for study are asked, "What does this passage mean to you?" or "What do you think this passage means?" The class becomes more of a "Talk Show" like many T.V. shows that simply explore human opinions, but never conclude with the positive biblical truth. The question is, "What thoughts did God intend to convey in this verse?" "How do those same thoughts apply to me?"

6. Acceptable Bible study must not be to search for passages which confirm a belief a person holds, but rather to find what God says on a given subject. Then one should accept what He says and forget what the reader may have mistakenly thought the Bible teaches.

7. One's attitude must be not only to **learn** what God expects, but also to **do** what He enjoins — not halfway, not half-heartedly or grudgingly, but rejoicing in gratitude for the wondrous blessings to be obtained through learning and obeying God's will.

8. One must not have the attitude that only scholars of Hebrew, Aramaic and Greek can understand the scriptures. God expected all

people to understand His word. That is why He spoke in the common language of the common people whom He addressed. He did not expect all to be scholars of special training and higher educational attainments. It is true that through a real understanding of these ancient languages, one may find a richer, deeper meaning in a word or phrase, but the general message to all humanity is understandable to all humanity.

Often the suggestion that one should spend more time in Bible study is met with the response, "I'd like to do so, but I just can't find the time." Now, just stop a minute and think about times you could study, but that you may have overlooked. Consider what one man did. He was a man with whom the present writer shared some personal experience in working for the Lord. I have read, though he did not himself reveal this to me, that in his younger days he was a busy farmer, and as he plowed his fields, he would stop his mule at the end of each long row, take a New Testament out of his pocket, read a verse a few times, put the book back in his pocket, proceed to the next row repeating the verse over and over until well memorized. Again and again this process continued, row after row and day after day. This young man later became a very dynamic and successful evangelist, leading countless numbers to knowledge and obedience to the gospel. His name was Gus Nichols.

Consider your daily routine. If you are a homemaker, with what is your mind engaged as you do household chores, dusting, dishwashing, vacuuming? Do you work to the tune of recorded music, radio or T.V. — whatever may be on? If you commute to a daily job, do you immediately turn on the radio as soon as you enter your car? Of course, memorizing scripture is not sufficient study, but having a store of such within the mind and heart provides material for meditation, analyzing and better understanding of other passages when one undertakes more prolonged study. Importantly, the proper scriptures come to mind when temptations arise and give one immediate answers to refuse Satan's inducements.

Of course it was not through memorizing alone that Gus Nichols achieved his knowledge of God's will. Memorizing was augmented by much study as Mr. Nichols labored during sixty-five years in the Lord's service. This study and learning continued through a lifetime. He would readily admit that as he neared life's end, after all these years of preaching the gospel, he was still learning, as should be true of all Christians.

Study in any specialized field requires much time, diligence, continuous and dedicated effort, and often is at the price of sacrificing the satisfaction of other desires deemed less important. Real Bible study, seeking to delve deeper and deeper into the treasures of biblical truths, is no different. I've often heard someone say, "I wish I knew the Bible as well as a certain person does." How to attain that wish should be evident, as shown by this appropriate reply: "If you would seek the opportunity and give as much time, effort and meditation as that person has, you could know as much."

The fact is that for a Christian, Bible study is not optional. Paul's instruction to the young Christian evangelist Timothy and applicable to all was:

> "Study to show thyself approved unto God, a workman that needeth not to be ashamed, rightly dividing the word of truth" (II Tim. 2:15 - KJV).

A newer translation of this passage expresses the same thought:

> "Give diligence to present thyself approved unto God, a workman that needeth not to be ashamed, handling aright the word of truth."

Our society has become one of avoiding hard tasks, unwillingness to labor if at all possible to avoid it. We want quick and easy ways of accomplishment: automatic dishwashers, washing machines and dryers, microwaves, central heating and air conditioning, constant entertainment via T.V., radio or recorded music, etc.

Some people admit: "I don't want silence while I am alone." They fail to realize that such time is an opportunity to meditate and consider life seriously. By inspiration David wrote:

> "Blessed is the man ... whose delight is in the law of the Lord and in His law he meditates day and night" (Ps. 1:1,2).

Common philosophy is: Why write a letter? It's easier to pick up a telephone. Why spend much time in food preparation when T.V.

dinners, minute rice, precooked or partially prepared foods are available, even though the finished product may be inferior to the quality and appeal of that which requires more time and effort? We want instant accomplishment.

This is not to say that these things mentioned as desired to save labor are bad within themselves, but they represent a widespread attitude of constantly avoiding tasks that are challenging or that require much thought or perseverance. This idea has been fostered and widely permeates the attitude of many, especially among the younger generations who are satisfied with mediocrity. Why work so hard to get an A in class when C is a passing grade? Why struggle to learn simple facts of addition and multiplication when a calculator will do it all? Why wait to buy those things I want? I have a credit card.

Too many people feel that they must have instant satisfaction. This is a dangerous philosophy. There is no easy way to learn all that a Christian needs to know and the things God expects one to know and do. Why else would He have given us the Bible and preserved it through the ages? One who truly desires salvation must be willing to put forth effort. Jesus' invitation was:

"Take My yoke upon you, and learn of Me ... " (Matt. 11:29).

A yoke is a means of control. The Christian must resolve and vow to be controlled by the Master's teaching. From whence or how can His teaching be known without study of His word? That is the only absolute, unquestionable source of the truths He has revealed. Bible knowledge cannot be acquired instantly or without a great deal of study and meditation. Without this knowledge and understanding the would-be Christian is unprepared to resist the allurements Satan keeps on constant display. Without Bible knowledge and understanding, the would-be Christian cannot recognize false teaching.

The dedicated Christian must realize the truth of which Paul wrote to the church at Ephesus:

"For our wrestling is not against flesh and blood, but against the principalities, against the powers, against the world-rulers of this darkness, against the spiritual hosts of wickedness in the heavenly places" (Eph. 6:12).

The Christian cannot successfully cope with these powerful enemies without help. From whence must that help come, and how can it be obtained? Paul answered these questions. He explained:

"Wherefore take up the whole armor of God, that ye may be able to withstand in the evil day, and, having done all, to stand" (Eph. 6:13).

Why put on the armor of God? Paul stated two reasons: (1) To enable one to stand firm, so as not be tossed about by every evil wind of doctrine. (2) To enable one to resist in the evil days.

When is the evil day? It is every time that the Christian is tempted to yield to Satan's lures. The evil day is every time the Christian is confronted with false teaching, teaching that does not harmonize completely with God's will as revealed in the New Testament.

Of what does this armor, that the Christian must wear, consist? The first consideration in meeting an enemy is self-protection. Therefore, Paul advised "girding the loins with truth," and putting on the "breastplate of righteousness" (Eph. 6:14).

While still on the earth, Jesus had said:

"... If ye abide in My word, then are ye truly my disciples; and ye shall know the truth, and the truth shall make you free" (John 8:31,32).

Thus, it is seen that through knowledge of the truth and righteousness the Christian is enabled to "stand firm" (Eph. 6:11). These principles are exemplified by Jesus, who soon after his baptism and forty day fast on the mountain, was confronted by Satan who sought to tempt Jesus through every avenue at Satan's command, through:

"the lust of the flesh ... lust of the eye, and the vainglory of life" (I John 2:16).

Totally righteous in heart and conduct, Jesus countered every thrust of Satan with a scripture. Jesus was wielding the "... sword of the Spirit, which is the word of God" (Eph. 6:17). Satan was defeated and Jesus was victorious. Thus truth and righteousness will also prevail in the life of the Christian.

The Christian must have at his command that "sword of the Spirit," the tool of defense, this ammunition needed to resist the fiery darts of Satan. That ammunition is a store of knowledge in mind and heart of God's word, for Paul said the "sword of the Spirit" is "the word of God" (Eph. 6:17). The psalmist wrote:

> "The sum of thy word is truth, And every one of thy righteous ordinances endureth forever" (Ps. 119:160).

> "Let my tongue sing of thy word; For all thy commandments are righteousness" (Ps. 119:172).

Since the only source of "the sum of God's word," and of all of His righteous commandments is the Bible, how necessary it is that Christians store within their minds and hearts the teachings of this precious book!

Paul further instructed regarding other parts of the Christian's armor which are necessary. The feet are to be:

> "shod ... with the preparation of the gospel of peace." (Eph. 6:15).

The feet are for the purpose of moving from place to place. Paul's words indicate that the Christian must be ready for action, having in his heart and mind the knowledge of the facts, exhortations and peaceful results of the gospel when it is allowed to work in the human heart and daily life. Then one is ready and anxious to carry that message to a lost world.

Another part of the Christian's armor is "the helmet of salvation" (Eph. 6:17). A helmet is designed to protect the head against possible danger such as the blows of an enemy. The enemy, Satan, attacks the head, the seat of the mind and direction-giving. Satan's weapons are false teachers who claim to be followers of Christ, but who

> "... will not endure the sound doctrine; but, having itching ears, will heap to themselves teachers after their own lusts; and will turn away their ears from the truth, and turn aside unto fables" (II Tim. 4:3,4).

These teachers who are threats to the purity of the church and to Christianity are further described as:

"holding a form of godliness, but having denied the power thereof ..." (II Tim. 3:5).

Regarding such persons, Paul further warned Timothy,

"... from these also turn away" (II Tim. 3:5).

Paul continued his instructions to the young preacher:

"But abide thou in the things which thou hast learned and hast been assured of, knowing of whom thou hast learned them; and that from a babe thou hast known the sacred writings which are able to make thee wise unto salvation though faith which is in Christ Jesus. Every scripture inspired of God is also profitable for teaching, for reproof, for correction, for instruction which is in righteousness: that the man of God may be complete, furnished completely unto every good work" (II Tim. 3:14-17).

Knowledge of the scripture, then, can impart the wisdom that leads to salvation. What more important reason could be given to emphasize the need for Bible study?

Noticing further the various parts of the armor on which the Christian must depend, Paul wrote:

"withal taking up the shield of faith, wherewith ye shall be able to quench all the fiery darts of the evil one" (Eph. 6:16).

Thus arrayed with the full armor of God to meet the onslaughts of Satan, the Christian is ready to do battle for the sake of his own salvation and the preservation of purity and complete compliance with God's instructions for Christian living and worship.

Long ago, God's people, upon whom He had lavished great blessings, care and special protection, insisted on turning away from allegiance to Him. He warned them repeatedly through his prophets of impending punishment, even to their being carried away into captivity. The prophets begged and pled with the nation to repent. Nevertheless, the people continued in their wicked ways, heedless of the prophets, so that eventually practically the entire nation was carried away into Babylonian captivity.

One of those prophets, whose words fell on deaf and heedless ears, was Hosea. He described the moral condition of the disobedient and immoral nation. Consider carefully Hosea's description of the moral decadence among those who had been God's chosen people.

> "... there is no truth, nor goodness, nor knowledge of God in the land. There is nought but swearing and breaking faith, and killing, and stealing, and committing adultery; they break out, and blood toucheth blood ... Yet let no man strive, neither let any man reprove; for thy people are as they that strive with the priest ... My people are destroyed for lack of knowledge: because thou hast rejected knowledge ... seeing thou hast forgotten the law of thy God, I also will forget thy children. ... Whoredom and wine and new wine take away the understanding. My people ask counsel at their stock, and their staff declareth unto them" (Hosea 4:1-12).

Do the conditions among society of Hosea's day bear any resemblance to conditions in modern society? "Swearing, deception, murder, stealing, adultery, violence, bloodshed and more bloodshed, harlotry, wine, turning from God to idols and diviners" (NASV). Compare with almost any T.V. newscast, or daily newspaper. It's all there! "Let no one find fault" (NASV). The victim's plight is downplayed, while the perpetrator is not at fault; he was himself victimized, so our juries decide. "Contend with the priest" (NASV). Refuse the counsel of God's instructor. He is trying to bind his personal beliefs upon society. He and his kind are narrow-minded bigots, denying others freedom to choose their own ways. Down with their kind! Close their mouths and their church doors!

Hosea said these people "counsel with their wooden idol and their diviners" (NASV). This country was founded by those fleeing religious oppression and whose purpose was to establish a nation which, while giving personal freedom to worship according to one's convictions, based its Constitution and laws on trust in the supreme God, Creator of the universe, as revealed in the Bible. The civil government of this nation was directed to be by the moral concepts given in God's word.

Yet, in this country, due to the influx of aliens, we actually have mosques and temples dedicated to idolatrous worship. We have multiple numbers of man-founded cults and religions claiming belief in Christ; but downplaying or perverting His role in man's salvation. We have hosts of individuals who dutifully consult their astrologists or diviners, who call themselves by various names, but all representing the occult. How similar is modern society to that of Hosea's day? Truly our nation is at risk, as well as the freedom of religious worship or public expression.

National leaders, educators and others vociferously bemoan social conditions and loudly protest that more money or philosophies of various kinds can produce the remedy, refusing to recognize the real cause of the degradation and moral stench of modern society.

Hosea plainly states the cause and makes evident the remedy. Look again at his words:

"My people are destroyed for lack of knowledge, because thou hast rejected knowledge."

"Thou hast forgotten the law of thy God."

It is not only in society in general that this deteriorating moral condition exists, but to a lesser degree, many spiritually immature Christians and even entire congregations are at risk for the same reason. God said through Hosea, "My people are destroyed for lack of knowledge." God's people then were the Jews. Today, God's people are the church. In many places across the land, we see God's people both individually and as congregations being destroyed spiritually through lack of knowledge. Knowledge comes through the study of God's word and putting that knowledge into active service in the Lord's vineyard. This contributes to one's personal spiritual growth and to the expansion of the Lord's church.

The apostle Peter admonished Christians to

"... grow in the grace and knowledge of our Lord and Savior Jesus Christ" (II Pet. 3:18).

I find it interesting to learn that by looking at the rings on a tree after it has been cut crosswise, one can distinguish between the years of drouth and the years of bountiful rainfall during the life time of the tree. Every year of the tree's life produces a ring of some kind, and a tree will grow as long as it lives.

In God's plan for the world of nature, everything must grow and thrive, produce fruit, or accomplish whatever God meant for it to perform. This is true of all plant and animal life, including humanity. How does this relate to a Christian?

Sad to say there are members of the Lord's church who resemble the fig tree which Jesus cursed and which completely withered at once (Matt. 21:19). The tree was covered with leaves, but it bore no fruit. It had the appearance of vitality and health, but it was not serving its God-given purpose for the fig tree should have produced fruit before producing leaves.

As with every living being of God's creation, the newborn Christian must grow in knowledge and spirituality. This growth should be manifest in bearing fruit, as Paul admonished. Christians should be "always abounding in the work of the Lord" (I Cor. 15:58).

If at the end of life, one could examine the growth rings in your or my spiritual life, what would be found? God does just that. I fear that in some lives, no rings would be discernible because they would barely exist. Too few of us grow as God desires, because we do not take enough spiritual nourishment from His words given in His holy book. Neither do some get enough spiritual exercise through Christian service and activity.

Just to be born into God's family through obedience to the gospel and remain in a state of spiritual infancy is even more sad than the condition of a human baby who never grows physically or mentally as God intended babies to grow. It is sad to say of some Christians who were born into the church many years ago that the same condition exists which the writer of the Hebrew letter described thus:

> "... ye are become dull of hearing. For when by reason of the time ye ought to be teachers, ye have need again that some one teach you the rudiments of the first principles of the oracles of God; and are become such as have need of milk, and not of solid food. For every one that partaketh of milk is with-

out experience of the word of righteousness; for he is a babe. But solid food is for fullgrown men, even those who by reason of use have their senses exercised to discern good and evil. Wherefore leaving the doctrine of the first principles of Christ, let us press on unto perfection; not laying again a foundation of repentance from dead works, and of faith toward God" (Heb. 5:11-6:1).

Every confessed Christian should assess his own spiritual growth often. Perhaps that was one of our Lord's purposes in planning that Christians meet each week in worship.

"Try your own selves, whether ye are in the faith; prove your own selves. Or know ye not as to your own selves, that Jesus Christ is in you? unless indeed ye be reprobate" (II Cor. 13:5).

The worship period should be not only a time to recognize the debt we owe our great Benefactor, and a time to praise Him, but it should be a time for internal spiritual evaluation. Note that in admonishing the Corinthians regarding their partaking of communion, Paul wrote:

"But let a man prove himself, and so let him eat of the bread, and drink of the cup" (I Cor. 11:28).

The Bible is the greatest, most precious and wonderful book ever produced. How often God's professed children neglect it, spurning its study by engaging in trivial, even questionable pursuits of worldly enjoyment. May I urge every child of God to be more diligent, more anxious and more determined to give God's service the time and attention needed by self-preparation, through knowledge of His word, to render to Him the respect, reverence and service He desires? If the battle to preserve the purity of the faith and practices of the New Testament church is to be maintained for this generation, and preserved for those of the future, every Christian soldier must arm himself for battle with Satan's host by putting on the whole armor of the Lord and standing true to His teachings, casting aside the arrows of unscriptural change constantly flying from the bows of Satan and his cohorts.

How Do You Read the Bible?

'Tis one thing, friend, to read the Bible through;
Another thing to read, to learn, to do.
'Tis one thing, too, to read it with delight,
And quite another thing to read it right.
Some read it with design to learn to read
But to the subject pay but little heed;
Some read it as their duty once a week,
But no instruction from the Bible seek.
Some read to bring themselves into repute
By showing others how they can dispute;
While others read because their neighbors do
To see how long 'twill take to read it through.

Some read the blessed Book, they know not why
It sometimes happens in the way to lie;
While others read it with uncommon care
But all to find some contradiction there.

One reads with Father's specs upon his head
And sees the things just as his father did;
Another reads through Campbell, Stone, and Scott
And thinks it meant just what they thought.

Some read to prove a pre-adopted creed,
Thus, understanding little what they read;
And every passage in the book they bend
To make it suit that all important end.

Some people read as I have often thought
To teach the Book instead of being taught.

— Author Unknown

CHAPTER SEVEN

GOD'S BLUEPRINT FOR A CHRISTIAN WOMAN

HIS PRIORITY IN CREATING WOMAN

Why is it that a woman, in the interest of fairness, should not expect to have the same opportunity to engage in any reputable enterprise as a means of livelihood that is open to a man? Why should not a woman be able to enter any field of activity, receive equal pay for equal time spent, climb the ladder of achievement to the highest office in a profession on the same basis as a man? Woman is equally capable as man!

So went the reasoning of many women, as well as men, when several decades ago efforts began to focus on passage of the "Equal Rights Amendment." It appeared to many as unfortunate that the long continued and concentrated efforts to pass this amendment failed. However, our nation is reaping the same damaging results as if the amendment had passed, because Satan, who instigated the idea of ERA, is well toward accomplishment of the real goal he hoped to accomplish through ERA. He has found other means to do his dastardly deeds. The primary goal of this evil being has always been to gain supremacy over God, to remove every godly influence and every vestige of Christian influence from the earth, and to establish his reign unhindered forever over mankind. When the hope through the amendment to attain Satan's wicked purposes failed, he turned to other less evident, but equally powerful allies working under cover of pretention of worthy purposes. He used organizations such as American Civil Liberties Union (ACLU), Planned Parenthood, National Education Association, advocates of "Pro Choice" regarding abortion and various radical feminist organizations. All of these alliances claim worthy objectives, but are in truth working toward Satan's goal of destroying the traditional home and influence of Christianity. Working with these organizations is a coalition of homosexuals and lesbians who not only seek personal freedom to live their sensuous and disgusting lifestyle but to bind it on society as acceptable, even desirable.

These evil forces have gone far in accomplishing their devastating role as is evident by the moral decay pervading society as seen in all of the following conditions: the alarming number of broken homes, neglected and otherwise abused children, in wide and open use of drugs, in multiplying and bulging prisons, in gang warfare endangering homes and streets, in a top-heavy and dysfunctioning judicial system, in prevalent dissatisfaction with our schools, in a government that has lost respect of the people and is conducted with greed, graft and inability to function as originally intended. The real objective of the women's liberation movement, beginning with ERA, was not equality but rather achievement of women's power over men, symbols of despotism and would-be dictators to these radical atheistic women. An overview of assembled legislators in Washington D.C. reveals the extent to which women having such views have infiltrated the government and helped to corrupt the highest political and governing powers in the land. Not stopping there, they are even invading the spiritual realm of personal conscience and moral behavior. Psychologically, these newly found positions of power in politics have produced within these women a "little Napolean" complex, which prompts them to seek recognition by their self-proclaimed loud protestations of wisdom, irrespective of the damage resulting in the lives of others throughout our society. Our country would greatly benefit if we could and would return the business and political arenas to the men while women take their rightful places in the home.

It does not take the wisdom of Solomon to see that all is far from well in our land. Why have the comparative peace and general well-being of a few decades ago given way to the alarming state of today's society where it is even dangerous to walk on the street at night, or to drive through the town in broad daylight without fear of being victimized by a casually aimed firearm or a car thief? Why can't our children walk to school safely or enter a school building without fear of gunshot or other assault? Why are our city streets littered with malcontents, drug addicts and homeless? Why are there not jobs enough to go around? Why do those jobs that exist often pay such low wages that it takes two wage earners to provide for a family's needs? Need we go on and on to describe the too familiar deplorable conditions existing in society today?

Perhaps you are asking, "How is all of this related to the subject at hand?" All of these sad circumstances go back in part to a primary consideration of what God intended the role of women, as well as of men, to be in this world and to understand how far away we have strayed. To understand this statement, it is necessary to investigate God's own instructions and revelations as to what He intended to be the role of each gender.

In the first place, note that man was not created to fulfill the needs of woman, but rather woman was created to fulfill the needs of man. Recall this incident that occurred after God made man:

> "And Jehovah God said, It is not good that the man should be alone; I will make him a help meet for him. And out of the ground Jehovah God formed every beast of the field, and every bird of the heavens; and brought them unto the man to see what he would call them: and whatsoever the man called every living creature, that was the name thereof. And the man gave names to all cattle, and to the birds of the heavens, and to every beast of the field; but for man there was not found help meet for him" (Gen. 2:18-20).

After viewing all animals on earth, a fact was evident to man that God already knew. Adam saw that no animal could fill the void that he felt inside him, a need for a companion that would truly be compatible with his need.

To be a help meet for man meant to be a helper suitable to satisfy or fulfill the needs of man. Today many people, especially women, give their pets a status of importance greater than that of their spouses, but though a faithful pet can often contribute to companionship or even to physical safety, no pet can reach the desirable status of a loving faithful spouse.

Because it was recognized by both God and Adam, after viewing all the animals, that no mere animal could perform the function of being a companion suitable for man's needs, God created woman and presented her to man, and she became his wife (Gen. 2:21-25).

Sad to say, although that first woman, Eve, was created to make one suitable for Adam's companionship, she proved herself also to be a liability because she, after having sinned by eating the God-forbidden fruit, led Adam to sin also. Both of them, as well as all following generations, thus became subject to Satan's temptations. Adam and Eve received certain punishments almost immediately after their sin. Note the punishment God pronounced upon Eve and all women. They were to be subjected to pain in childbearing. There was also a second penalty!

"... **in pain** thou shalt bring forth children; and thy desire shall be to thy husband, and **he shall rule over thee**" (Gen. 3:16).

However, along with the punishment, woman was to receive a particular blessing as seen in God's words to Satan:

"and I will put enmity between thee and the woman, and between thy seed and her seed: he shall bruise thy head, and thou shalt bruise his heel" (Gen. 3:15).

The seed of woman (Jesus) was to bruise the seed of the serpent (Satan). This was fulfilled when Jesus died, was buried and three days later rose victoriously from the grave.

Thousands of years later, Paul reminded Christians that

"... the woman is the glory of the man. For the man is not of the woman; but the woman of the man" (I Cor. 11:7,8).

God had in mind certain roles in life for both men and women. Through the apostle Paul, God stated:

"But I would have you know, that the head of every man is Christ; and the head of the woman is the man; and the head of Christ is God" (I Cor. 11:3).

These relationships are not a representation of progressive or retrogressive rank or value, but rather an expression of what God intended for the working out of His purposes for all mankind.

While on the earth, Jesus subjected Himself to God, as Jesus stated to His disciples:

> "I speak not from myself: but the Father abiding in me doeth his works" (John 14:10).

> "Who in the days of his flesh, having offered up prayers and supplications with strong crying and tears unto him that was able to save him from death, and having been heard for his godly fear, though he was a Son, yet learned obedience by the things which he suffered" (Heb. 5:7,8).

God intended that man, in turn, subject himself to Christ. Jesus said to His disciples:

> "... If any man would come after me, let him deny himself, and take up his cross, and follow me" (Matt. 16:24).

Likewise, God intended that woman be subject to man. Paul told Christians in Ephesus:

> "Wives, be in subjection unto your own husbands, as unto the Lord. For the husband is the head of the wife, as Christ also is the head of the church, being himself the saviour of the body. But as the church is subject to Christ, so let the wives also be to their husbands in everything" (Eph. 5:22,24).

In depicting this proper relationship between man and woman, Paul was not saying that man is more valuable in God's sight than woman or that woman is less capable or of less worth in this world than man. Contrary to those ideas, Paul stated the exact opposite to the Christians in Galatia:

> "There can be neither Jew nor Greek, there can be neither bond nor free, there can be no male and female; for ye all are one man in Christ Jesus" (Gal. 3:28).

Although men and women are of equal value as individuals in God's sight, and although women are due the same respect as men in the public's consideration, God created men and women to serve different functions for which He gave each the proper abilities and propensities to fulfill those functions. If each individual remains in that sphere of activity, as divinely intended, all will be happier, more contented, and more pleasing to God. The particularly sad problems such as now are making wreckage of our society would not develop.

It should be kept in mind that Paul's words regarding the marriage relationship were addressed to Christians. Continuing on, after the admonition to wives, Paul wrote:

> "Husbands, love your wives, even as Christ also loved the church, and gave himself up for it; that he might sanctify it, having cleansed it by the washing of water with the word, that he might present the church to himself a glorious church, not having spot or wrinkle or any such thing; but that it should be holy and without blemish. Even so ought husbands also to love their own wives as their own bodies" (Eph. 5:25-28).

Peter admonished Christian husbands thus:

> "Ye husbands, in like manner, dwell with your wives according to knowledge, giving honor unto the woman, as unto the weaker vessel, as being also joint-heirs of the grace of life; to the end that your prayers be not hindered" (I Pet. 3:7).

Note that the husband, who fails to honor, protect and provide for his wife in keeping with the divine admonition, will be so displeasing to God that God may not answer the man's prayers. Husbands should take care that they do not abuse their privilege.

Though wives are told to be submissive to their husbands, this is not to be a situation where the husband commands and the wife slavishly and meekly obeys. The divine plan is that the husband be responsible for providing the leadership, the direction in which the family proceeds, for stabilizing the marriage financially and morally. This is to be done in an attitude of cooperation, love and care for his wife and family. Husbands are commanded to love their wives, but wives are also taught to love their husbands (Titus 2:3,4). Wives are to appreciate their husbands for fulfilling this God-given role. Christian husbands, likewise, should prize and protect their Christian wives, for Solomon wrote that a worthy woman is more valuable than jewels and that she should be trusted by her husband. Read Prov. 31:10-31. When both husband

and wife lovingly and responsively accept these divinely appointed roles, a sincere, abiding and tender loving relationship results, whereby each regards the other with deep affection, desirous of nurturing and supporting each other, sharing all the experiences of life for the family's mutual happiness and well being. Each marriage partner gladly assumes the responsibility of the marriage relationship, happy to reciprocate devotion and service to each other. Each learns the real meaning and the joy of true love.

When these divine injunctions are obeyed by both husband and wife, this serves to accomplish two purposes intended by the mind of God:

I. In a marriage where the husband fulfills his place in the family, as God intended, and where there is the kind of wife God intended her to be, there exists the most nearly-perfect situation possible in this life for happiness, contentment, and self-fulfillment.

Husbands and wives who conform to God's plan find strength, encouragement and great satisfaction through the love, cooperative support, trust and respect each gives unquestionably to the other. Thus, each can go about fulfilling his or her own respective duties unhindered by doubting concern regarding those things to be done by the other spouse.

It was God's intention that with marriage, a man and woman embark on a lifetime commitment of homemaking. They become a team, each having a definite part to play in establishing and maintaining a home and family. Their functions are God-assigned and each has been given physical and emotional capabilities and strengths compatible with the kinds of duties that making a home imposes.

If a happy and truly God-fearing home is to result from the marriage of a man and woman, each must accept the particular responsibilities that naturally attend making a home. A properly functioning home is not a mere central station where each family member has headquarters from which he or she habitually goes separate ways, scarcely meeting in passing.

The role of wife and mother is not just to cook, sew, mend, clean, or perform other menial tasks, but rather to create in the home an atmosphere of love, support, and stability. She should be the hub around which the family moves. When she conducts the common activities of the household in an efficient, orderly manner, other members of the family are better enabled to regulate their affairs. When she goes about her tasks joyfully, optimistically, and makes a point of showing loving interest, cooperation and concern for all other family members, she sets the tone of a happy home that will forever linger in the memories of the participants.

On the other hand when the husband and father is fully aware of his responsibility of leadership as head of the family, he is invigorated emotionally and inspired to put forth his best efforts to fulfill his duties to his family. Traditionally, the spiritual training of children has rested primarily upon mothers, but God expects that fathers also cooperate in this matter, as explicit commands divinely given to fathers show.

The outward and habitual mutual display of trust, dependence and love between husband and wife is of great significance, not only to themselves, but also in teaching their children how to have happy homes of their own in their adult lives.

When both husband and wife are thus mutually motivated and the divine concept of home exists in reality, there is no more powerful force, other than the power of Christian teaching and influence, that can build and maintain a happy, peaceful and productive society.

II. God intended that the union of a Christian man and woman in marriage should be a beautiful and fitting symbol of the union of the church to Christ. The church is often represented in the New Testament as the bride of Christ. This symbolism begins to be revealed even in the Old Testament.

Because the people of Israel were those chosen of God from among whom Jesus, the God-man, was to come into the world, the Israelites were His people, "called out" of the world, symbolizing the church, "ecclesia" in Greek, meaning "called out" of the world. In a sense the Israelites were married to God as is shown by the many Old Testament statements referring to their frequent drifting into idolatry, which God's prophets called adultery. In spite of the many times that Israel fell away from pure worship and after repenting was restored to God's favor, He looked forward to the future of the Christian Dispensation when He would have a faithful people, the "called out," the church, a spiritual bride meet for God's Son, the Christ. Note these prophecies:

> "And the nations shall see thy righteousness, and all kings thy glory; and thou shalt be called by a new name, which the mouth of Jehovah shall name" (Isa. 62:2).

This prophecy was first fulfilled as stated by Luke:

> "... the disciples were called Christians first in Antioch" (Acts 11:26).

> "For as a young man marries a virgin, so shall thy sons marry thee, and as the bridegroom rejoices over the bride, so shall thy God rejoice over thee" (Isa. 62:5).

"Thy sons" is a reference to Christians because in becoming a Christian one becomes the adopted son of God.

> "but when the fulness of the time came, God sent forth his Son, born of a woman, born under the law, that he might redeem them that were under the law, that we might receive the adoption of sons. And because ye are sons, God sent forth the Spirit of his Son into our hearts, crying, Abba, Father" (Gal. 4:4-6).

> "For as many as are led by the Spirit of God, these are sons of God. For ye received not the spirit of bondage again unto fear; but ye received the spirit of adoption, whereby we cry, Abba, Father. The Spirit himself beareth witness with our spirit, that we are children of God: and if children, then heirs; heirs of God, and joint-heirs with Christ..." (Rom. 8:14-17).

Thus it can be seen that in Paul's presentation of proper attitudes and behavior of men and women in the marriage relationship, from the time even before God created the world and placed Adam and Eve in the garden, God looked forward to His plan of redeeming sinful mankind through the propitiatory offering of Jesus, God's Son. Those thus redeemed were to constitute His church, the saved, the bride of Christ.

While Jesus was on the earth, He made repeated references to this relationship of Himself as the groom and the church as His bride. Note the following:

In explaining to John's disciples why Jesus and his disciples did not fast, as did the Pharisees, Jesus said:

"... Can the sons of the bridechamber mourn, as long as the bridegroom is with them? but the days will come, when the bridegroom shall be taken away from them, and then will they fast" (Matt. 9:15).

Jesus told a parable about the coming of the kingdom of heaven being likened to a marriage feast. Ten virgins expected to attend the feast, but while waiting for the bridegroom's coming they fell asleep. At midnight they were awakened. The bridegroom was coming. Five virgins discovered that their lamps were going out for lack of oil. They had brought no extra oil. While they went to buy oil the bridegroom came. Five virgins, who had brought extra oil, continued with the bridegroom and entered the place where the feast was to be held. Then the door was closed. When the other five virgins had gotten more oil, they proceeded to the feast, but upon arriving they were denied entrance. They were too late. The marriage feast represents the second coming of Christ, which will be at a time unexpected. It will be the day of judgment. It will be the day when the marriage between Christ, the groom, and the church, His bride, will be consummated. The two will be together in that wonderful place where Jesus went to prepare an eternal home for His bride. The parable shows not only the symbolism of the marriage of Christ and the church, but the importance of complete preparation in the hearts and lives of those who profess to be followers of Christ.

Women are not merely enjoined to be in subjection to their husbands, but are told the reason why they are thus commanded. Symbolically, the church, the bride of Christ, owes its very being to Christ who bought it with His own precious blood. It is His; it belongs to Him; only through His atoning sacrifice can the members of His church be saved eternally. Marriage was intended to be a beautiful symbol of the tender, abiding and supportive relationship between Christ and the church.

When viewed as such, why should a Christian wife object to the idea of being in subjection to a caring, protective Christian husband, who loves her as devotedly as Christ who loved His bride enough to purchase her with the sacrifice of Himself on the cruel cross of Calvary?

Admittedly, this may be because some husbands have not understood their exact role, or else have been unfaithful in exhibiting proper love and respect for their wives, being despotic or dictatorial, also because some wives have not taken their responsibilities seriously.

However, it is very evident that a chief reason for some women to resent the kind of marriage relationship described by Paul is because of the adverse influence in recent decades of the militant and radical elements of the women's organizations who seek to destroy the status of men and women's relationships as intended by God. Success of women in the professional world has been applauded, at the same time implying that being "just a homemaker" is belittling to a woman. This has resulted in many wives and mothers feeling of little worth without having some other "career," but this attitude and its consequences, of necessity, result in neglecting or short-changing of husbands and children of their rightful expectations, at least to some extent, and at most, to disaster in marriage or in the lives of their children. At the same time, these changing attitudes have been confusing to many men as to what their role should be, and have caused them to develop wrong attitudes regarding their behavior.

The large number of women holding positions in the professional fields, formerly confined chiefly to men, has increased the number of people in the work force, while the number of jobs needed has not increased proportionately. Hence, many are without employment and because of the increased numbers of workers, pay levels are lowered. If women had remained in the homes, fulfilling their God-given role of wives, caretakers and mothers, there would be less unemployment for men and pay schedules for men would be higher, thus making it unnecessary for wives to be gainfully employed. Children would be tended by loving, teaching mothers rather than left alone unsupervised or under the care of those who may provide for physical needs, but who cannot replace the loving bond, affection and concerned spiritual guidance of a godly mother.

It is unquestionably true that for many of the evil, disruptive, immoral and life-threatening conditions now corrupting American society, women's so-called liberating organizations must bear considerable blame. Volumes of data supporting this truth could be written, but suffice it here to say that the whole concept of the feminist movement is anti-Biblical and anti-Christian.

These statements concerning women in the workplace are not made with the intention of downgrading those faithful Christian wives and mothers who, because of circumstances beyond their control, are forced to work outside the home in order to provide life's necessities.

However, many professional women have chosen to work in order to provide more luxurious living rather than out of necessity. Others have chosen to give a career greater priority, having succumbed to the feminist view that the woman who spends her days at home has less contact with "intellectuals" and "higher pursuits," therefore she is inferior in intellectual quality and achievement. How blind are they who accept this standard!!! For one thing, it is indeed questionable whether or not a career in the public arena denotes association with intellectuals, and I am sure that in God's eyes, there is no higher pursuit for women than faithfully fulfilling the role of a Christian wife and mother. The ideal role of the Christian woman as it is set forth in God's word is primarily to be a caretaker, a physical and spiritual source of assistance, nurturing husband, children and self toward successful Christian living and service to God and fellow man. Therein lies true happiness and laudable achievement. There is no higher calling for any woman, and it is important that every woman, young and old, realize this important truth. Some career women do not have children, but most of them, sooner or later, feel a strong desire to rear children. This is a natural God-given part of being a woman. The following quotation is in keeping with God's plan for womankind. Whether her own children, or for the multiplied homeless children, any woman desiring to do so can fulfill this mission.

"The most important occupation on earth for a woman is to be a real mother to her children. It does not have much glory in it; there is a lot of grit and grime. But there is no greater place of ministry, position or power than that of a mother."

— Philip Whisenhunt in American Opinion

It is important to note that the militant feminists do not speak for the majority of women, though the militants speak loudly and are gaining in number due to the lack of proper education of youth in the last two or three decades. I have read statements from many lonely professional women who have reached the top of the ladder in their professions. They admit quickly that they would surrender all the plaudits of their success to find themselves as a vital part of a family with an adoring husband and loving, respectful children. Women who have experienced life as God intended it to be for them are heartily in agreement with the words of the following unknown writer.

I Am A Tired Woman

I AM A TIRED WOMAN ... tired of being told that I am not happy and that any illusions I might have to the contrary are indicative of a low mentality or at least a lack of originality or imaginative thinking.

I AM A TIRED WOMAN ... weary of those married females who made a shambles of their own marriages, who tell us that the institution of marriage won't work, who, having found themselves unequal to the task of finding happiness in marriage, intimate that we are less than adequate if we do not find fulfillment outside of marriage.

I AM A TIRED WOMAN ... and full of pity for those who complain of being the playthings of men, while they strut around in broad daylight in such a state of undress that they leave no doubt whatever as to what they consider their primary function in this life is.

I AM A TIRED WOMAN ... tired of watching those who never learned the art of grace in being a woman, yet seek to undermine everything that is feminine, trying to make men and women into carbon copies of each other, not for the betterment of mankind, but for the sole purpose of satisfying their own selfish desires.

I AM A TIRED WOMAN ... fed up with those who are so interested in their own so-called "rights" that they actually want to pass a law making it illegal to treat us like women, thus stomping on the rights of those of us who have found fulfillment in being women, who know what it really means to be women and to be treated like women. I AM A TIRED WOMAN... yes, but I AM A WOMAN, and I like it that way!!!

GOD'S PLAN FOR WOMEN IN THE WORSHIP ASSEMBLY

"... As in all the churches of the saints, let the women keep silence in the churches: for it is not permitted unto them to speak; but let them be in subjection, as also saith the law. And if they would learn anything, let them ask their own husbands at home: for it is shameful for a woman to speak in the church" (I Cor. 14:33-35)

"I desire therefore that the men pray in every place, lifting up holy hands, without wrath and disputing... Let a woman learn in quietness with all subjection. But I permit not a woman to teach, nor to have dominion over a man, but to be in quietness. For Adam was first formed, then Eve; and Adam was not beguiled, but the woman being beguiled hath fallen into transgression: but she shall be saved through her childbearing, if they continue in faith and love and sanctification with sobriety" (I Tim. 2:8-15).

In the above scriptures, Paul was using the term "in the church" or "churches" as referring to the meeting together of Christians to worship in the general assembly when the family of God, constituting the church, meets to engage in formal worship. This is the obvious conclusion when serious consideration is given to the following facts.

In the Greek New Testament, the word EKKLESIA means church. In many instances it refers to the totality of the family of God. In other passages, translated into English simply as church, the Greek EKKLESIA is preceded by EN. When EN EKKLESIA appears in the Greek, the reference is to the church as a body when its members are assembled as a congregation. Some instances of the appearance in the

Greek text of EN EKKLESIA are: After both Ananias and Sapphira claimed that the contribution placed at Peter's feet was the total money received from a property sale, thus affirming a lie, God struck them dead instantly. This happened during an assembly of the church. Of that occasion, Luke wrote:

> "And great fear fell upon the whole church ... [EN EKKLESIA]" (Acts 5:11).

Other references to similar passages are here noted:

- "For first of all, when ye come together in the church [EN EKKLESIA], I hear that divisions exist among you ..." (I Cor. 11:18).

The author of Hebrews quoted a prophetic psalm, here translated congregation, but which could as properly be translated "church," according to the original writing.

- "... I will declare my name unto my brethren, In the midst of the congregation [EN EKKLESIA] will I sing thy praise" (Heb. 2:12)

Paul sent his letter to the church at Colossea by Tychicus and Onesimus. In closing Paul wrote:

- "And when this epistle hath been read among you, cause that it be read also in the church [EN EKKLESIA] of the Laodiceans ..." (Col. 4:16).

There is another reason making it apparent that when Paul taught women to be "silent in the church" he was speaking only of an occasion when all of the congregation was assembled. This reason in seen in the fact that a Christian woman in one sense is always "in the church" wherever she goes or whatever she does. She is always a part of God's family. She has been born into it through compliance to the gospel message. To apply the rule of silence generally to a woman would sentence her to becoming entirely speechless. She could not even pray aloud in her home.

Christians can and should worship often, but when they assemble for the formal participation in the specified worship on the Lord's day, they are obligated to follow the divinely-prescribed pattern of worship commanded in the New Testament or exemplified by the early church under the guidance of the inspired apostles.

Women are not expected by our Lord to be passive participants in the worship service — far from it, but their voices are not to be vocal except in the song service where their voices are blended with other voices of all present. In this instance there is no usurping of authority.

Women can pray as fervently as men by joining in sentiment with the spoken prayers of the men. If, on occasion, a woman cannot hear the prayer, she can breathe a silent prayer.

Women should participate just as men do in giving attention to and meditating on what the preacher or speaker says. Some women, as well as men, receive benefit by referring to scripture citations immediately when given by the speaker. Others may receive more benefit by making notes of the scriptures and key points taught, and thoughtfully considering these things later. Still others prefer to listen quietly and simply concentrate carefully on what is being said.

And just as men should partake of the Lord's communion service by observing certain precautions as given in Paul's letter (I Cor. 11:27-30), women should realize their obligation to do likewise, but for a woman to serve the bread and fruit of the vine to the congregation would be to disobey a forbidden injunction, not to usurp the place of leadership belonging to men. Recall that it was a man, though a God-man, who first served the bread and fruit of the vine and instituted the memorial service.

In this connection, the consideration of the worship assembly, there arises the questionable act of having special a capella musical renditions, such as a solo, a duet, or quartet involving women. The only possible claim to scriptural authority that might be used to substantiate a claim of the propriety of such might be the exhortation:

> "Let the word of Christ dwell in you richly; in all wisdom teaching and admonishing one another with psalms and hymns and spiritual songs, singing with grace in your hearts unto God" (Col. 3:16).

The same expression is used in Ephesians 5:19. But "teaching and admonishing one another" is always done in congregational singing except in songs of praise to God, and there it is possible to teach.

On the other hand, there are valid reasons which indicate a conclusion that it is not wise for such special renditions to be used. For one thing, persons who take part in duets, quartets, etc., especially women, are faced with the temptation of becoming unduly proud of their special ability or the temptation of being overly concerned with their personal appearance. By the same token, listeners are tempted to center their attention on the ability of the persons singing or on their physical appearance rather than engaging their minds on the sentiments expressed in personal devotion while listening. There is always the danger that the occasion may be considered more as entertainment than of reverent worship and therefore offend fellow-Christians, as well as God.

There is also another danger. If it is proper to have such songs by a small limited number of singers occasionally, why is it not proper to do so regularly? And if it is proper to have one, two, or four sing alone, why not a whole chorus? And if an occasional chorus is proper, why not have a regular choir, which eventually involves a very limited amount of all Christians' active participation?

We see all of these things happening in all of the mainstream denominations. These choirs have developed through the extension of a few singers to a regular group whose activities become, in the minds of many, more entertainment than worship. The audience often applauds following a performance, exhibiting admiration as for any other entertainment. In addition, it is becoming increasingly common in mainstream denominations to see the wearing of special robes, giving way to Catholic tradition of separating clergy and laity, and also to more of an appearance of entertainment, rather than worship.

These conclusions will not be in accord with the ideas of many, but they are safe conclusions. We know that such activities are not essential in order to please God. If they are even slightly questionable, why take the risk of displeasing God?

In a similar situation, suppose one were offered a choice between a five-dollar gold coin and a piece of paper currency labeled "Five

Dollars" of which the donor suggested that it might be counterfeit, although he had no real reason for thinking so. Which choice would a reasonable person make?

GOD'S PLANS FOR OTHER ROLES OF CHRISTIAN WOMEN IN AREAS OF SERVICE

In all manners of Christian growth and service, God's word makes no distinction between men and women. Each is to work toward the growth of Christian character and development of Christian virtues. In addition to the constant striving to arrive upon a higher plain of spiritual thinking and actions in one's personal spiritual meditations and actions, both genders should always be consciously active in letting the light of Christianity shine through their words and deeds so as to reflect the glory, majesty and love of Christ and His gracious offer of salvation to all who will heed His word and follow Him. Paul wrote:

"... whatsoever ye do, do all to the glory of God" (I Cor. 10:31).

In recent years, the feminist movement has resulted in many religious institutions beginning to license women to fulfill official capacities formerly limited by their various religious creeds to men. Even Catholics have begun to appoint women priests. Of course, priests, in the manner that Catholic priests serve, as professed meditators between sinners and God, are not scriptural even for men. But in the church of our Lord, from its very inception, not only all men, but all women also, are priests. Peter, writing to both genders of Christians, said:

"ye also, as living stones, are built up a spiritual house, to be a holy priesthood, to offer up spiritual sacrifices, acceptable to God through Jesus Christ" (I Peter 2:5).

Under the Mosaic Dispensation, in the tabernacle the church was typified by the Holy Place and heaven was typified by the Most Holy Place, the place where God said His presence would abide among His people. At that time only priests could enter the Holy Place, and only the high priest could enter the Most Holy Place. He could do so only twice on the Day of Atonement each year.

Peter declared that every Christian is a priest. This includes both men and women. The Mosaic priests, ministering in the Holy Place — as they tended the lamps, the altar of incense, and the table of showbread —typified the Christian's worship service in the church through shining the gospel message by means of teaching, offering of prayers, and participation in the communion service. But it was the high priest who typified the ministry of Christ as the mediator between man and God. The high priest carried the blood from the lamb on the altar of burnt offering in the outer court (which typified the world) into the Most Holy Place, putting it on the ark of the covenant, thus typifying the atonement through Christ's blood shed on the cross for sins of the nation. Since the blood of animals could not take away the sins of the world, but could only roll them forward, Jesus — the Lamb of God — gave His life on Calvary to make it possible for the sinners of the world to be redeemed.

It is significant that when Christ died on the cross, the veil in the temple, which had replaced the tabernacle, was "rent asunder" (Matt. 27:51). The veil had separated the Holy and Most Holy Places. The renting asunder proclaimed the fact that Jesus' atoning sacrifice had opened the way for the priests to enter the Most Holy Place, therefore making it possible for every Christian to do as Peter said:

"to offer up spiritual sacrifices acceptable to God through Christ."

The Israelites needed priests to intercede with God on their behalf. Now each Christian can go directly to God. However, this is true only because Jesus is now the Christian's high priest, always available to intercede between God and man. Therefore our prayers are directed to God through Jesus Christ, our heavenly mediator.

WOMEN'S SPECIAL WORK: In working out His purposes, God has always used faithful women as an important part. Although faithful Abraham was chosen to father God's chosen nation, Christ was distinctively to be born as the seed of woman, just as God had in a prophecy, vague to Eve, foretold (Gen. 3:15). So it was that the Hebrew writer recorded:

> "By faith even Sarah herself received power to conceive seed when she was past age, since she counted him faithful who had promised" (Hebrews 11:11).

Rahab lived in Canaan at the time when God was ready to allow His people, after forty years of wilderness wandering, to enter the promised land. Although Rahab lived among idolatrous people and was a common prostitute, often a part of idolatrous worship, when she learned of the miracles God performed in providing miraculous safe passage on dry land for His people when crossing the Red Sea and later crossing the flooded Jordan River, she accepted Him as the true God. Turning away from her sinful past, she rejected loyalty to her wicked city and saved the lives of the Israelite men sent by Moses to spy out the land of Canaan, thus receiving the privilege of having her name recorded in the sacred book along with other Old Testament worthies:

> "By faith Rahab the harlot perished not with them that were disobedient, having received the spies with peace" (Hebrews 11:31)

It was many years after Rahab that the following incident occurred. Naomi, her husband and two sons had fled from Israel into Moab because of a famine in Israel. The two sons married women of Moab. Naomi's husband and sons died. Supposing her daughters-in-law preferred to remain in Moab, Naomi planned to return to Israel. However, Ruth, one of Naomi's daughters-in-law, was determined to stay with Naomi. Evidently Ruth had been so impressed with the godly conduct of Naomi and what she had learned from Naomi and her family that Ruth, a Moabitess, made this memorable statement:

> "... for whither thou goest, I will go; and where thou lodgest, I will lodge; thy people shall be my people, and thy God my God; where thou diest, will I die, and there will I be buried" (Ruth 1:16,17).

God did not fail to heed the faithfulness of this woman. He saw that it was by faith that Ruth, though a Moabitess by birth, was willing to leave her homeland and cast her fate with that of Israel. She was rewarded of God by being in the ancestry of David through whose lineage Jesus, future king of the eternal heavenly kingdom, would be born.

Another faithful woman used of God was Hannah. Having reached an age too old to conceive a child, and even though she had always been barren, Hannah prayed and wept in great distress because she so greatly desired a child. She did not give up. Her faith was so great that she continued to pray fervently, even in the temple of God, that He would give her a child vowing that, if her prayer were answered, she would give him to the Lord's service all the days of his life (I Sam. 1:10,11). God heard her prayer. She bore a son and as soon as He was weaned, he was left with Eli the priest. Under Eli's care this boy, Samuel, began at an early age to be used of God to proclaim His messages. Samuel served as a prophet and as a righteous judge over Israel for many years. He anointed the first two kings of Israel.

Another woman of Old Testament times was one whose name is not even given. She is known simply as the "widow of Zarephath," but God used her to perform a very important function, to care for the sustenance of the faithful prophet Elijah, who was in hiding from King Ahab and his wicked wife Jezebel, who sought Elijah's life because he had condemned their idolatry and killed their false priests. Elijah was waiting until the three-year drought, brought upon Israel because of its idolatry, was to end. Since the widow was willing to share her last morsel of food with God's prophet and provide an abiding place for him, God blessed her faith with a continual supply of food during the famine and also blessed her in other ways. See I Kings 17.

Hundreds of years after these women who have been mentioned lived, another faithful young woman appeared on the scene. Her people, the Jews, were scattered throughout a foreign nation whose natives hated the Jews. This young woman, Esther, risked her life on two occasions out of faith in God, which she had learned through her faithful uncle. Through her efforts on these two occasions, the lives of all her people in that nation were saved. Read this beautiful and powerful story of faith and selflessness in the Old Testament book of "Esther."

Other women of Old Testament times were used of God in carrying out His plans, but these examples cited attest to the value that God places upon women and to the fact that their special functions are just as important in His sight as are men's.

Continuing on through several hundred years of Old Testament history, we come to the New Testament and to some events fulfilling past prophecies where women were used of God. One of these was Elizabeth whose husband was Zachariah.

> "And they were both righteous before God, walking in all the commandments and ordinances of the Lord blameless. And they had no child, because that Elizabeth was barren, and they both were now well stricken in years" (Luke 1:6,7).

God selected these two people as those through whom an ancient prophesy was to be fulfilled. He chose Elizabeth to bear the child of prophecy who was to be the forerunner of Jesus. This child was John, later called "The Baptist."

Only fifteen months after Elizabeth conceived, God used a virtuous young woman Mary to bear the Christ-child, the person of prophecy, first foretold after the sin of Eve and Adam (Gen. 3:15).

Not only during the period of Old Testament history did women serve very important functions in God's service, but during the lifetime of Jesus and continuing through the history of the apostolic period, women were prominent in carrying on God's work.

During the three and a half years of Jesus' earthly ministry, women as well as men became his disciples and sometimes traveled through the country with Him.

> "... he went about through cities and villages, preaching and bringing the good tidings of the kingdom of God, and with him the twelve, and certain women who had been healed of evil spirits and infirmities: Mary that was called Magdalene, from whom seven demons had gone out, and Joanna the wife of Chuzas Herod's steward, and Susanna, and many others, who ministered unto them of their substance" (Luke 8:1-3).

Among Jesus' disciples Mary and Martha are often mentioned, being first introduced by Luke, chapter 10:38-42. They were among Jesus' dearest friends.

While on earth Jesus did not confine his ministry to men, although it was they who received his strongest denunciations. He exhibited a sense of respect and sensitivity to women's pains and sorrows as well as to those of men. One time a woman taken in adultery was brought before Him by the accusing, murderous Pharisees seeking to try Him. His quiet response, after stooping to the ground in humility before His Father, as well as outward compliance with His accuser's Pharisaic assumption of piety and authority, said simply "He that is without sin among you, let him first cast a stone at her." Defeated in their hypocritical attempt to entrap Jesus, the Pharisees quietly departed, one by one, leaving Jesus still writing on the ground — on the same level physically as the humiliated and doubtless frightened and contrite woman. Rising, Jesus refused to condemn her. He knew her heart and also perhaps, with His divine knowledge of her past, knew that she may have been guilty under conditions which she was unable to control. Nevertheless, whatever the circumstances, He spoke words of consolation to her:

"... Neither do I condemn thee: go thy way; from henceforth sin no more" (John 8:11).

On another occasion, as Jesus and His disciples were on their way to a ruler's home to raise his daughter from death,

"... a woman, who had an issue of blood twelve years, came behind him, and touched the border of his garment: for she said within herself, If I do but touch his garment, I shall be made whole" (Matt. 9:20,21).

"But Jesus turning and seeing her said, Daughter, be of good cheer; thy faith hath made thee whole. And the woman was made whole from that hour" (Matt. 9:22).

Although the purpose of Jesus in performing miracles was to establish His claim to divinity, His love and compassion for all mankind including woman, is evident in the raising from the dead the only son of the widow of Nain. Jesus, as He was entering the city, met the funeral procession carrying the body to be buried.

"And when the Lord saw her, he had compassion on her, and said unto her, Weep not. And he came nigh and touched the bier: and the bearers stood still. And he said, Young man, I say unto thee, Arise. And he that was dead sat up, and began to speak. And he gave him to his mother" (Luke 7:13-15).

Jesus was not ashamed to associate with sinners, but it was for the purposes of healing their sinsick souls, not to engage with them in their evil practices. One day he accepted an invitation to eat with a Pharisee. As they sat down to eat, a woman of the city, who was known for her sins, entered the house, bringing

> "... an alabaster cruse of ointment, and standing behind at his feet, weeping, she began to wet his feet with her tears, and wiped them with the hair of her head, and kissed his feet, and anointed them with the ointment" (Luke 7:37,38).

Jesus read the minds of the Pharisees present and answered their thoughts by telling a parable about two debtors. One owed five hundred shillings and one owed only fifty. The generous lender forgave both, and Jesus asked the Pharisees, "Which of these debtors will love their benefactor most?"

The critical Pharisees could only answer, "He, I suppose, to whom he forgave the most." Jesus drew the parallel, explaining that the Pharisees had not even extended the usual customs of that time in greeting into their home a guest. He said:

> "Thou gavest me no kiss: but she, since the time I came in, hath not ceased to kiss my feet. My head with oil thou didst not anoint: but she hath anointed my feet with ointment. Wherefore I say unto thee, Her sins, which are many, are forgiven; for she loved much: but to whom little is forgiven, the same loveth little" (Luke 7:45-47).

Then, turning to the weeping woman,

> "... he said unto her, Thy sins are forgiven. And they that sat at meat with him began to say within themselves, Who is this that even forgiveth sins? And he said unto the woman, Thy faith hath saved thee; go in peace" (Luke 7:48-50).

On another occasion Jesus was in Bethany, eating in the house of "Simon the leper." A woman entered with an alabaster cruse of ointment of pure nard, a very costly substance. She broke the cruse and poured the liquid over Jesus' head. Some of those present were indignant that she had, according to them, wasted what could have been sold to feed the poor. But Jesus defended her. Knowing that His death was at hand and recognizing the deep love being exhibited toward Himself, Jesus said:

> "... Let her alone; why trouble ye her? she hath wrought a good work on me. For ye have the poor always with you, and whensoever ye will ye can do them good: but me ye have not always. She hath done what she could; she hath anointed my body beforehand for the burying. And verily I say unto you, Wheresoever the gospel shall be preached throughout the whole world, that also which this woman hath done shall be spoken of for a memorial of her" (Mark 14:6-9).

John wrote that the woman thus commended by Jesus was the sister of Lazarus of Bethany.

> "And it was that Mary who anointed the Lord with ointment, and wiped his feet with her hair, whose brother Lazarus was sick" (John 11:2).

On still another occasion, Jesus sat in the temple near the treasury and watched as people placed their offerings. Many rich people put large sums into the coffer, but Jesus saw a poor widow cast in two mites, the least valuable coin. He knew that she placed into the treasury all that she had. He said to His disciples:

> "... Verily I say unto you, This poor widow cast in more than all they that are casting into the treasury: for they all did cast in of their superfluity; but she of her want did cast in all that she had, even all her living" (Mark 12:43,44).

Which one would you have preferred to be — the rich person or the poor widow, a woman?

One time as Jesus traveled through Samaria from Judea to Galilee, He encountered a woman who came to draw water from the well where He had stopped to rest while His disciples went to a nearby village to procure food. Although Jews usually felt it beneath their dignity to converse with a Samaritan (a half-breed Jew), Jesus engaged this woman in a fairly lengthy conversation during which she told Him, as he already knew, that she had had five husbands and was then living with another man, though not married to him. Jesus' words and manner of speaking so impressed the woman that she went into the nearby city and brought crowds of people to hear Jesus.

They were intensely interested and at their request Jesus stayed there two days teaching them. Of this occasion John wrote:

> "And many more believed because of his word; and they said to the woman, Now we believe, not because of thy speaking: for we have heard for ourselves, and know that this is indeed the Savior of the world" (John 4:41,42)

What a ministry this woman performed in bringing souls to Christ!

Although Jesus condemned many men for their sinful behavior, we have no record of His personal condemnation of any particular woman during His ministry on earth except for a mild, loving rebuke to Martha (Luke 10:40,41).

At last, after undergoing the miseries of His last few hours of earthly ministry, Jesus, bearing His cross, was led along the way toward the place of crucifixion,

> "And there followed him a great multitude of the people, and of women who bewailed and lamented him" (Luke 23:27).

And as He suffered on the cross,

> "... the women that followed with him from Galilee, stood afar off, seeing these things" (Luke 23:49).

It was faithful men who took the body of Jesus, lovingly and sorrowfully anointing it before placing it in the tomb. But it was the women who had followed Jesus from Galilee who first found the empty tomb and to whom special messengers from heaven appeared and first announced Jesus' resurrection. Among these women were Mary Magdalene, Joanna, and Jesus' mother, Mary. (Luke 24:1-10.)

> "And on the Sabbath they rested according to the commandment. But on the first day of the week, at early dawn, they

came unto the tomb, bringing the spices which they had prepared. And they found the stone rolled away from the tomb. And they entered in, and found not the body of the Lord Jesus. And it came to pass, while they were perplexed thereabout, behold, two men stood by them in dazzling apparel: and as they were affrighted and bowed down their faces to the earth, they said unto them, Why seek ye the living among the dead? He is not here, but is risen: remember how he spake unto you when he was yet in Galilee, saying that the Son of man must be delivered up into the hands of sinful men, and be crucified, and the third day rise again. And they remembered his words, and returned from the tomb, and told all these things to the eleven, and to all the rest. Now they were Mary Magdalene, and Joanna, and Mary the mother of James: and the other women with them told these things unto the apostles" (Luke 24:1-10).

After the church was established, women still played important roles in the furtherance of the gospel. It is recorded that Philemon's house was the meeting place of the church (Philemon 1:2) and likely the homes of other Christians were used thus. When Peter was miraculously delivered from prison, he went to the house of Mary, mother of John Mark, where Christians were gathered as they engaged in prayer.

"And when he [Peter] had considered the thing, he came to the house of Mary the mother of John whose surname was Mark; where many were gathered together and were praying" (Acts 12:12)

Paul, Barnabas, Timothy and Luke went to Philippi, a Grecian city. Since Jews had no synagogue there, these men supposed some Jews might be gathered near the riverside outside the city gate. Going there, they found Lydia, a worshipper of God with her household, but they were not Christians. When these Christian men joined the women and began to teach them about Christ, they responded by obeying the gospel message. Afterward, Lydia was very useful in the promotion of the gospel by providing a home for these missionaries as long as they stayed in Philippi, setting an example of Christian hospitality for Christian women of today. Read Lydia's story in Acts 16:14,15.

Some other Christian women are mentioned by name as being useful in carrying on the work of the church. Paul mentioned Phoebe, who it seems was going to Rome. Paul said of her,

> "I commend unto you Phoebe our sister, who is a servant of the church that is at Cenchreae: that ye receive her in the Lord, worthily of the saints, and that ye assist her in whatsoever matter she may have need of you: for she herself also hath been a helper of many, and of mine own self" (Romans 16:1,2).

In his letter to the Philippians, Paul mentions Euodia and Syntyche who had labored with him "in the gospel" and of whom he said:

> "... whose names are in the book of life" (Phil. 4:3).

Calling her a sister (in Christ), Paul mentioned Apphia in the beginning of his letter to Philemon.

Here is the example of another way that Christian women are peculiarly fitted to serve Christ:

> "Now there was at Joppa a certain disciple named Tabitha, which by interpretation is called Dorcas: this woman was full of good works and alms deeds which she did" (Acts 9:36).

This good woman died, but her fellow-Christians in Joppa called Peter to go to Joppa for aid. Upon arriving, he was taken to where her body lay,

> "... and all the widows stood by him weeping, and showing the coats and garments which Dorcas made..." (Acts 9:39).

You probably know the story. Through Peter, God brought Dorcas back to life.

Are not these multiplied examples of God's use of women, in working out His plans, abundant evidence that women's importance in the church is not overshadowed or minimized by her role being different than that of men's roles? Each gender is peculiarly provided by God with the abilities and qualities to perform best in the sphere designated by God's word.

WOMEN'S ROLE AS TEACHERS

Paul told Titus to teach older Christian men that they should have developed certain qualities of character such as temperance, gravity, sober-mindedness, soundness in faith, love and patience. They are told to be teachers and examples to younger men:

> " the younger men likewise exhort to be sober-minded: in all things showing thyself an ensample of good works; in thy doctrine showing uncorruptness, gravity, sound speech, that cannot be condemned ... " (Titus 2:6-8).

Older Christian women should also have these same characteristics. They are also to be "reverent" in demeanor, not gossipers, or given to wine. They should teach younger women, both verbally and by example. Paul instructed that older women were to teach in order

> "that they may train the young women to love their husbands, to love their children, to be sober-minded, chaste, workers at home, kind, being in subjection to their own husbands, that the word of God be not blasphemed" (Titus 2:4,5).

Women's teaching activities are not confined to teaching younger women. They may teach anyone in any place other than the general assembly when the congregation is assembled. They may teach by written word in books, private letters, magazine articles, pamphlets, etc. Women who teach are not necessarily restricted to those who are older, but all Christian women who have a true knowledge of the word and are mature as Christians have a teaching responsibility as they have opportunity. All Christian mothers certainly are expected to teach their children from their earliest ability to learn. One cannot discount the magnitude of the result of faithful teaching and example of godly mothers. Consider the influence of Lois and Eunice. In writing to Timothy, Paul was rejoicing over the unfeigned faith of Timothy.

> " ... which dwelt first in thy grandmother Lois, and thy mother Eunice; and, I am persuaded, in thee also" (II Tim.1:5).

None can begin to count the number of souls that were converted through Timothy's labors as a preacher and his and their continued influence throughout the ensuing centuries.

Women may properly teach even a man privately. Consider the following New Testament example: Priscilla's influence in helping to instruct a great preacher through whom her influence touched countless others.

Apollos was "an eloquent man" and "mighty in the scriptures." He was "fervent in spirit," a preacher who "taught accurately the things concerning Jesus," but he knew "only the baptism of John" (Acts 18:24). Perhaps this was because he was not a resident of Palestine where almost all of Jesus' ministry was performed. Apollos was "an Alexandrian by race."

It was some time after the church had been established in Jerusalem that Apollos went to the city of Ephesus and began to preach there in the synagogue of the Jews. Residing in Ephesus was a man, Aquila, and his wife, Priscilla. They were well taught concerning the church.

> "and he [Apollos] began to speak boldly in the synagogue. But when Priscilla and Aquila heard him, they took him unto them, and expounded unto him the way of God more accurately" (Acts 18:26).

In Luke's account of this occurrence, he mentioned the name of Priscilla before that of Aquila, perhaps indicating that she played a major role in the teaching of Apollos. However, it must be noted that the teaching was done in privacy. The adequacy of that teaching is shown by Apollos' further great ability to preach the gospel:

> "for he powerfully confuted the Jews, and that publicly, showing by the scriptures that Jesus was the Christ" (Acts 18:28).

Though a woman, Priscilla's influence in helping to instruct a great preacher played a major role in countless others' eternal salvation.

Is it not evident, after noting the foregoing facts, that women should not feel that they have a lesser involvement in promoting Christianity than do men? God's plan was simply that they act in a different sphere of growth. As far as worship is concerned, they participate in every activity. Although it is a man who formally and publically directs the proclamation of God's word, the woman — through attentive listening and application to the written word of God — actively participates, as well as when she is active in her own assigned areas of activity.

Say It Again, John

In the furor which the women's liberation movement has raised, the words of John Ruskin some generations ago are worth recounting:

"We are foolish, and without excuse foolish, in speaking of the superiority of one sex to the other, as if they could be compared in similar things! Each has what the other has not; each completes the other; they are in nothing alike; and the happiness and perfection of both depend on each asking and receiving from the other what the other only can give."

— Author Unknown

CHAPTER EIGHT

CHRISTIANS AND THE WORLD

In the Dec. 16, **1993** weekly bulletin of the Sixth & Izzard St. Church of Christ of Little Rock, Ark. the following article appeared as a quotation by Bill McDonough from Dr. Mac Lynn of David Lipscomb University who stated that "the churches of Christ in America have grown by only .16% per year in the past ten years." It was not always that way however. By comparison, note the following article which appeared in **1863** in one of the country's leading newspapers. Note the contrast between the growth of the church as the Restoration Movement in America moved swiftly forward.

American Restoration Movement

"The growth of this body of Christians, sometimes called Campbellites, is unparalleled in religious history. They had their origin in this country only 40 years ago but they number now in the United States alone over 600,000 communicants while they are growing rapidly in Great Britain, Canada, the West Indies and Australia. As a denomination they have always been devoted to the interest of education and the diffusion of general intelligence, and they have now under their control 13 first-class colleges, a large number of quarterly, four weekly and 11 monthly papers, academies and seminaries of higher learning and innumerable tracts and pamphlets have been published. Their statistics show they have 4,200 preachers in the field in this country, many of whom are men of high intellectual culture and talent. Their great strength lies in the valley of the Mississippi, the state of Kentucky having 13,000 persons in this church alone. They claim no creed but the Bible, call things by Bible names, and say they occupy the ground held by primitive Christians. However much in error their doctrinal tenets may be regarded by their religious friends, the facts cannot be discarded that during the past 30 to 40 years they have made more rapid growth than any other denomination in the United States."

— Baltimore American 1863

Note that this article was written, not by a member of the Church of Christ but, by someone connected with the newspaper. This explains use of the word "Campbellites" and it also explains the fact that the author refers to the origin of the church being in America. It did not begin in America. Its origin in Jerusalem was in 33 or 34 A.D.

The emphasis of the article was on the phenomenal growth of the church during a forty-year period. Contrast this rate of growth by the year 1863 with Dr. Mac Lynn's statement of the present rate of growth. How can this tremendous difference be explained?

As the Restoration Movement came to a climax resulting in religious bodies identified under the name of church of Christ, its members have since been known generally for their strict doctrinal orientation regarding the scriptures and their personal different lifestyle. This was true because from the time when the church in the 19th century, which began after the great apostasy to identify itself simply by this name of biblical origin, its members consisted chiefly of persons who left various denominational churches out of a realization that, after carefully examining their particular doctrines, they were found to be conflicting in various ways with the tenets that resulted from an effort to be guided strictly by the Bible, to worship God only as biblically authorized. This principle crystallized in the motto "Where the Bible speaks, we speak; where the Bible is silent, we are silent." Until recent years practically all mature members of churches of Christ could defend all principles of their faith by Biblical citations. A large percentage could give off-hand book, chapter and verses upon which their doctrines and practices were founded. Because of this, the church's stand on the necessity of New Testament authorization for its differences from denominations, it has often been caricatured by such phrases as "those people who don't believe in music" or "those people who believe in water salvation." As thus stated, both of these assessments are misrepresentations resulting from lack of understanding on the part of the speaker.

Sadly true, as was minutely discussed in a previous chapter, this situation, in too many instances, is not still the case. Even when church doctrines are plainly specified in public preaching and teaching, it is evident that they, too often, do not carry over into personal application in the every-day behavior of many church members. Consequently, we see many church members whose behavior, as seen by their associates outside the church, is no different than that which it was before becoming Christians, or as no different from that of the world in general. The attitudes and actions of one who accepts the Lord's invitation to follow Him involve acceptance of new duties and responsibilities as well as changes in lifestyle. Examine the lives of early converts to Christ in the apostolic age. Immediately, they began efforts to involve others in their newly-found joy at the prospect of the blessings and promises of Christianity to the righteous. These new converts met often for mutual instruction and encouragement. They changed their hopes and aspirations from those which were formally mere quests for satisfaction through gain of material possessions, fleshly satisfactions, worldly fame or power. Instead, the new converts began to turn from those things which satisfy fleshly lust, passion and worldly satisfaction to the pursuit of spiritual qualities exemplified in Christ and taught by Him and the Holy Spirit inspired apostles. These Christians left no doubt among their associates as to their Christian identity. The newly born Christians began to follow the sincere plea of Paul who wrote:

> "And be not fashioned according to this world: but be ye transformed by the renewing of your mind, that ye may prove what is the good and acceptable and perfect will of God" (Romans 12:2).

True Christianity changes the heart and all aspects of living because one begins to realize the magnitude of the changed situation. When one has received the promise of escape from the disappointments that would have followed him when, in the literal though not self-recognized servitude to Satan, the most evil of all creation—that recipient can look forward with faith toward eternal happiness. The faithful believer is delivered from the powerful rule of the one who presides over the power of darkness. Through obedience to the gospel of redemption, the Christian is translated into the kingdom of the Son of God, thus becoming a potential instrument for His service. But this means that the recipient of God's bountiful grace, claimed through obedience to the gospel, must yield himself readily and willingly, in spite of surrounding pressures, perhaps from friends as well as foes, to make himself ready and willing to reject his worldly impulses and fleshly appetites, yielding himself whole-heartedly to God's purposes. His entire Christian lifestyle, daily behavior, ambitions, ideals and hopes must be directed from a completely different viewpoint. He must form a mental assessment of the true meaning of living a Christian life. Depending on his former lifestyle, he may have to make changes in practically every aspect of his life.

One becomes a Christian only after He has been made aware of his guilt and the punishment that would be in store for him without the benefit of forgiveness. He has acknowledged that guilt and received forgiveness through the provisions made possible by acceptance of the offer extended through God's loving grace in giving His Son to provide the only acceptable sacrifice of Jesus Christ.

Having become a Christian, one must reject his worldly scale of values, replacing them with those values set forth in God's word. Moral judgments of the past, by which the new Christian's life was previously governed, must be examined in the light of divinely revealed principles and changed accordingly. The sincere new-born Christian, truly desiring to live a life pleasing to God, hungers and thirsts for further instructions to guide him in every activity of life. He is so thankful for his new state of being an adopted child of God that the young Christian will seek to grow in virtuous conduct worthy of Christ. From the very beginning of his Christian life, one must endeavor to grow toward spiritual maturity. He will never reach perfection in this world, but as long as he strives in that direction, God will be pleased and the Christian will be happy, even if being a Christian involves hardships.

This task of change in lifestyle is harder for some than for others, but none can achieve the desired result without God's help. However, through the very act of rebirth, the infant in Christ is promised the assistance needed. He has thus received, not only forgiveness for past sins but, the "gift of the Holy Spirit," that indwelling influence that will help guide the new Christian when he allows this to happen as he studies God's revealed word and strives to comply with its instructions.

Since the Christian has taken the Bible, and the Bible only, as the authoritative guide providing patterns and principles of conduct, he must carefully apply these to every phase of his life, to all his relationships with others, whether in family, social, business, recreational or religious activities. These cannot be departmentalized, but must be integrated into his whole thinking processes, his total character.

It is sad to note that, especially beginning some two or three decades ago, many individual Christians began to drift away from this vital concept of Christianity until, at the present time, in a sweeping survey of the church in general, evidences of widespread worldliness are seen within the body of Christ. This is true, not only in the lives of certain dissatisfied and poorly-informed individuals, but also in the attitude of many who may not themselves be participants in worldly activities, but who are prone to blindness in recognizing the extreme seriousness of certain existing circumstances. Even church leaders, preachers and elders sometimes fail to recognize and sound the alarm and warnings against worldly activities. Seemingly, to some in the church, these worldly behaviors of some fellow-Christians are excusable in light of the changing attitudes of modern society.

These immoral attitudes of society today, concerning the sanctity of marriage, Biblical authority and the validity of various lifestyles, have been creeping into the behavior of some would-be or professed Christians. From its very beginning, and continuing until two or three decades ago, it was not only within the churches, but throughout society in general, that the Judeo/Christian values were accepted as the guiding principles of proper behavior. Our country was established by those who sought a place where all would be free to worship according to their conscience and convictions. Our Constitution and civil laws were based on these biblical principles. Within the past thirty years, this society has gradually developed a proliferation of crime, violence, and sexual immorality which would formerly have been unthinkable. These conditions are of such proportions as to surpass even the imagination of the earliest settlers in this land. Among contributors to this situation have been (1) the influx of mothers into the market place, leaving them less time and energy to teach and nourish their children spiritually; (2) the withdrawal of teaching of biblical moral values in the public schools; and (3) the introduction into the classrooms of behavioral ideas contrary to Judeo/Christian beliefs, often even ridiculing them as outmoded and no longer valid.

Without these restraints on moral conduct, a vast number of children of the last two generations have grown up with little or no spiritual guidelines and consequently have been easily vulnerable to the fleshly temptations common to human nature and constantly set forth by Satan.

As a result, young people, even of Christian parentage, have fallen prey to the peer pressure of their schoolmates and friends who think nothing of cheating, violence to achieve their desires, or of promiscuous sexual activity. Often even these "Christian" parents are themselves the victims of peer pressure. This influence may begin and be thoughtlessly encouraged in the home. The child demands name-tag brand clothing because without such, he is left out of the crowd. Girls commonly wear mini-skirts, tight skirts, short shorts, skimpy looking bathing suits and other immodest attire. Of course, Susie has to be in style, no matter that God explicitly forbids immodest clothing or actions that may excite lustful passions. Someone aptly described people who succumb to peer pressure as having "a banana complex." They have to be a part of the bunch. This has always been a temptation for God's people. The Israelites demanded of Samuel that instead of being led by judges, as previously, the people wanted a king because they wanted to be like other nations. God said that this attitude was a rejection of Him (I Sam .8:7). It is just as true today as it was then. Being part of the "in crowd" amounts to rejecting God.

Likewise, any attempt by Christians to be like the world amounts to rejecting God. One cannot follow both Christ and the world:

> "Ye adulteresses, know ye not that the friendship of the world is enmity with God? Whosoever therefore would be a friend of the world maketh himself an enemy of God" (James 4:4).

Those who want to follow the crowd are just as thoughtless and foolish as are sheep, of which a young shepherd wrote. He said that he used to amuse himself by holding a stick across a gateway that the sheep had to pass through. After the first few sheep had jumped over the stick, it was withdrawn, but all the other sheep followed leaping through the gateway over an imagined barrier. Sheep are not alone in having that tendency. In our modern society, almost all are prone to do what other peers do, accepting without question the actions of the crowd.

James called those who enjoy friendship with the world adulteresses. Adultery and fornication are in the same category in God's sight. Note what Paul said of such sin:

> "Flee fornication. Every sin that a man doeth is without the body; but he that committeth fornication sinneth against his own body. Or know ye not that your body is a temple of the Holy Spirit which is in you, which ye have from God? and ye are not your own; for ye were bought with a price: glorify God therefore in your body" (I Cor. 6:18-20).

Writing to the Christians in Rome, Paul exhorted:

> "Let not sin therefore reign in your mortal body, that ye should obey the lusts thereof: neither present your members unto sin as instruments of unrighteousness; but present yourselves unto God, as alive from the dead, and your members as instruments of righteousness unto God" (Rom. 6:12,13).

God expects the Christian to be as faithful to Him as a wife should be to her husband. Christians who flirt with and love the world are guilty of spiritual adultery.

Of course there is a difference between being in the world and of the world. Of necessity Christians must associate with the world, but when, in doing so, Christians lay their spiritual values aside, they are showing their "banana bunch" attitude.

Just before going to the garden where He was to be betrayed and arrested to face trials and crucifixion, Jesus prayed fervently. On behalf of His apostles, He said,

> "I pray not that thou shouldest take them from the world, but that thou shouldest keep them from the evil one" (John 17:15).

Although Christians must live in an unholy world, modern society places extraordinary temptations and a pervasive display of sensuality, religious intolerance, bold and shameless examples for the young and untaught. James says that an important part of true religion is to "keep oneself unspotted from the world" (James 1:27). How must Christians respond when confronted with the unrelenting pressures of this sinful world? God certainly did not intend that we withdraw from society, as did the monks of long ago. Jesus answered this question when He said that His disciples are to be "the light of the world" and the "salt of the earth" (Matt. 5:13,14).

It is sad that some in the church seem to see no harm in certain worldly activities, such as attending dancing parties (especially high school proms) or in frequenting, and even carrying their children, into fancy-eating places that also provide music and space for dancing, as well as bars. They see no harm in an occasional social drink, so long as they are temperate, notwithstanding the fact that in so doing they may influence others, including their own children, to drink which might lead to their becoming alcoholic. These people of "banana instinct" think little of participating in public or mixed swimming, wearing indecent and scanty clothing, or even in allowing their children to do so. "Everybody does it," they say. Do these "Christians" think that in such places they can let their light shine, glorifying Christ as He commanded? Or can such participation provide the preserving power of salt to the purity of society?

When Christians conform to the world, the very distinctive qualities of Christian virtue are lost. Like Peter, who three times denied Christ, those who want to be a part of the crowd may even resort to profanity to prove themselves part of "the bunch." Of the Christian who refuses to partake of sinful worldly activities, those in the popular crowd may even "think it strange that ye run not with them into the same excess of riot" (I Pet. 4:4). The "bunch" may even ridicule and try to put the Christian to shame for his manner of life, for his willingness to accept Christ as supreme guide of his life, but the dedicated Christian knows what Jesus said, that since His enemies persecuted Him, His disciples could expect the same.

Much has been said about the power of peer pressure, meaning the pressure brought to bear by one's associates to do as they do. If that peer pressure conforms to Christian standards, it can be a good thing, but the most prevalent peer pressure today, as always, is the pressure of those whose behavior is of a worldly nature, that which appeals to the lower instincts of the flesh.

Wherein lies the tremendous force of peer pressure? It is in the feeling of emotional insecurity felt by many who have a poor concept of their own self worth. Those affected are not only the young, but among many of those who should have reached a more mature status, sometimes even the parents of the young.

And why is this feeling of emotional insecurity so prevalent? It is because so many people have not from their earliest years lived in an environment where they learned reverence for God and the importance of respecting His word in all areas of conduct. They have not learned that acceptable behavior in God's sight must be different from that of the world in general. They have not achieved the self confidence and assurance resulting from the satisfaction that comes when one can feel that his life and conduct meet with God's approval.

The dedicated Christian realizes that to be different from the world is not a sign of inferiority deserving disapproval, but rather a distinguishing mark by which one feels a steady anchor to Christ and the consequent eternal blessings to be received after this life. Such a person, rather than developing a poor self-image, will have a great sense of self-esteem and satisfaction. With this realization of the superiority of his choice over that of his worldly peers, the confident Christian is happy, and is in a position to serve as a leader of his peers and others rather than becoming an unthinking follower of them. To those who are tempted to accept the values of their peers, Solomon advised:

> "... if sinners entice thee, consent thou not ... walk not in the way with them ... refrain thy foot from their path ..." (Proverbs 1:10-15).

The story is told of a grizzly bear that broke into the cabin of some hunters who had departed, leaving a fire still burning in a heavy pot-bellied stove. Seeing the red-hot stove and mistaking it for an enemy, the grizzly ran toward it clasping it in a bear hug. Feeling the burning heat, and thinking that his enemy was fighting back, the bear squeezed harder and harder until he caught aflame and was destroyed.

Many would say, "What a dumb animal!" Yes, he paid dearly for his stupidity, but many, even among those claiming to be Christians, behave in a similar way that leads to that which is far worse than physical destruction. They continue to embrace the common attractions of the world that lead to immorality in this life as well as eternal destruction. In spite of biblical instruction and warning from others, these people continue in their worldly ways of lying ("just little white lies"), stealing ("IRS is unfair to me"), immodest dress ("I have to be in style"), drinking alcoholic beverages ("— just a few social drinks"), gambling ("only in the lotteries. After all, they're legal"), dancing ("I don't see any harm in it"), and so, on and on.

Sins of the world have become so commonplace that without efforts to hide their actions, or without reticence or shame, many young people, professing to be Christians and attending religious services, blatantly engage in close physical conduct with those of opposite sex, cuddling, embracing, girls sitting on boys' laps, etc. with no evident thought of impropriety. As a natural consequence, often in private these actions lead to more intimate-adulterous relations. I have witnessed behavior in some aspects of these actions among young couples even in the presence of their professing Christian parents. Conversation between young men and women often sinks to the level of joking or mention of the most private areas of physical functions with no seeming realization of the invasion of moral decency. Such blatant flaunting of one's insensibility to the chaste virtuous behavior which should characterize Christians is sadly lacking. These

"... proclaim their sin like Sodom, they do not hide it" (Isa. 3:9).

Fellow Christians, do you not often note the permissive way in which the church quietly tolerates the worldly views and actions evident within the church?

How many church members do you know that, as they go about their professional duties, are quickly and easily identified by their associates as Christians? How many church members' conversation is so similar to that of the world that in a casual encounter with a stranger, or even a longer association, the Christian would never be recognized as different from the world at large? How many church members do you know who form their closest friendships with non-Christians rather than from within the church? How many Christians do you know who can rattle off the names of the leading figures of current and past popular movie hits or of soap-opera characters, as well as relate the theme of these productions? Can these same Christians tell you as much about Bible characters such as Aaron, Caleb, Deborah, Miriam, Ahab, Jeremiah or many others? Do you know Christians that spend as much or more money and time relating to their enjoyment of golf, movies, ski trips, sporting activities, vacation expenses and other entertainment than they contribute on Lord's day? Do you know Christians that can find time for many such activities as those just mentioned as well as T.V. viewing, but who can't find time for dedicated extended Bible study? Do you know Christians that can tell you all the things the preacher, the elders, and "they" should be doing, who find little time to devote regularly to actual personal service to Christ and others?

These observations are not to say that clean sports, vacations, and certain other things are evil within themselves. The problem is that it is very easy to let them take priority over other things of greater importance. They must not rob one of time, money, effort and concern for those spiritual activities necessary to faithful Christian service.

Many who say they are Christians have been deceived into thinking they can keep themselves unspotted from the world while associating with worldly friends, frequenting worldly activities and participating in what the world calls pleasure, not realizing that in so doing their spiritual values become eroded, their consciences become seared, their possible influence for Christ is sacrificed, and Christ is dishonored. Christian, do not be deceived! You cannot serve Jesus while walking in the ways of the world. Jesus said:

> "No man can serve two masters: for either he will hate the one, and love the other; or else he will hold to one, and despise the other. Ye cannot serve God and mammon" (Matt. 6:24).

It is impressively evident that in living a Christian life one must not only "put away" undesirable traits of character, worldly thinking and activities. He is also to "put on" Christian ways of thinking; one must practice the ways of righteousness and holiness.

Paul tells Christians to:

"... Abhor that which is evil; cleave to that which is good" (Rom. 12:9).

While traveling toward their own destruction, sinners often invite others to join them. The Christian must refuse to participate in the sinners' worldly ways. Refuse to be drawn into their web. Accept rejection by some as the price one must pay in order to achieve a better way of life, one that offers lasting rewards with no evil consequences. Seek friends among those who have Christian ideals and purposes, friends that will be a moral support, rather than drag one into a moral morass of corruption. Don't fret about those who may ridicule you. Be sorry for them because they have no conception of the superiority of your choice of behavior.

The Christian must continue to build a reverent and trusting relationship with Christ, thus rendering oneself invulnerable to the appeal of Satan's advocates. This refusal to compromise with the world builds self-esteem and true Christian character. It results in a life of satisfaction and contentment during one's earthly sojourn, but even of greater value is the promise of life eternal in the presence of God.

Christians, if they live truly in accord with biblical principles, cannot hide their lights as if ashamed of being different, but they must shine the precious light of the gospel making evident the corruption of the world's spiritual darkness. It is only to Christ's followers that He has given the sole responsibility of disseminating the gospel by which righteousness can be preserved in the world. Christians must resist worldly influences and live according to divine instruction if they are to live eternally and help others to do likewise.

> 'Tis not enough to say, I'm sorry and repent,
>   And then go on from day to day, just as we always went.
> Repentance is to leave the sins we loved before,
>   And show that we in earnest grieve by doing them no more.
>
> — Author Unknown

When Jesus was raised from the dead, He was given a place to sit at the right hand of God, "in the heavenly places far above all rule, all authority and power, and dominion, and every name that is named, not only in this world, but also in the world to come" (Eph. 1:20-21). He rules today in His earthly kingdom, the church (Eph. 1:22). Many individuals who have accepted the gospel invitation and were thus added to the church, without realizing their actions, are attempting to follow Christ, but in reality are trying to divide their allegiance between Christ and Satan, who is the "prince of this world" (John 16:11).

The Church Walking With The World

"The Church and the World walked far apart
    On the changing shores of time,
The World was singing a giddy song,
    And the Church a hymn sublime.
"Come, give me your hand," said the merry World,
    "And walk with me this way!"
But the good Church hid her snowy hands
    And solemnly answered "Nay,
I will not give you my hand at all,
    And I will not walk with you;
Your way is the way that leads to death;
    Your words are all untrue."

"Nay, walk with me but a little space,"
    Said the World with a kindly air;
The road I walk is a pleasant road,
    And the sun shines always there;
Your path is thorny and rough and rude,
    But mine is broad and plain;
My way is paved with flowers and dews,
    And yours with tears and pain;
The sky to me is always blue,
    No want, no toil I know;
The sky above you is always dark,
    Your lot is a lot of woe;
There's room enough for you and me
    To travel side by side."

Half shyly the Church approached the World
    And gave him her hand of snow;
And the old World grasped it and walked along,
    Saying, in accents low,
"Your dress is too simple to please my taste;
    I will give you pearls to wear,
Rich velvets and silks for your graceful form,
    And diamonds to deck your hair.
The Church looked down at her plain white robes,
    And then at the dazzling World,
And blushed as she saw his handsome lip
    With a smile contemptuously curled.
"I will change my dress for a costlier one,"
    Said the Church, with a smile of grace;
Then her pure white garments drifted away,
    And the World gave, in their place,
Beautiful satins and shining silks,
    Roses and gems and costly pearls;
While over her forehead her bright hair fell
    Crimped in a thousand curls.

"Your house is too plain," said the proud old World
    "I'll build you one like mine;
With walls of marble and towers of gold,
    And furniture ever so fine."
So he built her a costly and beautiful house;
    Most splendid it was to behold;
Her sons and her beautiful daughters dwelt there
    Gleaming in purple and gold;
Rich fairs and shows in the halls were held,
    And the World and his children were there.
Laughter and music and feasts were heard
    In the place that was meant for prayer.
There were cushioned seats for the rich and the gay,
    To sit in their pomp and pride;
But the poor who were clad in shabby array,
    Sat meekly down outside.

"You give too much to the poor," said the World.
    "Far more than you ought to do;

If they are in need of shelter and food,
    Why need it trouble you?
Go, take your money and buy rich robes,
    Buy horses and carriages fine;
Buy pearls and jewels and dainty food,
    Buy the rarest and costliest wine;
My children, they dote on all these things,
    And if you their love would win
You must do as they do, and walk in the ways
    That they are walking in."
So the poor were turned from her door in scorn,
    And she heard not the orphan's cry;
But she drew her beautiful robes aside,
    As the widows went weeping by.

Then the sons of the World and the Sons of the Church
    Walked closely hand and heart,
And only the Master, who knoweth all,
    Could tell the two apart.
Then the Church sat down at her ease, and said,
    "I am rich and my goods increase;
I have need of nothing, or aught to do,
    But to laugh, and dance, and feast."
The sly World heard, and he laughed in his sleeve,
    And mockingly said, aside,
"The Church is fallen, the beautiful Church;
    And her shame is her boast and her pride."

The angel drew near to the mercy seat,
    And whispered in sighs her name;
Then the loud anthems of rapture were hushed,
    And heads were covered with shame;
And a voice was heard at last by the Church
    From Him who sat on the throne,
"I know thy works, and how thou hast said,

'I am rich,' and hast not known
That thou art naked, poor and blind,
And wretched before My face;
Therefore from my presence cast I thee out,
And blot thy name from its place."

— Matilda C. Edwards

If you have been making this futile attempt to divide your allegiance, give Christ a chance to see what a change He can make in your life. You will be pleased with the results.

The Touch of the Master's Hand

'Twas battered, scarred, and the auctioneer
Thought it scarcely worth his while
To waste his time on the old violin,
But held it up with a smile.
"What am I bidden, good folks," he cried,
Who will start the bidding for me?
A dollar, a dollar?"—then, "Two!" "Only two?
Two dollars, and who'll make it three?
Three dollars once; three dollars, twice;
Going for three—" But no,
From the room, far back, a gray-haired man
Came forward and picked up the bow;
Then, wiping the dust from the old violin,
And tightening the loose strings,
He played a melody pure and sweet
As sweet as a caroling angel sings.

The music ceased, and the auctioneer,
With a voice that was quiet and low,
Said "What am I bidden for the old violin?"
And he held it up with the bow.
"A thousand dollars, and who'll make it two?
Two thousand! And who'll make it three?
Three thousand, once; three thousand, twice;
And going, and gone!" said he.

The people cheered, but some of them cried,
"We do not quite understand
What changed its worth?" Swift came the reply,
"The touch of the master's hand."

And many a man with a life out of tune
And battered and scattered with sin,
Is auctioned cheap to the thoughtless crowd,
Much like the old violin.
A "mess of pottage," a glass of wine;
A game—and he travels on.
He's "going" once, and "going" twice,
He's "going" and "almost gone."
But the Master comes and the foolish crowd
Never can quite understand
The worth of a soul, and the change that's wrought
By the touch of The Master's Hand.

— Myra Brooks Welch

Nazareth

Nazareth was a poor town
    And Nazareth was small;
Not a house in Nazareth
    Was spacious, fine or tall;
The rooms were dark and uncomfortable;
    The table fare was lean;
Yet out of a meager Nazareth
    There comes the Nazarene.

        — Betty Jean Favre

CHAPTER NINE

CHURCH LEADERSHIP

PRESIDING HEAD

> "... the God of our Lord Jesus ... that ye may know what is the hope of his coming ... the riches of the glory of his inheritance ... and the exceeding greatness of his power ... which he wrought in Christ, when he **raised him from the dead,** and made him to **sit at his right hand in the heavenly places**, far above all rule, and authority, and power, and dominion, and every name that is named, not only in this world, but also in that which is to come: and he **put all things in subjection under his feet**, and **gave him to be head over all things to the church, which is his body** ..." (cmphasis added) (Eph. 1:17-23).

Unlike those who look to the pope, their "Lord God on earth," and unlike the congregations who group themselves as a body under a man-made organization of authority, the church which Jesus built looks to Christ alone as its only authority. Unlike those denominations, whose beliefs are based on man-made creeds listing the doctrines on which their adherents base their hopes of eternal life, members of the church of Christ base their beliefs and hopes for eternity on the words of the New Testament penned by men inspired and directed by the Holy Spirit who was sent as their guide by Jesus, according to the promise He made to His apostles shortly before his death (John 16:13,14).

Although Christ, having fulfilled His earthly ministry ascended "far above all the heavens," He did not leave His followers without instruction and guidance. The New Testament writings provide in tangible form all information necessary for Christian living and for the preservation of Jesus' church, His spiritual body, His earthly kingdom, over which He reigns supreme on a heavenly throne. In addition to His written word, He made other provisions for the building up of the church through certain earthly ministrations.

> "And he gave some to be apostles; and some, prophets; and some, evangelists; and some, pastors and teachers; for the perfecting of the saints, unto the work of ministering, unto the building up of the body of Christ: till we all attain unto the unity of the faith, and of the knowledge of the Son of God, unto a fullgrown man, unto the measure of the stature of the fulness of Christ" (Eph. 4:11-13).

Paul named apostles, prophets, evangelists, pastors and teachers as those who were to serve being commissioned by Christ to oversee, teach and encourage the church on earth. The apostles and prophets, specially endowed with knowledge of divine inspiration, actively served the church only through the apostolic age — that is, until all of the thirteen apostles appointed by Jesus were dead and the church had in its possession the inspired words now embodied in the New Testament.

Since then, evangelists, pastors and teachers are to be the earthly leaders responsible to God for the care and direction of His church, always within the guidelines of biblical instruction. Note that the purpose of all of these special servants of the church was specifically the "building up of the body of Christ," the church, to "attain unto unity of the faith" and to "the knowledge of God" that Christian character might grow toward the maturity "of a fullgrown man" in the likeness of "the fulness of Christ." We shall note the New Testament instructions regarding each of these special ministries.

EVANGELISTS

When Paul named those who were to serve in special ministries within the church (Eph. 4:11) after "apostles" and "prophets," "evangelists" were named next in rank. An evangelist is a preacher, a proclaimer of the gospel message that was first revealed through the Holy Spirit on the day of Pentecost following Christ's ascension into heaven.

How do men become evangelists? Apostles and prophets were individually and specially called of God into His service. Evangelists, however, do not become so because of a direct and evident divine appointment. Today, any man so desiring can take upon himself the position of evangelist or preacher. This is his own personal decision. This is not to say that God may not, through unseen ways of His providence, influence individuals to make this decision.

I have heard very dedicated preachers, however, relate experiences, not meaning evident higher intervention, but of a definite time or situation when the individual felt so overcome with the desire to devote his main purpose in life to the ministry of proclaiming the gospel that a definite decision was made at that time to do so, a decision henceforth soon initiated and continued throughout a lifetime of ministry.

Also, a well known preacher gave this advice to young men. "If you can give your life wholeheartedly to some other profession and feel fully satisfied that in it you can make your greatest contribution to society, don't become an evangelist." His intention was not to discourage one from this ministry, but rather to pinpoint the degree of strong compulsion by which one must make such a decision.

Contrary to the denominational world, evangelists in the church of Christ, which endeavors to be guided by biblical example alone, are not confirmed or ordained by some over-all organization or even by a congregation. One who has prepared himself to perform this ministry through study of God's word and personal dedication may preach for any congregation which desires to use his services, or he may go to some area with no congregation, start preaching and build a congregation of the church.

However, it is the prerogative and duty of every congregation to investigate and scrutinize the character and teaching of any professed evangelist before giving him the privilege and obligation of further teaching in that particular congregation. It is also the duty of a congregation which, having secured the services of an evangelist and having found him unsound in doctrine or unholy in practice, either to see that he is further and properly instructed and needed changes made in his teaching or behavior, or else to remove him from the position of leadership and make known to the brotherhood his false teaching or unholy conduct, if he cannot be brought to penitence and changes of behavior. If necessary, the evangelist must be disciplined by the eldership and entire congregation, just as is the case with any other Christian guilty and impenitent of such sin.

To the man thinking of becoming an evangelist, it is important to realize that the work of an evangelist should not be considered a profession in the same sense as that of lawyers, physicians, etc. Rather, evangelism should be a calling arising out of a deep devotion to God, combined with love and concern for sinners doomed to eternal destruction. It is only when that love and desire to save others is so strong that it forces a dedicated believer of the gospel to be willing to spend and be spent for the good of others that he should become an evangelist.

Financial Support of Evangelists: It is the obligation of each congregation if possible to support financially its evangelist, in order that he may be able to spend his time entirely in activities by which the church is edified, instructed and involved in soul-saving. It is reasonable to expect the amount of that support to be sufficient to care for all the basic needs of the evangelist, but it is not reasonable to expect that the amount of support should be so great as to allow the evangelist and his family to live in a luxurious lifestyle incompatible with that of the congregation as a whole.

Until recent years, evangelists were usually paid low or moderate salaries, often barely adequate for the needs of his family. But at the same time, the majority of church members is made up of average or low wage-earners. It was not for the financial return that the evangelist labored, but rather for the opportunity of serving. In humility and gratitude, most evangelists accepted, without further demands, what the congregation offered.

Any evangelist, who is asked to serve a congregation where he sees for himself the opportunity to gather a great harvest of souls and encourage growth and active participation in Christian service, and who refuses so to serve for the sole reason that the congregation cannot or will not meet his self-specified salary, is questionable, if not surely unworthy, to be an evangelist for the Lord Jesus Christ.

This writer, having spent over seventy years personally as a member of the Lord's body, sixty-two years of which were as the wife of an evangelist, in looking back over the history of the church, realizes that she lived during the latter part of the period during which the church experienced its greatest growth. The church of Christ was growing more rapidly than any denomination during the period following the advent and climax of the Restoration Movement. These years include the years of the great depression. Preachers were poorly supported financially. Few people in the church had a lot of this world's goods. I recall the time when a preacher returned home from holding a gospel revival meeting lasting ten days, the likes of which were common in those times. Usually they were well attended with much zeal and enthusiasm manifested by the church and community, and many souls obeyed the gospel. This preacher received pay in the form of home-canned fruits, vegetables and live chickens.

Many regular preachers of good-sized congregations found it necessary to augment their salaries by working also at some other work. The apostle Paul likewise found this necessary at times, even though some churches sent him financial support while he did mission work in several cities. Later, while in prison, Paul wrote to the church in Philippi, recalling that work which he had done some years earlier and the help that he had received from Philippi.

> "And ye yourselves also know, ye Philippians, that in the beginning of the gospel, when I departed from Macedonia, no church had fellowship with me in the matter of giving and receiving but ye only; for even in Thessalonica ye sent once and again unto my need" (Phil. 4:15,16).

Nevertheless, Paul defended the rights of himself and Barnabas, as well as of all who spend their full time in service to Christ and the church, to lead a normal life like all other Christians. Paul wrote:

> "Have we no right to eat and to drink? Have we no right to lead about a wife that is a believer, even as the rest of the apostles, and the brethren of the Lord, and Cephas? Or I only and Barnabas, have we not a right to forbear working? What soldier ever serveth at his own charges? who planteth a vineyard, and eateth not of the milk of the flock?" (I Cor. 9:4-7).

Paul was here appealing to common reason. But, as he continued, speaking according to divine revelation, he reminded his readers that God had announced this truth by telling Moses:

> "... Thou shalt not muzzle the ox when he treadeth out the corn. Is it for the oxen that God careth, or saith he it assuredly for our sake? Yea, for our sake it was written: because he that ploweth ought to plow in hope, and he that thresheth, to thresh in hope of partaking"
> (I Cor. 9:9,10).

Paul was using the examples of material functions, but he pointed out that the same principal applies to spiritual matters:

> "If we sowed unto you spiritual things, is it a great matter if we shall reap your carnal things? If others partake of this right over you, do not we yet more? Nevertheless we did not use this right; but we bear all things, that we may cause no hindrance to the gospel of Christ"
> (I Cor. 9: 11,12).

> "Even so did the Lord ordain that they that proclaim the gospel should live of the gospel" (I Cor. 9:14).

This principle of financial support applies, not only to preachers, but also to elders and others who give their full time to labors for Christ. Writing to Timothy, Paul applied the same scriptures.

> "Let the elders that rule well be counted worthy of double honor, especially those who labor in the word and in teaching. For the scripture saith, Thou shalt not muzzle the ox when he treadeth out the corn. And, The laborer is worthy of his hire" (I Tim. 5:17,18).

Having established the fact that he and other ministers who give their efforts particularly to their ministries should be financially supported, Paul explained that he chose not to avail himself of that right in Corinth.

> "If others partake of this right over you, do not we yet more? Nevertheless we did not use this right; but we bear

all things, that we may cause no hindrance to the gospel of Christ" (I Cor. 9:12).

Paul said that his defense of a preacher's right to receive pay for his ministry was not in order to get the Corinthian church to pay him. He said that if he preached the gospel for pay, he had done nothing more than render service as an employee, "for necessity is laid upon me." He was happy in knowing that he was giving of himself beyond merely doing his duty.

> "... if I do this of mine own will, I have a reward: but if not of mine own will, I have a stewardship intrusted to me. What then is my reward? That, when I preach the gospel, I may make the gospel without charge, so as not to use to the full my right in the gospel" (I Cor. 9:17,18).

With Paul, these were not empty words. At times Paul did work physically to support the needs of himself and fellow workers. This was true when he went to Corinth. Upon arrival there, he was alone, having left his companions in other cities of Macedonia to strengthen new congregations they had just established. But Paul found a couple, Aquila and his wife Priscilla, who had been forced, because they were Jews, to leave Rome.

> "... and he (Paul) came unto them; and because he was of the same trade, he abode with them, and they wrought; for by their trade they were tentmakers. And he reasoned in the synagogue every Sabbath, and persuaded Jews and Greeks" (Acts 18:2-4).

Corinth was not the only place mentioned where Paul and his fellow-laborers worked for their own support while preaching. At a later time he wrote to the church in Thessalonica saying:

> "neither did we eat bread for nought at any man's hand, but in labor and travail, working night and day, that we might not burden any of you: not because we have not the right, but to make ourselves an ensample unto you, that ye should imitate us" (II Thess. 3:8,9).

It is sad to note that today, during a period when the church of Christ is experiencing an exceedingly low lack of substantial growth, some congregations spend such large amounts for salaries and local expenses that very little money is left to support what God intended to be the main function of the gospel — the saving of souls. In some cases preachers of unusual oratorical abilities and dynamic personalities have gained wide-name recognition and popularity; and taking advantage of these, they demand and are granted exorbitant salaries. I suggest that such an attitude of demand, or even acceptance of such a salary far exceeding the average church member, is demeaning to the image of dedication, which should characterize a truly sincere minister, striving to set an example of humility and willingness to sacrifice for the cause of Christ as did Jesus Himself and Christian ministers of New Testament times. All evangelists should show themselves willing to follow Paul's advice to Timothy, a young evangelist:

> "But be thou sober in all things, suffer hardship, do the work of an evangelist, fulfil thy ministry" (II Tim. 4:5).

> Someone once asked Francis of Assisi how he was able to accomplish so much. He replied, "This may be why: The Lord looked down from Heaven and said, 'Where can I find the weakest, littlest man on earth?' Then He saw me and said, 'I've found him. I will work through him, and he won't be proud of it. He'll see that I am only using him because of his insignificance.'"

> — From Our Daily Bread

Special Functions of Evangelists: The New Testament includes three short epistles written by the apostle Paul to two young evangelists, Timothy and Titus. By carefully examining these, one can arrive at a clearer understanding of what God intended for His evangelists to do. We have already noted that they are to work toward "the perfecting of the body of Christ" (Eph. 4:11). We know also that — like all who have believed that Jesus was God's Son, that have repented of their sins and have been baptized in the name of the Father, Son and Holy Spirit — evangelists seek to teach others how to avail themselves of the precious blessings available through God's wondrous grace. But evangelists do much more. They minister to the whole congregation. Paul instructed Timothy that he should:

> "Hold the pattern of sound words which thou hast heard from me, in faith and love which is in Christ Jesus. That good thing which was committed unto thee guard through the Holy Spirit which dwelleth in us" (II Tim 1:13,14).

> "And the things which thou hast heard from me among many witnesses, the same commit thou to faithful men, who shall be able to teach others also" (II Tim. 2:2).

> "But abide thou in the things which thou hast learned and hast been assured of, knowing of whom thou hast learned them" (II Tim. 3:14).

> Paul's admonition to Titus and to all who would speak for God:

> "... speak thou the things which befit the sound doctrine" (Titus 2:1).

> "in all things showing thyself an example of good works; in thy doctrine showing uncorruptness, gravity, sound speech, that cannot be condemned; that he that is of the contrary part may be ashamed, having no evil thing to say of us" (Titus 2:7,8).

The reader should bear in mind that the early evangelists had no New Testament written texts as do evangelists of today. The early evangelists were to keep in mind those teachings gleaned from listening to the word of God's inspired apostles and prophets.

No doubt, it was God's intention that these letters from Paul to Timothy and Titus benefit not only the original recipients, but that they should provide instruction for future generations of evangelists and teachers. Therefore, these letters contain teachings on certain subjects not given so explicitly elsewhere.

1. Instructions regarding prayer (I Tim. 2:1-5).

2. Instructions to women as to personal appearance and conduct in the worship assembly (I Tim. 2:9-15).

3. Qualifications and conduct of elders, deacons and certain women (I Tim. 3:1-13; 5:1,19,20; Titus 1:5-9).

4. Responsibilities of the church and kinsmen for the care of elderly widows and directions for their personal conduct (I Tim. 5:2-16).

5. Propriety of payment to "those who labor in the word and in teaching" (I Tim. 5:17,18).

6. Conduct of Christian servants and masters (I Tim. 6:1,2; Titus 2:9-10).

7. Proper attitude toward riches (I Tim. 6:6-10).

8. Admonitions to aged men and women (Titus 2:2-6).

9. Miscellaneous admonitions (Titus 3:10).

10. The most emphasized charge, judging from the space devoted to it, was the responsibility of guarding the church against false teachings. The outstanding false teaching of the apostolic age was concerned with the Jewish rite of circumcision, whether or not it was bound upon Christian Gentile converts. This was settled eventually and is no longer a controversy. There were also other old wives' tales, genealogies, etc. against which Timothy was warned to give no heed. Today, false teaching is still a great danger to the church, but these teachings are of a different character. In relation to what Paul mentioned in his charge to evangelists to refute unholy teaching and false doctrine, his words not only apply to the particular sins of every generation, but to those sins which are prevalent in our modern society and which are strongly condemned by God. These sins which are particularly devastating to our present civilization were explicitly named:

> "as knowing this, that law is not made for a righteous man, but for the lawless and unruly, for the ungodly and sinners, for the unholy and profane, for murderers of fathers and murderers of mothers, for manslayers, for fornicators, for abusers of themselves with men, for menstealers, for liars, for false swearers, and if there be

any other thing contrary to the sound doctrine" (I Tim. 1:9,10).

"But the Spirit saith expressly, that in later times some shall fall away from the faith, giving heed to seducing spirits and doctrines of demons, through the hypocrisy of men that speak lies, branded in their own conscience as with a hot iron; forbidding to marry, and commanding to abstain from meats, which God created to be received with thanksgiving by them that believe and know the truth. For every creature of God is good, and nothing is to be rejected, if it be received with thanksgiving: for it is sanctified through the word of God and prayer" (I Tim 4:1-5).

"But know this, that in the last days grievous times shall come. For men shall be lovers of self, lovers of money, boastful, haughty, railers, disobedient to parents, unthankful, unholy, without natural affection, implacable, slanderers, without self-control, fierce, no lovers of good, traitors, headstrong, puffed up, lovers of pleasure rather than lovers of God; holding a form of godliness, but having denied the power thereof: from these also turn away. For of these are they that creep into houses, and take captive silly women laden with sins, led away by divers lusts, ever learning, and never able to come to the knowledge of the truth. ... But evil men and impostors shall wax worse and worse, deceiving and being deceived" (II Tim. 3:1-7, 13).

All church leaders, whether elders, preachers, or teachers, must always be on guard against false teachers and the doctrines they proclaim. It is often easy for those in the flock, who are to be guarded and properly taught, to be misled. False doctrines are often, when first seen, seemingly insignificant, interesting ideas, although they are actually insidious and if ignored they will grow like the tiny mustard seed into huge devastating proportions in their fatal consequences.

"A little leaven leaveneth the whole lump" (Gal. 5:9).

Paul was saying that false teaching is like leaven or yeast in bread dough. Unnoticed, false teaching spreads quietly and rapidly through the brotherhood, ultimately destroying true faith and the purity of the church, resulting eventually in complete apostasy of both individual and church.

The confrontation of error set forth by false teachers is the responsibility of the church which, as Paul told Timothy, is "the pillar and ground of the truth" (I Tim. 3:15). As representatives of the church, *elders* must see that the congregation, where they exercise oversight, must not provide a forum for false teaching. *Preachers* must present the truth which refutes false teaching, and *teachers* are responsible for knowing and upholding the truth as opposed to error.

When our Lord appeared to John while he was exiled on the isle of Patmos, giving him letters to deliver to seven churches, one of those letters was to the church at Thyatira. In this letter the Lord commended the love, faith, ministry, patience and past wholesome activity of that church. Nevertheless, He pronounced on its members strong condemnation for tolerating gross immoral corruption within the membership. All church leaders, especially, should hear and heed the solemn message given to this church.

> "But I have this against thee, that thou sufferest the woman Jezebel, who calleth herself a prophetess; and she teacheth and seduceth my servants to commit fornication; and to eat things sacrificed to idols. And I gave her time that she should repent; and she willeth not to repent of her fornication. Behold, I cast her into a bed, and them that commit adultery with her into great tribulation, except they repent of her works. And I will kill her children with death; and all the churches shall know that I am he that searcheth the reins and hearts: and I will give unto each one of you according to your works" (Rev. 2:20-23).

> "Now I beseech you, brethren, mark them that are causing the divisions and occasions of stumbling, contrary to the doctrine which ye learned: and turn away from them. For they that are such serve not our Lord

Christ, but their own belly; and by their smooth and fair speech they beguile the hearts of the innocent" (Rom. 16:17,18).

"A factious man after a first and second admonition refuse; knowing that such a one is perverted, and sinneth, being self-condemned" (Titus 3:10,11).

"because that for the sake of the Name they went forth, taking nothing of the Gentiles. We therefore ought to welcome such, that we may be fellow-workers for the truth. I wrote somewhat unto the church: but Diotrephes, who loveth to have the preeminence among them, receiveth us not. Therefore, if I come, I will bring to remembrance his works which he doeth, prating against us with wicked words: and not content therewith, neither doth he himself receive the brethren, and them that would he forbiddeth and casteth them out of the church. Beloved, imitate not that which is evil, but that which is good. He that doeth good is of God: he that doeth evil hath not seen God" (III John 7-11).

"The great causes of God and Humanity are not defeated by the assaults of the Devil, but by the slow crushing, glacier-like masses of thousands and thousands of indifferent nobodies."

— George Adam Smith

God's people today must take every precaution lest they become as they were in Israel prior to that nation's being carried away into captivity in a foreign land. Of those people the prophet Jeremiah sadly lamented:

"A wonderful and horrible thing is come to pass in the land: the prophets prophesy falsely, and the priests bear rule by their means; and my people love to have it so..." (Jeremiah 5:30,31).

As important as it is to recognize and refute false teaching, it is important to differentiate between (1) the proclaiming of error in an effort to change true doctrine, and (2) the fellow-Christian who is struggling with personal convictions because of spiritual immaturity, misunderstanding, or lack of biblical literacy. Toward such an uninformed and spiritually weak member, church leaders and stronger Christians must exercise brotherly love and patient assistance.

> "And we exhort you, brethren, admonish the disorderly, encourage the fainthearted, support the weak, be long-suffering toward all" (I Thess. 5:14).

Clear distinction must be made then between the weaker but conscientious Christian brother and the proclaimer of false doctrine for the purpose of refuting divinely revealed truth, and introducing a doctrine which creates a divisive party or division into the church.

> "Now I beseech you, brethren, mark them that are causing the divisions and occasions of stumbling, contrary to the doctrine which ye learned: and turn away from them. For they that are such serve not our Lord Christ, but their own belly; and by their smooth and fair speech they beguile the hearts of the innocent" (Rom. 16:17,18).

> "but shun foolish questionings, and genealogies, and strifes, and fightings about the law; for they are unprofitable and vain. A factious man after a first and second admonition refuse; knowing that such a one is perverted, and sinneth, being self-condemned" (Titus 3:9-11).

> "Whosoever goeth onward and abideth not in the teaching of Christ, hath not God: he that abideth in the teaching, the same hath both the Father and the Son. If any one cometh unto you, and bringeth not this teaching, receive him not into your house, and give him no greeting: for he that giveth him greeting partaketh in his evil works" (II John 9-11).

According to John's words, even to receive one who sows discord and causes factions among the brotherhood into your home, or even to give him brotherly greeting, involves you in his sin. One must not only refuse to fellowship the false teacher, but his errors must be quickly brought to light and condemned. The church must not allow silence on such a matter, thus implying approval or indifference to the false teaching. It has been well said that all that is needed for evil to prevail is for good to be silent or indifferent.

As an example of the strong bearing the infirmities of the weak, consider this situation found among early Gentile converts to Christianity. Most of them had a background of idolatry and paganism. For this reason, these new Christians' experiences posed a particular problem which Paul addressed in his first letter to the Corinthian church and later in his letter to Christians in Rome. [For more details, see I Cor. 10:23-32 and Rom. 14:13-23.] The problem arose because after idolaters in the community had used animals or parts of animals in their idolatrous rites, the remaining meat was often sold to the meat markets where the meat from idolaters was included in that offered for sale to the public. Knowing this occurred, some Christians could not conscientiously eat the meat and they judged as wrong-doers those Christians who did buy and eat the meat, being unconcerned about its previous use. Paul explained that for those who gave no thought to the meat's previous use, it was not in itself wrong to eat the meat:

> "Whatsoever is sold ... eat, asking no question for conscience' sake" (I Cor. 10:25).

> "I know, and am persuaded in the Lord Jesus, that nothing is unclean of itself: save that to him who accounteth anything to be unclean, to him it is unclean" (Rom. 14:14).

However, Paul counseled:

> " ... he that doubteth is condemned if he eat, because he eateth not of faith; and whatsoever is not of faith is sin" (Romans 14:23).

In other words, Jesus has made no restrictions on what is lawful or unlawful for Christians to eat, but if one's conscience condemns him for eating any particular thing, it would be sinful for him to violate his conscience and eat it.

The point of this discussion is twofold: First, the Christian who is more well-grounded in the faith must respect and encourage the weaker brother. Second, even if doing something is not wrong in itself, if one believes it to be wrong, he sins if he violates his conscience and commits the action anyway.

> "Now we that are strong ought to bear the infirmities of the weak, and not to please ourselves" (Romans 15:1).

To the stronger brother, Paul said:

> "Let us not therefore judge one another any more: but judge ye this rather, that no man put a stumbling block in his brother's way, or an occasion of falling" (Rom. 14:13).

Paul explained: If your eating meat causes grief to your brother who believes this to be wrong and if you continue to do so, you are not exhibiting love for your fellow-Christian. You must not in this way destroy the faith of your brother for whom Christ died.

> "Overthrow not for meat's sake the work of God...." (Romans 14:20).

This eating of meat well illustrates the commission of any act which is lawful in God's sight, but which appears as an offense to the conscience of another brother who is zealously seeking to serve God. Paul says the doer of the act should refrain from thus exercising his liberty in Christ in order not to cause another Christian to perform the same act when in doing so he violates his own conscience. In summation Paul concludes:

> "Give no occasion of stumbling, either to Jews, or to Greeks, or to the church of God: even as I also please all men in all things, not seeking mine own profit, but the profit of the many, that they may be saved" (I Cor. 10:32,33).

Proper attitude and activities of evangelists: Paul gave evangelists certain charges and instructions of which all should be aware and strive to accomplish. All should be motivated by love, conscience and faith:

> "But the end of the charge is love out of a pure heart and a good conscience and faith unfeigned" (I Tim. 1:5).

> "This charge I commit unto thee, my child Timothy, according to the prophecies which led the way to thee, that by them thou mayest war the good warfare" (I Tim. 1:18).

> "Let no man despise thy youth; but be thou an example to them that believe, in word, in manner of life, in love, in faith, in purity" (I Tim. 4:12).

> "I charge thee in the sight of God, and Christ Jesus, and the elect angels, that thou observe these things without prejudice, doing nothing by partiality" (I Tim. 5:21).

> "O Timothy, guard that which is committed unto thee, turning away from the profane babblings and oppositions of the knowledge which is falsely so called" (I Tim. 6:20).

> "Give diligence to present thyself approved unto God, a workman that needeth not to be ashamed, handling aright the word of truth" (II Tim. 2:15).

Modern preachers' actions and obligations in obeying this injunction go beyond those of Timothy and Titus because today all of the New Testament scriptures are easily available for reading and providing material for reflection, materials Titus and Timothy did not have. Paul told Timothy to:

> "... give heed to reading, to exhortation, to teaching. ... Be diligent in these things; give thyself wholly to them; that thy progress may be manifest unto all" (I Tim. 4:13-15).

For reading, Timothy had the Old Testament scriptures and the letters written to him by Paul. Also, like all Christians, but especially one who serves as an evangelist and necessarily becomes a very evident example to others, Timothy had a special obligation, which Paul expressed in this way:

> "... neither be partaker of other men's sins: keep thyself pure" (I Tim. 5:22).

After warnings to all of those who are "minded to be rich," Paul warned Timothy:

> "But thou, O man of God, flee these things; and follow after righteousness, godliness, faith, love, patience, meekness. Fight the good fight of the faith, lay hold on the life eternal, whereunto thou wast called, and didst confess the good confession in the sight of many witnesses" (I Tim. 6:11,12).

> "But flee youthful lusts, and follow after righteousness, faith, love, peace, with them that call on the Lord out of a pure heart. But foolish and ignorant questionings refuse, knowing that they gender strifes" (II Tim. 2:22,23).

Evangelists should proclaim the whole truth boldly, heedless of likely personal opposition, but their preaching must be spoken in a spirit of love, patience and kindness, not with barbed insinuations or spiteful epithets:

> "And the Lord's servant must not strive, but be gentle towards all, apt to teach, forbearing, in meekness correcting them that oppose themselves; if peradventure God may give them repentance unto the knowledge of the truth, and they may recover themselves out of the snare of the devil, having been taken captive by him unto his will" (II Tim. 2:24-26).

As a general summation of Paul's charges to Timothy and all gospel evangelists, Paul laid on them this inclusive and meaningful obligation:

> "preach the word; be urgent in season, out of season; reprove, rebuke, exhort, with all longsuffering and teaching" (II Tim. 4:2).

Note that every word of this admonition is fraught with deep urgency, great necessity, and consuming loving passion for the salvation of others. And that the evangelist might keep this charge faithfully, God has provided the means of doing so:

> "Every scripture inspired of God is also profitable for teaching, for reproof, for correction, for instruction which is in righteousness: that the man of God may be complete, furnished completely unto every good work" (II Tim. 3:16,17).

Special teaching needful today: There are countless numbers of subjects upon which an evangelist can dutifully expound in public preaching before the general assembly. This makes it necessary for him to choose to give special attention to those matters most relevant to prevailing situations existing at the time the selection of subjects is made. Considering the fact that at present one of the most troubling matters for elders and preachers is the widespread sweeping sentiment across the Christian brotherhood, the cry for making changes in the manner of conducting the activities in the general assembly for worship each Lord's day, this subject needs to be properly addressed. The evident reason for such a demand is the scriptural illiteracy among great numbers of individuals who have been taught and have responded to the gospel plan of salvation. They have accepted Jesus as the divine Son of God; they have repented of past sins in a general sense (often not really realizing the extent or full nature of those sins), and they have been scripturally immersed in the waters of baptism. They have begun to attend church services. They have, too often with a ritualistic attitude, engaged outwardly in the activities of worship as carried on in the assembly.

At the same time, these persons have not really understood all that was involved in their actions. Many do not realize the basic differences between Christ's church and all churches of various denominations which claim belief in Christ, even though among them are beliefs and doctrines which are in complete contradiction to each other. A big problem now is that many of the untaught newborn Christians are attracted by certain practices among the denominations that appear harmless because the world has been so accustomed to them. Examples of some of these things for which some spiritually immature Christians are clamoring for their adoption into the worship service are using women in active roles of public worship, of introducing dramatic skits to teach rather than only "dry sermons," special musical numbers by gifted groups or individuals, musical instruments as accompanying congregational singing or as separate renditions and such like. These advocates of change do not understand that these practices are relics of the great apostasy that remain because many in the religious world have failed to recognize the evils of their use, even though many other fallacies of the medieval church have been corrected by these churches.

With these understandings of the reasons for demands for change in mind, evangelists today should give considerable attention to making sure that newborn Christians and others receive full and adequate instruction on matters which seem to be so lacking in the general knowledge of Christians. Instead of continuous preaching on those subjects of morality regarding which most congregations even in various denominations agree, evangelists should make sure that they are feeding their congregations balanced spiritual nourishment. I would challenge each evangelist to answer and consider the importance of these matters: How long since you have preached one or more lessons on any or all of these subjects?

1. What evidences can you give that support an unquestionable faith that God exists? Or that the Bible is the inspired word of God?

2. Unmistakable evidences that Jesus was the Christ.

3. Why are the virgin birth of Jesus and the certainty of His resurrection of utmost importance?

4. What reliable evidence exists that verifies the virgin birth of Jesus and His resurrection?

5. Detailed historical data explaining and describing the great apostasy culminating in the medieval church. [This is necessary in order that one understand how denominations came into existence.]

6. Events and importance of the Reformation Movement.

7. Details and importance of the Restoration Movement. [This knowledge makes possible a clear understanding and intelligent appreciation of the distinctiveness of the church of Christ.]

8. Why the church of Christ does not use instrumental music.

9. Why the church does not believe in continual divine revelations today.

10. Why members of the church of Christ believe and practice the memorial of Jesus' death by partaking of bread and fruit of the vine each Lord's day.

11. Scriptural descriptions of immodest attire and behavior and God's injunctions for its necessity.

These are some of the subjects which evangelists seem to take for granted that all understand, but this is not true; and the church is suffering because of this lack of understanding. When every Christian fully understands these subjects relating to his professed Christian faith, he will be able to heed Peter's injunction:

> "but sanctify in your hearts Christ as Lord: being ready always to give answer to every man that asketh you a reason concerning the hope that is in you, yet with meekness and fear: having a good conscience, that, wherein ye are spoken against, they may be put to shame who revile your good manner of life in Christ" (I Pet.3:15,16).

The challenge to evangelists of today: In reality, the challenge is the same as that at the time when the first sermons were preached, but many today are evading it. They are giving in to the demands of modern society, trying to soothe the "itching ears" that do not want their own actions condemned. Paul warned Timothy about these, saying:

> "For the time will come when they will not endure the sound doctrine; but, having itching ears, will heap to themselves teachers after their own lusts; and will turn away their ears from the truth, and turn aside unto fables" (II Tim. 4:3,4).

How was Timothy to respond toward these people? Paul advised:

"But be thou sober in all things, suffer hardship, do the work of an evangelist, fulfil thy ministry" (II Tim. 4:5).

Timothy's ministry, as should be that of every evangelist, was described in this charge worthy of repetition which was so important that Paul called on God and Christ to witness it:

"I charge thee in the sight of God, and of Christ Jesus, who shall judge the living and the dead, and by his appearing and his kingdom, **preach the word**; be urgent in season, out of season; **reprove, rebuke, exhort**, with all longsuffering and teaching" (II Tim. 4:1,2).

Effective preaching must be with boldness, that is with straightforward decisive language, regardless of to whomsoever it may apply. In modern parlance the truth must be told like it is, letting it hit where it falls. Stephen exhibited boldness in declaring the appropriate message, even though it cost him his life. He was emulating Jesus, the master teacher and master preacher. Many prophets of Old Testament times told it like it was and many thus became martyrs. John, the baptizer, told it like it was and was imprisoned and then decapitated for it.

When modern preachers really exhibit the boldness in proclaiming truth, the whole truth, from their pulpits, many changes will take place throughout the brotherhood. The outcry of boredom, prevalence of unfaithfulness in marriage and consequent divorce, worldly behavior, indecently dressed girls and women, lack of respect for God, for parents, for civil authority and decency will be noticeably affected. The church may decrease in number, but it will be fortified by loss of the chaff and there will be stronger fortitude and stability within, therefore the church will be capable of greater accomplishments.

The story is told of a Quaker who discovered a thief in his house, and taking down his grandfather's old fowling piece, the Quaker quietly said: "Friend, thee had better get out of the way for I intend to fire the gun right where thee stands."

Gospel preaching should be fired in the same way. Read the Bible and you will be impressed that this is God's way of preaching and combating error. When this kind of preaching becomes common, the light of the gospel will begin to shine forth and the saving quality of salt will begin taking effect in the preservation of purity in personal characters and in the church as a body.

The evangelist lacking boldness will listen to such pleas as the following:

To The Preacher

Preach about yesterday, Preacher!
    The time so far away:
When the hand of the deity smote and slew,
And the heathen plagued the stiff-necked Jew;
Of when the Man of Sorrow came,
And blessed the people who cursed his name—
Preach about yesterday, Preacher,
    Not about today!

Preach about tomorrow, Preacher!
    Beyond this world's decay:
Of the sheepfold Paradise we priced
When we pinned our faith to Jesus Christ.
Of those hot depths that shall receive
The goats who would not so believe—
Preach about tomorrow, Preacher,
    Not about today!

Preach about the old sins, Preacher!
    And the old virtues, too!
You must not steal nor take man's life,
You must not covet your neighbor's wife,
And woman must cling at every cost
To her one virtue, or she is lost—
Preach about the old sins, Preacher!
    Not about the new!

Preach about the other man, Preacher!
    The man we all can see!
The man of oaths, the man of strife,
The man who drinks and beats his wife,

Who helps his mates to fret and shirk
When all they need is to keep at work,
Preach about the other man, Preacher!
Not about me!

— Charlotte Perkins Gilman

PASTORS, ELDERS, BISHOPS, PRESBYTERS

Who are they? All of these are different terms applying to the same office within the church. Those holding this office are appointed officials that exercise authority and direction in the church. Each congregation has its own elders, chosen by the congregation.

The New Testament does not give specific instructions for the selection of men to fill this office, except to list qualifications by which they are to be selected within each local congregation, which is the only realm in which they have authority. During the apostolic age, we are told how they were selected in some instances. Paul and Barnabas appointed elders in Iconium, Lystra and Derbe (Acts 14:21-23). Their appointment was accompanied by fasting and praying. On another occasion, the young preacher Titus was told by Paul to appoint elders among certain congregations where Paul and Silas had previously established congregations of the church.

> "For this cause left I thee in Crete, that thou shouldest set
> in order the things that were wanting, and appoint elders
> in every city, as I gave thee charge" (Titus 1:5).

In the absence of further biblical instruction regarding the appointment of elders, and since we do not have evangelists who have special gifts from God as did Paul — and perhaps Silas — evangelists today are not given the privilege of appointing elders. The general practice among churches, since the apostolic age, has been that used by the Jerusalem church (Acts 6:1-6) as directed by the apostles in the selection of men who were to serve in the capacity of deacons. Having been told the qualifications necessary in these men, members of the congregation were asked to select men having these qualities, who were then appointed by the apostles.

However, the church is not a democracy where these officials are chosen by popular vote. Since God has revealed the characteristics necessary to qualify a man to serve in this capacity, members of the congregation are asked, with these qualifications in mind, to consider which men in the membership appear to have attained these qualities. After due consideration, if such men are found, they are appointed in an official and public way making their appointment known to all, providing that these men selected are totally willing to accept the heavy responsibilities inherent to that service as pronounced in God's word.

The selection of elders is an enormous responsibility for any congregation and should not be done without careful and enlightened consideration. Some congregations have not adhered carefully enough to the particular characteristics divinely given for selecting elders, and have made some erroneous selections relative to the eldership that have had catastrophic results within the congregation.

Because a man has an outgoing personality and is loved and appreciated by all, or the fact that a member holds an important status in his community, does not necessarily fit him to serve as an elder, although these qualities may be assets to his position. If he is to serve well in his very special appointed position, he must fit the description given and recorded by divine revelation.

When consideration is given to the work of elders, it is evident that men chosen for this office must be full of love for others and for the church, men willing and able to give unsparingly of their time and effort on behalf of their heavy responsibility. They need not only to have developed the general Christian values, graces and virtues which are constantly to be sought by all Christians, but elders must have developed these qualities to a degree of maturity beyond that of the average young child of the faith. The particular characteristics needful for qualified elders are enumerated by Paul to two young preachers under his tutelage, Timothy and Titus.

Specified scriptural qualifications: Paul gave Timothy a long list of these qualifications (I Tim. 3:1-7). To Titus Paul likewise named certain qualifications (Titus 1:6-9) and Peter elaborated especially on the elders' comparison to shepherds (I Pet. 5:1-4).

Combining the lists of spiritual qualifications from the three accounts, we see that they name spiritual qualities such as every Christian should be striving to develop.

Perfection in all of these cannot be expected, even of elders, but each qualification must be present in recognizable quantity in elders. An elder must be "without reproach," "of good testimony from those without" — in more everyday language, an elder must have a good reputation. He must be "temperate" or "sober-minded" — that is not given to excesses of any kind. He must be "orderly" — that is, able to think systematically and reasonably. He must be "no brawler," "no striker" — that is, "not contentious," but "gentle" and "considerate." He must not be "self-willed" or "soon angry" — not determined to have his own way always. The elder must be a "lover of good" and consequently a hater of evil.

Aside from these personal spiritual characteristics, there are two requirements that are peculiar to the eldership. An elder must be married, "the husband of one wife." This means one wife at a time. If a man has married and his wife dies and then the man marries again, he is still the husband of only one wife, because death has severed the first relationship. This requirement, of course, precludes a woman being an elder.

The second requirement peculiar to an elder is that he must have children. These children must be old enough to have become believers and must in truth, be believers. These children must be obedient to their parents, not accused of riot or unruliness. The elder must be "one that rules his own house, having his children in subjection with all gravity." The reason given for this is: "if a man knows not how to rule his own house, how can he take care of the church of God?"

The elder is to be "not a novice," that is one who has been a Christian for a very short time, not long enough to qualify being "apt to teach," and fully equipped with knowledge of the scriptures and their applications to Christian living. Paul explained this to Titus saying that an elder should be

> " ... given to hospitality, a lover of good, sober-minded, just, holy, self-controlled; holding to the faithful word which is according to the teaching, that he may be able

both to exhort in the sound doctrine, and to convict the gainsayers. For there are many unruly men, vain talkers and deceivers, specially they of the circumcision" (Titus 1:8-10).

Of those traits of character for which all Christians should strive constantly to develop to greater and greater intensity is the right attitude toward money. The elder must not be a "lover of money" or, expressed differently," not given to filthy lucre." He must be "blameless as God's steward" — that is, he habitually gives generously and cheerfully of his financial means toward the progress of Christianity. He must set a worthy example in this as well as in other aspects of life. He is to exhibit a love of hospitality toward others in every sense of the word.

In Peter's letter to Christians, he expands on the role of the eldership, comparing it to the role of a shepherd as it was in the culture of those times. Jesus, Himself, often spoke of his disciples as sheep and of Himself as a shepherd.

Jesus spoke regarding the church as if it were a sheepfold. He said,

"I am the door; by me if any man enter in, he shall be saved..." (John 10:9).

"I am the good shepherd: the good shepherd layeth down his life for the sheep" (John 10:11).

"I am the good shepherd; and I know mine own, and mine own know me, even as the Father knoweth me, and I know the Father; and I lay down my life for the sheep" (John 10:14).

This symbolism was even used in the revelations made to Isaiah, who wrote prophetically of the coming of Christ and His promised salvation:

"He will feed his flock like a shepherd, he will gather the lambs in his arm, and carry them in his bosom, and will gently lead those that have their young" (Isaiah 40:11).

In John, chapter 21, read about an occasion when, after Jesus' resurrection and before His final ascension to heaven — there to remain until the end of time, when He shall return to judge the world — He appeared to several of the disciples near the sea of Tiberias. Among those present was Peter, the apostle who had on the night of Jesus' betrayal thrice denied being a disciple of Jesus, but who later deeply repented of this grievous sin. When Jesus appeared on the seashore, after the disciples recognized Him and shared a meal of fish and bread, Jesus asked Peter three times if he loved Jesus and three times Peter responded that he did love Jesus. After each affirmation of Peter's love, Jesus told Peter, "Feed my sheep" or "Feed my lambs." The record of how Peter continued after this to obey Christ is recorded in the New Testament. Peter was true to his profession of love for Christ, demonstrating this by spending the remainder of his life to tending the church.

In Peter's letter, written many years after the foregoing incident, he said, "I am a fellow-elder." He explained to elders how they should go about their duties as elders:

> "Tend to the flock of God which is among you, exercising the oversight, not of constraint, but willingly, according to the will of God; nor yet for filthy lucre, but of a ready mind; neither as lording it over the charge allotted to you, but making yourselves examples to the flock. And when the chief Shepherd shall be manifested, ye shall receive the crown of glory that fadeth not away" (I Peter 5:2-4).

In the land where Jesus grew up as a child, there were many sheep. They were lovingly and carefully tended by shepherds. In Jesus' symbolic language referring to Himself as the "good Shepherd" and calling His disciples sheep, He knew His hearers would see the applications. Peter said that elders were to care for the church as the shepherd cares for his sheep.

Perhaps one of the best known Bible passages is the 23rd Psalm, written by the shepherd boy David.

A few years ago Charles Smith wrote an article, which appeared in "The Way of Truth." The article was entitled "A Shepherd's

Interpretation of the 23rd Psalm." The article has many good points and I would like to share a few with you.

"The Lord is my shepherd" — Each sheep knows his master, and the master knows his sheep. They know his voice and they follow him.

"He leadeth me beside still waters" — Sheep will not drink gurgling water. The shepherd leads the sheep to a "still" place, a little pool, or else he will fashion such a place with his hands in a shallow area.

"Valley of shadow of death ... thy rod and staff comfort me." This valley, well known by the shepherds, was a valley of about four and a half miles long. Its walls were some 1500 feet high. The floor is full of gullies seven or eight feet deep. Some places on the path are so narrow that a sheep cannot turn around.

In the valley there are wild animals which try to prey on the sheep. But the shepherd is there, and with his staff he drives the animals away! The shepherd protects his sheep!

"Thou preparest a table in the presence of my enemies." One of the greatest enemies of the sheep is poisonous weeds. Before the shepherd allows the sheep into a new field he "goes before" and gathers up the poisonous weeds and burns them. The sheep are then safe to feed on the good grasses.

"Thou anointest my head with oil..." At every sheepfold there is a large bowl of olive oil. The shepherd examines his sheep, one by one. If any scratches are found he immediately applies the oil, anointing the injury.

"Surely goodness and mercy shall follow me all the days of my life; and I shall dwell in the house of the Lord forever."

David knew of God's loving kindness! He knew of His protection! Shouldn't this encourage us as well? And shouldn't it encourage the elders, shepherds of the congregation of God's people to be better shepherds?

Duties and responsibilities of elders: The elder must recognize that the authority of the eldership in making decisions regarding the church is not vested in him solely as an individual, but rather in his official capacity in conjunction with other elders. The eldership always refers to a plurality. A congregation should have elders, not an elder. Furthermore, one elder is not to take or be given precedence over the other elders. Elders may sometimes have differences in judgment where divine authority is not explicit. If their work is to be fruitful and pleasing to God, there must always be a spirit of humility, gentleness, brotherly love and willingness to consider the various viewpoints of each elder. Their deliberations and decision-making should not be accompanied by bickering evidences of jealousy and seeking prominence. Sad to say such un-Christian conduct sometimes occurs and results in detrimental consequences to the congregation. The future of any congregation is largely determined by the caliber of its eldership. A congregation will not progress farther than the vision of its leaders. Their assignment is not just an honor to show the respect and trust of their congregation. Rather, it is a major undertaking requiring commitment to a great amount of effort, time, reflection and prayer, as well as actual activity. Being an elder should not be a task assumed lightly, but recognized as a personal commission from the Lord, Himself. For this reason, Paul wrote to Timothy, "If a man seeketh the office of a bishop, he desireth a good work" (I Tim. 3:1). That is, if a man desires to serve in this capacity, this is a worthy ambition. Paul was not saying, however, that one should so desire the office that he campaigns for it with a contentious attitude such as that of one man that I knew who so desired the office that he threatened, "If I'm not appointed, I'm leaving." His very statement showed his lack of proper qualification. On the other hand, one should not be appointed as elder unless he is truly willing to shoulder the heavy burden of responsibility.

Although conforming to the strict qualifications divinely given, this does not mean that an elder will be perfect. In fact, such is not possible among mere humans. All men are subject to weaknesses at times;

all men are targets for Satan's arrows. If on occasion an elder makes a mistake in judgment, that does not merit open season on him for condemnation and criticism. Paul gave instructions to the young preacher Timothy as to the way in which such situations should be handled.

> "Rebuke not an elder, but exhort him as a father... "
> (I Tim. 5:1).

In cases where an elder may have become involved in actual wrongdoing, Timothy was thus advised:

> "Against an elder receive not an accusation, except at the mouth of two or three witnesses. Them that sin reprove in the sight of all, that the rest also may be in fear"
> (I Tim. 5:19,20).

The elder must realize that his task is not always easy. The courageous leader must face the facts. He knows that he will have to face decisions which may be criticized, misunderstood, and sometimes defeated. He knows that he has to define and communicate objectives. An elder, like all Christians, but perhaps to a greater degree, must be concerned with his placement of priorities: his professional means of livelihood, his family, his personal needs, and the church. He knows his behavior will be subjected to much scrutiny, as will that of his family. And he knows that ultimately he will be subjected to the greatest strictness of all, the final rendering of his account for the way he handled his task of guiding and guarding his flock.

Like all humanity, the elder sometimes wrestles with emotions of indecision, frustration, discouragement, inaction and inertia. But let it also be remembered that the courageous leader experiences the thrill of moral victory. He knows the joy in lasting achievement of eternal good accomplished in the lives of others.

There is no greater responsibility within the church than that which rests upon elders of the church. They have a commission from God to serve as shepherds of His flock in a particular locality. As the literal shepherd of a flock of sheep must see that they are provided with proper pasture for physical food, elders of the church should see that proper spiritual food is put before the congregation regularly. As the good shepherd tends a sheep which has been injured or is ill, the good elders seek to watch over individual lives where spiritual illness exists or is threatened and to render such assistance as is possible.

The loving shepherd of Bible days carefully gathered his flock at the close of the day and if a sheep or lamb was missing, the shepherd left his flock in the fold or a place of safety and searched diligently for the lost ones. Likewise, concerned elders become familiar with each individual of the congregation and if one is repeatedly absent from the assembly, or is involved with some special spiritual threat or other problem, the elders make efforts to help the troubled Christian cope with the cause or causes.

If elders had only to care for the souls of the faithful, serving as elder would not be a difficult task. But elders are charged with the task of caring for all kinds of persons who make up the body of the church. There are the hardy faithful, but also the weak, worldly, the imprudent, the biblical illiterate, the egotist, the lukewarm, the prejudiced, even the hypocrite. The church is a collection of all kinds of individuals from different walks of life. But they have one important thing in common. All were at one time sinners. All have had their past sins forgiven through obedience to the gospel, made possible through the atoning sacrifice of Christ. All are striving in varying degrees of intensity to obtain an eternal home with God after this earthly life is over.

Beyond this common bond, each individual has entered the church with a different personal legacy from his past life. Some have many more weaknesses to overcome than others. Some have scars and wounds from past bouts with Satan that can easily add difficulty to living the Christian life and therefore these persons may need special attention and encouragement, as well as compassionate understanding and assistance.

A still further and heavy responsibility of elders, like that of the shepherd of literal sheep is guarding the flock against wolves, a natural enemy of sheep.

Even before the church was established, in His early ministry, Jesus warned:

"Beware of false prophets, who come to you in sheep's clothing, but inwardly are ravening wolves. By their fruits ye shall know them. Do men gather grapes of thorns, or figs of thistles? (Matt. 7:15,16).

Referring to the day when Jesus shall return to judge the world, He said:

"Not every one that saith unto me, Lord, Lord, shall enter into the kingdom of heaven; but he that doeth the will of my Father who is in heaven. Many will say to me in that day, Lord, Lord, did we not prophesy by thy name, and by thy name cast out demons, and by thy name do many mighty works? And then will I profess unto them, I never knew you: depart from me, ye that work iniquity" (Matt. 7:21-23).

At one time during His earthly ministry, Jesus sent the twelve apostles to go out among the villages performing miracles in His name and preaching "The kingdom of heaven is at hand." Read Matthew, chapter 10. Conditions in society regarding spiritual values then were similar to present conditions. Jesus warned:

"Behold, I send you forth as sheep in the midst of wolves: be ye therefore wise as serpents, and harmless as doves" (Matt. 10:16).

After the church had been established, the apostle Paul, having spent years in laboring to save souls and having established many congregations of the church over a widespread area, was on his way to Jerusalem. He knew that he was to experience trials and hardships there and would probably never be able to visit again the church in Ephesus where he had previously labored, amid persecution, for three years.

Paul was pressed for time then because he was anxious to be in Jerusalem by the day of Pentecost. The ship on which he was traveling docked on its way at Miletus, not far from Ephesus. Paul arranged for the elders from Ephesus to meet him at Miletus. He desired to warn them about the serious dangers that would confront the church, againstwhich he was instructing the elders that they recognize these false teachings when they appeared and withstand their influence in order to protect the church. Note Paul's warnings:

> "For I shrank not from declaring unto you the whole counsel of God. Take heed unto yourselves, and to all the flock, in which the Holy Spirit hath made you bishops, to feed the church of the Lord which he purchased with his own blood. I know that after my departing grievous wolves shall enter in among you, not sparing the flock; and from among your own selves shall men arise, speaking perverse things to draw away the disciples after them. Wherefore watch ye, remembering that by the space of three years I ceased not to admonish every one night and day with tears. And now I commend you to God, and to the word of his grace, which is able to build you up, and to give you the inheritance among all them that are sanctified. I coveted no man's silver, or gold, or apparel" (Acts 20:27-33).

Paul emphasized the gravity of the elders' responsibility. They held their office because the Holy Spirit had bestowed it upon them, not directly through some miraculous intervention of the Holy Spirit, but because they had been appointed as elders and had assumed that authority and influence over the congregation. The same is true of the eldership in all congregations.

Paul's exhortation to these elders was the same in meaning as that Jesus had given to Peter, "Feed my sheep" — "Feed the church." The church must be assured of proper and complete spiritual nourishment, consisting of a full dispensation of God's word. It is only through such foresight that Christians can be prepared to have the spiritual strength to do battle with the evil forces of the perverse teachings set before them by the wolves "in sheep's clothing" that barge their way into the fold.

Note that the "grievous wolves" that do the most damage are not those avowed enemies of the church, but those (as Paul said):

> "... from your own selves shall men arise, speaking perverse things, to draw away the disciples after them" (Acts 20:30).

In view of such certain impending dangers to the church, Paul's fervent admonition to the elders was to "watch," to be on guard, to follow Paul's example when he was among them,

> "... remembering that by the space of three years I ceased not to admonish every one night and day with tears" (Acts 20:31).

False teaching, however minor it may appear to some, cannot and must not be ignored. It must be recognized, refuted, and its influence eliminated from the church. Elders and evangelists may try to ignore it, hoping it will go away. However, teaching that which does not agree with definite divinely revealed truth is a tool of Satan. If such teaching is ignored or receives only a slap rather than a death-blow, the erroneous doctrine will grow and spread rapidly, eventually destroying all in its path.

Someone has likened false teaching to crab grass growing in the cotton field. One might think the crab grass would die after it has been chopped away. But with the next rain, the plant will revive, take root and in only a few days be as strong as ever. The truth is that the entire roots must be dug from the earth, turned up to full exposure to the sun, by which they will, after a few days, be entirely dead and unable to grow again.

False teaching must likewise be fully exposed to the light of truth as revealed in God's word. This course of action is simply following the example of apostolic days. Brethren, teaching their own false conception of Christianity that would bind the Jewish rite of circumcision upon Christians, tried to bind this doctrine upon the churches of Galatia. These same men, advocating this false doctrine, opposed Paul, Barnabas and Silas because they had been preaching to Gentiles without demanding of their converts acceptance of circumcision. Regarding these, Paul wrote:

> "... of the false brethren privily brought in, who came in privily to spy out our liberty which we have in Christ Jesus, that they might bring us into bondage: to whom we gave place in the way of subjection, no, not for an

hour; that the truth of the gospel might continue with you" (Gal. 2:4,5).

Like the crab grass, this false teaching about circumcision did not just dwindle away after one encounter. Advocates of this same false doctrine even went to the strong church in Antioch claiming to have been sent from Jerusalem, where the apostles, the recognized authority, were. These false teachers condemned the church in Antioch because it had sent Paul and others out to preach to the Gentiles and did not demand their adherence to the Jewish rite of circumcision. As a consequence, Paul — although an apostle himself, knew the truth, but for the sake of finally settling the question — went to Jerusalem where the apostles and elders were gathered together to consider this matter. Here it was finally settled by the united testimony of the apostles and elders that the Jewish law did not apply to Christians. This was such an important decision that the judgment was written and circulated throughout the churches. Read Acts 15:1-28. This incident is a great example of the way to deal with false teaching. Go to the recorded word of God and accept its authority, thus settling the question.

Every elder should read and consider carefully the divine instrucions given by the Old Testament prophet Ezekiel, as recorded by the prophet himself. See Ezek. 3:17-21. God was sending Ezekiel to be a watchman over His people, just as elders are set as watchmen over the church, to instruct and to warn against apostasy, worldly behavior and false teachings that can lead to eternal condemnation.

When the watchman fails to warn the wicked of the danger of his actions, both the wicked and the watchman will be punished, but if the watchman sounds the warning and the wicked fail to heed, the wicked will suffer his punishment, but the watchman will be justified.

On the other hand, if a righteous man sins, and the watchman does not warn him, the righteous man's former righteousness is canceled in God's sight and both he and the watchman will be accountable because of the sin of the once righteous man. If, however, the righteous man who sins hears and heeds the watchman's warnings, both shall escape punishment.

The faithful watchmen, elders over the Lord's church, can know the satisfaction of a job well done when they have diligently seen to the proper tending of their flocks, nurturing each member with the whole word of God, watching lest wolves in sheep's clothing wreak their destructive influence by leading the church away from the simplicity and beauty of the gospel. These faithful servants of God can look forward with a special delight to hearing at last, these words from Jesus, the righteous judge:

> "... Come, ye blessed of my Father, inherit the kingdom prepared for you from the foundation of the world" (Matt. 25:34).

Attitude of other church members toward elders: Not only do elders have a responsibility toward the congregation, but the members also have responsibilities toward the elders. Christians need to pray for their elders, give them encouragement for their dedication, time and efforts. Church members need to cooperate in actively supporting activities planned by the elders for the furtherance of the gospel. The writer to the Hebrew Christians gave Christians this exhortation:

> "Obey them that have the rule over you, and submit to them: for they watch in behalf of your souls, as they that shall give account; that they may do this with joy, and not with grief: for this were unprofitable for you" (Heb. 13:17).

Remember the example of Nehemiah. He returned from Persia to Jerusalem zealous to rebuild the city's walls that had been destroyed long ago when its people were carried away captive, but Nehemiah could not do it alone. So it is with elders who have zealous plans for advancing the cause of Christ in their community. Rebuilding Jerusalem's walls was such a tremendous undertaking that governors of surrounding provinces scoffed in ridicule at Nehemiah's efforts, but God's people in and around Jerusalem had a mind to work, and through united, zealous and constant perseverance, the wall was built. May this example inspire elders to lead and congregations to cooperate, thus accomplishing much for the kingdom of Christ.

Performing the duties of eldership requires strong faith, courage and boldness when occasions arise for personal encounters with erring Christians, but this must not prevent positive action on the part of the eldership when needful.

When elders deem it necessary to seek to strengthen, instruct or reprimand a member of the flock, for some action unbecoming to a Christian, that person should not take offense and consider the elders advice or reproof as being out of place. The erring Christian should examine carefully his behavior that is called in question, thankfully realizing that the elders' reproof or admonitions are not motivated by criticism felt personally, but are rather an effort to fulfill the obligations the elders assumed in accepting the responsibility of their office. Such reproof or admonitions as are given are prompted by brotherly love and concern for a fellow Christian who has succumbed to Satan's enticement and has therefore become guilty of sin as well as bringing reproach on the church.

There are occasions when a church member may be living in open sin, defiant of strict and explicit rules of behavior unquestionably unacceptable to divine approval. In such instances very strict disciplinary measures must be taken as in the case within the church at Corinth. Paul described the blatant sin existing there.

> "It is actually reported that there is fornication among you, and such fornication as is not even among the Gentiles, that one of you hath his father's wife" (I Cor. 5:1).

Attention was drawn to the repulsive nature of the sin on the part of the individuals involved. But the sin included all of the congregation as shown by Paul's further words:

> "And ye are puffed up, and did not rather mourn, that he that had done this deed might be taken away from among you" (I Cor. 5:2).

Paul went on to explain the wide effect of sin within the church.

> "Your glorying is not good. Know ye not that a little leaven leaveneth the whole lump? Purge out the old leaven, that ye may be a new lump, even as ye are

unleavened. For our passover also hath been sacrificed, even Christ" (I Cor. 5:6,7).

Throughout the Bible the writers have used leaven as an appropriate symbol of sin. The symbolism, as mentioned before, lies in the rapidly spreading growth of yeast when placed in dough causing it to rise, to increase in bulk. So it is with sin. The church is the body of Christ. It must be kept pure. The seriousness of the sin of incest between two people in the church or any other type of illicit sexual involvement must be exposed and the guilty ones must be held responsible. Therefore, the congregation as a body must take action by withdrawing fellowship from those involved in this sin. Paul called this action "delivering those guilty to Satan for the destruction of the flesh." In other words, they were cast out of the church into the world where Satan reigns, with the hope of the church that this would bring the guilty ones to a realization of the serious consequences of their sin, thus bringing each one to repentance "that their spirits might be saved in the day of the Lord Jesus."

This public act of discipline was meant to accomplish its goal or reaching its ultimate purpose through being enforced by each Christian's actions in refusing to have any further contact with those who had been guilty. Paul further commanded:

> "but as it is, I wrote unto you not to keep company, if any man that is named a brother be a fornicator, or covetous, or an idolater, or a reviler, or a drunkard, or an extortioner; with such a one no, not to eat" (I Cor. 5:11).

The instructions for the discipline of the grievous sinners in the Corinthian church were included in the first letter that Paul wrote to them. Evidently, the guilty person responded to the action of the church in its withdrawal, because in a later letter written to the same church, Paul wrote:

> "Sufficient to such a one is this punishment which was inflicted by the many; so that contrariwise ye should rather forgive him and comfort him, lest by any means such a one should be swallowed up with his overmuch

sorrow. Wherefore I beseech you to confirm your love toward him" (II Cor. 2: 6-8).

This withdrawal of fellowship involved every activity of life, even sitting and eating at the same table.

Note that the disciplinary action was not an act of the church leaders alone, but each member joined in condemnation of the guilty ones by withdrawing association as in the past. This was necessary in order to serve the desired purpose of the disciplinary action. Those involved in the sin had formerly enjoyed regular activities and fellowship with all the other Christians. This complete withdrawal of all fellowship emphasized the seriousness and gravity of the sin, so that God's purpose might be accomplished. However, the effort would have failed if the guilty ones had not habitually first enjoyed the former close asssociation with their fellow-Christians, thus feeling strongly the later withdrawal of that uplifting, encouraging and caring atmosphere of Christian associations.

The incident of withdrawal of fellowship in Corinth is the most explicit example of church discipline recorded in the New Testament. Paul also made reference to another case, but no details are given other than Paul's statement to Timothy.

> "This charge I commit unto thee, my child Timothy, according to the prophecies which led the way to thee, that by them thou mayest war the good warfare; holding faith and a good conscience; which some having thrust from them made shipwreck concerning the faith: of whom is Hymenaeus and Alexander; whom I delivered unto Satan, that they might be taught not to blaspheme" (I Tim. 1:18-20).

In order for the teaching and practices of Jesus' church to be preserved, and for false teachings and sinful practices confronting the church to be overcome there must be **recognition, refutation and rejection of the teaching as false**. To tolerate false teaching or overt sin among members instead of revealing and rejecting the sin amounts to giving sanction and encouragement to that which is wrong.

DEACONS

Deacons are not listed among the offices named by Paul (Eph. 4:11) because those named there were to serve the special purpose of:

> "... perfecting of the saints, unto the work of ministering, unto the building up of the body of Christ: till we all attain unto the unity of the faith, and of the knowledge of the Son of God, unto a fullgrown man, unto the measure of the stature of the fulness of Christ" (Eph. 4:12,13).

Whereas elders, evangelists and teachers are to minister specifically to the spiritual growth and welfare of the church, deacons serve particularly in matters regarding the physical or material growth and welfare of the church.

The only New Testament record of deacons being appointed in the church concerns those of whom we read in Acts 6. They are not called deacons in our English translation of this passage, but the word deacon, DIAKONOS in the Greek rendition, simply means "servant" as rendered in John 5:9 and Matt. 22:13, where the same word appears in the Greek text.

The first deacons appointed were to oversee the benevolent work of the early church in providing food to the needy among the large group of Christians, many of whom were away from their homes having come to Jerusalem to observe the Jewish Pentecost and having been converted to Christ while there, they stayed in Jerusalem longer than first intended, learning more from the apostles and enjoying their new-found fellowship. The deacons were needed because the apostles, who were first overseeing this work, explained:

> "And the twelve called the multitude of the disciples unto them, and said, It is not fit that we should forsake the word of God, and serve tables. Look ye out therefore, brethren, from among you seven men of good report, full of the Spirit and of wisdom, whom we may appoint over this business. But we will continue stedfastly in prayer, and in the ministry of the word" (Acts 6:2-4).

The apostles were not saying that they were above serving in such a ministry of benevolence, but rather that their work of teaching was so important that they should not spend their time in doing what others could do as well because the apostles had been especially called to preach.

Deacons serve in many capacities as appointed by the elders to do so, and as needs arise. Those being appointed to be deacons are expected to meet certain God-given specifications.

After listing a number of qualifications needful for men to serve as elders, Paul wrote to Timothy:

"Deacons in like manner must be grave, not double-tongued, not given to much wine, not greedy of filthy lucre; holding the mystery of the faith in a pure conscience" (I Tim. 3:8,9).

It is noticeable that the list of qualifications to be met by deacons is a shorter list than that of elders. However, in many ways these two lists are similar. Since elders are more likely to be older men, it is reasonable to expect that their growth toward maturity of the virtues listed would be more advanced than that of the deacons. Paul's introductory words to the list of deacons' qualifications, following the list given of elders' qualifications are "in like manner," implying that deacons should be advancing toward development, seeking to attain the same degree of maturity in the spiritual virtues, in which the elders have already attained a higher development.

A specific quality mentioned as needed by deacons is gravity, signifying solemn, serious, dignified behavior. They are not to be "double-tongued." Such a person is hypocritical, saying one thing to one person, and the opposite to another.

A third qualification, "not given to much wine" should be understood as related to the culture of the people at that time, rather than to the modern concept of social drinking. This admonition indicated moderation in drinking wine as it was used then, and still is, in countries of the Mediterranean areas. Wine usually accompanied their meals and it was often fermented since there was no way of long-preservation of grape juice at that time. Wine was diluted with water, rather than drunk at full strength. Only excessive use of such wine would result in drunkenness, which would certainly disqualify one from service as a deacon. Such was condemned by Paul as he instructed all Christians:

> "And be not drunken with wine, wherein is riot, but be filled with the Spirit" (Eph. 5:18).

In those days, wine was also used for medicinal qualities. In the story of the good Samaritan, Luke wrote that, after finding the man who had been robbed, stripped and beaten until half-dead, the Samaritan:

> "... bound up his wounds, pouring on them oil and wine..." (Luke 10:34).

In like manner, Paul advised Timothy to:

> "... use a little wine for thy stomach's sake and thine often infirmities" (I Tim. 5:23).

Like elders, deacons were not to be "greedy of filthy lucre." They were to be "husbands of one wife" and should be "ruling their children and their houses well."

Interspersed among the listing of deacons' qualifications is inserted:

> "Women in like manner must be grave, not slanderers, temperate, faithful in all things: (I Tim. 3:11).

There is not agreement among Bible scholars as to whether "women" here refers to wives of the deacons and elders or to women known as deaconesses. The Greek word, GUNAIKAI, can be translated properly either "wife" or "woman."

We read of "... Phoebe our sister, who is a servant of the church that is at Cenchrea" (Rom. 16:1). Here in the Greek text the feminine form of the word meaning deacon or servant is used. In one sense every woman who renders service to the church is a servant or deaconess, but this does not necessarily mean that such a service was actually commissioned by the elders, though it might well be. For instance, Dorcas was a servant of Christ and the church when she made and dispensed garments to the poor in the name of Christian service. See Acts 9:36-43.

Since verse 11 is inserted among other qualifications of deacons, it seems most reasonable to believe that Paul was referring especially to the wives of deacons, for beyond a doubt, for either deacon, elder, or preacher, the character of their wives, their influence, and their support of their husband's activities have a great bearing on the efficiency and effectiveness of the husband's accomplishments. In many instances, such as the special work of deacons in dispensing food and clothing in deeds of benevolence, their tasks can be greatly augmented by the help of faithful women's ministrations.

Paul ended his consideration of deacons with this statement:

"For they that have served well as deacons gain to themselves a good standing, and great boldness in the faith which is in Christ Jesus" (I Tim. 3:13).

They that "serve well as deacons" receive two rewards. First, they achieve "good standing," a reference to recognition of an assignment well done. Second, they have demonstrated "great boldness in the faith" toward Jesus Christ. Many deacons later become elders, after having shown their reliability and their steadfastness in the faith. Service as a deacon provides a basis of self confidence for a person naturally shy or timid. He learns to proceed with boldness toward the accomplishment of the activity assigned to him. He experiences the joy of active participation in service to Christ.

Serving as a deacon provides an effective field for Christian growth, perhaps toward the eldership, or to becoming a preacher, as did two of the first deacons appointed in Jerusalem. Stephen became the first Christian martyr after giving a very powerful discourse against the enemies of Christ. Philip preached in Samaria (Acts 8:12). He preached to and converted the Ethiopian eunuch (Acts 8:26-38). Philip also preached in cities along the sea coast between Gaza and Caesarea, where he made his home (Acts 8:40).

CHAPTER TEN

THE TEACHING MINISTRY

THE TEACHING ROLE

Paul wanted each Christian to realize to the fullest measure of his capabilities the magnitude of what Christ did to establish His church.

> "Now this, He ascended, what is it but that he also descended into the lower parts of the earth? He that descended is the same also that ascended far above all the heavens, that he might fill all things" (Eph. 4:9,10).

Yes, before Jesus was ready to ascend into heaven to take His place at the right hand of God to rule over His spiritual earthly kingdom, He first had to descend into death itself. Fifty days later, having risen from the tomb, Jesus sent the Comforter, who was the Holy Spirit, the very Spirit of truth, to guide the apostles, according to His promise made on the night of His betrayal (John 14:16,17,26). This baptism of the Holy Spirit was received only by the apostles and it enabled them, while speaking in their own language, to be understood by all who heard in their own languages. By this enabling of the Holy Spirit, Peter preached the first gospel sermon, proclaiming the terms upon which any sinner might have his sins forgiven and receive the gift of the Holy Spirit. The result was that three thousand sinners responded in obedience to the commands of the gospel. Thus, the Lord's church was established in the world and the Christian era began (Acts 2).

Jesus would no longer walk the earth in bodily form, but He made provisions for the expansion of the church, its proper instruction and care. He placed the treasure of the gospel message into the hands of men, humble earthen vessels (II Cor. 4:7). And in order that each member live in the way befitting a child of God, each must be taught:

> "... to walk worthily of the calling wherewith ye were called, with all lowliness and meekness, with longsuf-

fering, forbearing one another in love; giving diligence to keep the unity of the Spirit in the bond of peace" (Eph. 4:1-3).

It was Jesus' desire that every Christian understand, appreciate, and work toward maintaining unity in His church. Paul explicitly named the fundamental aspects of unity that characterized the Lord's church.

> "There is one body, and one Spirit, even as also ye were called in one hope of your calling; one Lord, one faith, one baptism, one God and Father of all, who is over all, and through all, and in all" (Eph. 4:4-6).

Our Lord planned that in the church there should be certain caretakers, certain persons to see that His work was accomplished through the church. He named the positions of these administrators of His will:

> "And he gave some to be apostles; and some, prophets; and some, evangelists; and some, pastors and teachers" (Eph. 4:11).

In the previous chapter the work of the apostles, prophets, evangelists and pastors was discussed. Let us now consider the work of teachers.

It has already been noted that all five of these different ministries are to work toward the same purpose:

> "... the perfecting of the saints, unto the work of ministering, unto the building up of the body of Christ: till we all attain unto the unity of the faith, and of the knowledge of the Son of God, unto a fullgrown man, unto the measure of the stature of the fulness of Christ" (Eph. 4:12,13).

All Christians should understand that when they accepted Jesus, truly believing that He was God's Son, when they then repented of all their past sins and were buried in baptism into Christ, they became newborn children of God. But they were infants spiritually. They needed to be fed the milk of God's word that they might develop spiritually and grow to spiritual manhood. This growth demanded that they receive spiritual nourishment. The prophets and apostles fulfilled their God-given mission when they proclaimed God's words orally and also recorded them for all future generations, being guided in doing so by the Holy Spirit. Now they, too, have departed from this earth, leaving the work to be done by evangelists, pastors, and teachers. When each of these co-laborers works harmoniously together, God's purpose will be fulfilled. These babes in Christ will grow toward full-grown, mature Christians in varying degrees of maturity, but if they have been fully nourished acquiring the knowledge of God's will and have exercised proper Christian activity, they will no longer be weak babes but spiritually strong and capable of wider accomplishments. They are

"... no longer children, tossed to and fro and carried about with every wind of doctrine, by the sleight of men, in craftiness, after the wiles of error" (Eph. 4:14).

These mature Christians will be recognized by their "speaking the truth in love," each having become a participating identity, a part of that spiritual

"... body fitly framed and knit together through that which every joint supplieth, according to the working in due measure of each several part, maketh the increase of the body unto the building up of itself in love" (Eph. 4:16).

What a perfect picture of unity! The church is seen as a strong force, the entire body of Christ working as a beautiful unit, with every member fitting perfectly into his place and functioning as God intended under the direction of Christ.

It is sad to note, however, that viewing the church today, we do not always see this beautiful picture, as envisioned by Christ, because in many congregations there is little sense of unity. There is seen unrest, dissension, brother criticizing brother, professed Christians trying to serve God — yet living much like the world, lack of evidence of deep reverence in the presence of God immediately before and during the worship where He has promised to be present when two or three are gathered in His name, rebellion against His restrictions in attempting to gain human approval by efforts to revamp the meaning of God's instructions by changing the manner of worship to conform to man's ideas and desires.

Why do we see such a difference between Christ's ideal body and His body as it is often seen today? Is not the answer to this question found in the sacred words written to the Hebrews when they were thus reprimanded?

> "Of whom we have many things to say, and hard of interpretation, seeing ye are become dull of hearing. For when by reason of the time ye ought to be teachers, ye have need again that some one teach you the rudiments of the first principles of the oracles of God; and are become such as have need of milk, and not of solid food. For every one that partaketh of milk is without experience of the word of righteousness; for he is a babe. But solid food is for fullgrown men, even those who by reason of use have their senses exercised to discern good and evil" (Hebrews 5:11-14).

The writer accused some of the Hebrew Christians of being "dull of hearing." No, they were not physically deaf, but they had lost the gratitude and joy first felt when, after baptism, they accepted God's forgiveness of past sins and later had settled into complacency, forgetful or unmindful of the fact that they had not yet achieved eternal salvation, although it had been promised as the eventual expectation that could be attained at the end of physical existence. They were like one who enrolled in the Olympic races, but having once entered the arena where the race was being run, casually walked toward the destination, turning aside to examine each inviting sight on either side of the race track, sometimes being so entranced by what was found that the would-be runners lost track of time and their purpose for entering the race.

Paul told the Corinthian Christians:

"... Even so run; that ye may attain" (I Cor. 9:24).

Paul wanted them to realize that to win the race one must "strive," that is, put forth every possible bit of strength. Also, he must "exercise self-control" in order to reach the goal. Paul said of himself:

"but I buffet my body, and bring it into bondage; lest by any means, after that I have preached to others, I myself should be rejected" (I Cor. 9:27).

Even after many years of hard service suffering under persecution as Paul had preached the gospel and thus had led many to Christ, and even though he was in prison at that very time of writing for having done so, he made the foregoing statement. He said further:

"Not that I have already obtained, or am already made perfect: but I press on, if so be that I may hold on that for which also I was laid hold on by Christ Jesus. Brethren, I count not myself yet to have laid hold: but one thing I do, forgetting the things which are behind, and stretching forward to the things which are before, I press on toward the goal unto the prize of the high calling of God in Christ Jesus" (Philippians 3:12-14).

If Paul, after all he had accomplished for Christ, could not relax and take life easy, who among the church today can risk living casually, pursuing all the pleasures offered by the world, enduring little sacrifice of time and effort for Christ? Many seem almost oblivious to the moral state of our present society, judging by their lackadaisical attitude toward serious personal endeavor to change it. Are we "dull of hearing" as were those so accused in the letter to the Hebrews?

Paul told the Philippian Christians that they should walk as he was walking, disregarding those who acted as though "dull of hearing." The faithful Christians were to

"... mark them that so walk even as ye have us for an example. For many walk, of whom I told you often, and now tell you even weeping, that they are the enemies of the cross of Christ: whose end is perdition, whose god is the belly, and whose glory is in their shame, who mind earthly things" (Philippians 3:17-19).

The Hebrew Christians were told that enough time had elapsed between the time when they became Christians and the present, that they should have grown and matured spiritually so much that they would be capable of teaching instead of having to be taught. They should now be ready to receive deeper harder things to understand. Instead they needed to be taught again the very basic truths of the gospel, which the writer called the "first principles of the oracles of God." These Christians were like newborn babies who must at first be nourished with milk. Only after growth and more maturity would they be capable of digesting "solid food" (Heb. 5:12).

The "first principles," of course, are the facts concerning (1) the lost condition of humanity; (2) the virgin birth of Jesus, making of Him a God-man (one both human and divine); (3) the death, burial and resurrection of Jesus, by which He provided the only possible sacrifice through which atonement for the sins of humanity was made possible; and (4) the glorious gospel of grace, by means of which eternal salvation can be achieved through obedience to the gospel invitation to believe, repent and be baptized in the name of the Father, the Son, and the Holy Spirit, thus receiving forgiveness for past sins and "the gift of the Holy Spirit."

How many Christians, who have been in the church for many years, if asked to go to some non-Christian and teach that person the gospel in order that he might be converted, would decline saying something to this effect, "Oh, I don't feel able to explain it well enough. Why don't you go?" or "Brother or Sister So and So can do it much better." In my experience such has been common. Is such a person ready to go on to a "solid food" diet, or does he or she still need teaching regarding "first principles"?

The Hebrew writer was not discounting the importance of teaching first principles, but to those who once learned these, Paul said:

> "... let us press on unto perfection; not laying again a foundation of repentance from dead works, and of faith toward God, of the teaching of baptisms, and of laying on of hands, and of resurrection of the dead, and of eternal judgment. And this will we do, if God permit" (Heb. 6:1-3).

Yes, of course, we should continue teaching first principles, but these are for those who are outside the body of Christ. The new Christian has already heard and obeyed these first principles. He is a spiritual newborn. As newborn human babes must for a while be nourished with milk before becoming able to digest solid food, just so, the young Christian needs to be taught the simpler truths embodied in Christian living, thereby gaining spiritual strength. As he is able to receive more and more solid spiritual food, he grows stronger and stronger in faith and resistance to evil until by reason of time, teaching and spiritual exercise, he reaches a level of maturity capable of receiving with understanding, appreciation and gratitude the deeper meanings of Christianity.

In this study of the teaching ministry in the church, the preceding thoughts have dealt with its importance and the fact that not every member of the church is qualified or capable of assuming the role of teacher in a public way any more than that every man in the church is qualified to serve as an elder or evangelist in the church. Yet, it has not been uncommon in my experience to hear an announcement from the pulpit or to see in a church bulletin a statement similar to this: "If any one is interested in teaching a class, please see ... ," or "If you will volunteer to teach a class in the Bible school, please contact..." Such statements seem to indicate very little consideration to the qualifications of an effectual teacher. Parents, would you want your children to attend a public school in which teachers were placed so carelessly and indiscriminately?

As you read God's word and read about those whom He selected to do His work, how much use did He make of volunteers? Go to the Old Testament. Read the account of God sending Moses to lead the Israelites out of Egypt, or the story of Gideon's defeat of the Midianites, or the call of Jeremiah to be God's spokesman urging God's people to repentance. None of these leaders volunteered. They even remonstrated with God and tried to evade God's call, but God knew who had the capacity to do the task He wanted done.

Go to the New Testament. Whom did He call to be His special teachers? They already had work to do. Matthew was busy collecting taxes. Peter, James and John were busy at their profession as fishermen. Surely God's ministry of teaching in His church requires those of spiritual maturity, those willing to work at the task as one of great importance, deserving the full use of the time, effort, and dedication due it.

THE REGULAR SUNDAY BIBLE CLASSES

The elders have a great responsibility in overseeing the eligibility of those chosen to teach in every class. Likewise, their's is the responsibility for what is taught in these classes.

Teachers should be chosen who are recognized as Christians who are faithful in attendance, who are known to have full knowledge of scripture content and basic Christian doctrine. They should be persons of recognized high moral caliber, especially for teaching children through adolescence. It is not enough for one to know the material which is to be taught, but the teacher must know how to present the subject in a way that will attract attention and continued interest among the various members of the class. It has proven a worthwhile endeavor for congregations to provide special programs occasionally where recognized superior and experienced successful teachers assist would-be teachers in learning techniques of successful teaching.

Patterned after the beloved writing of Paul in I Cor. 13 concerning love are two following selections, the authors of which are unknown, but the sentiments expressed regarding the Bible school teacher are worthy of much thought by those serving as teachers.

> Though I have all the Elmer's Glue and scissors and have read the lesson five times and have not love, I am not a teacher. And though I have all the construction paper, glitter and Bible posters, puzzles and unit activities and have been in special planning sessions and have not love, I am not a teacher. For being a teacher is more than being on time, present, Bible brought and lesson prepared. It's even more than faithfully attending the services.
>
> A teacher is kind and smiles a lot. A teacher looks neat and is not easily provoked when something is wrong with the heating or cooling system. A teacher is not envious of other's talents, but uses his/her own creativity and talents to the best of his/her ability.
>
> A teacher seeketh not for his/her name to be praised, but works for the glory of God. They beareth the problems, believeth and hope the best for all the students

they teach, for a teacher's work is in vain unless he/she has true interest in people.

Where there be magic markers — they shall dry up. Where there be chalk and blackboards — they shall crumble. Where there be printed literature — it shall fade. But a right relationship to God will endure forever, as it is shared in the lives of your students. All work is a result of His love. And now abideth planning, preparation, and love, these three, but the greatest of these is LOVE.

Teachers — Listen

If I read all the books that men have written about teaching, but have not love for teaching, I am only making a sound.

And if I have a magnajector, and understand the use of all visual aids, and if I have all energy as to make a new poster every week, but have not love for teaching, I am not a teacher.

If I use all that I have; give all my time to decorating my classroom, but have not love for teaching, my students have profited nothing.

When I was a child, I spoke and understood and thought like a child. When I became a teacher, I put away childish things, but I did not forget what it was like to be a child.

And now abides the teacher's knowledge, and teacher's aids, and the teacher's love; and the greatest of these is the teacher's love.

Although both children's and adult's Bible classes are important, the main thrust of the comments following immediately concern the teaching of children of all ages.

A poet, whose name I do not know, expressed vividly the true significance of spiritual training of the young:

> "I took a piece of plastic clay
> And idly fashioned it one day,
> And as my fingers pressed it still,
> It moved, and yielded to my will.

> I came again when days were passed;
> The bit of clay was hard at last,
> The form I gave it still it bore,
> But I could change that form no more.
>
> I took a piece of living clay
> And touched it gently day by day,
> And molded with my power and art
> A young child's soft and yielding heart.
>
> I came again when years were gone;
> It was a mind I looked upon;
> That early imprint still he wore,
> And I could change that form no more."

Repeated exhortations throughout the Old Testament exhort continuous teaching of children in the home regarding God and responsibility toward Him. The same instructions continue through the New Testament. While on earth Jesus taught the value of children and demonstrated His love and respect toward them. On one occasion, His disciples asked Him about who would be greatest in the kingdom of heaven, Jesus instructed them thus:

> "... Verily I say unto you, Except ye turn, and become as little children, ye shall in no wise enter into the kingdom of heaven. Whosoever therefore shall humble himself as this little child, the same is the greatest in the kingdom of heaven. And whoso shall receive one such little child in my name receiveth me: but whoso shall cause one of these little ones that believe on me to stumble, it is profitable for him that a great millstone should be hanged about his neck, and that he should be sunk in the depth of the sea" (Matt. 18:3-6).

While this duty of instruction should be carefully observed by parents, beginning as soon as the child is able to understand words, it remains a duty of the congregation to reinforce the teaching of Christian parents as well as to instruct them further, also to teach many other children who can be brought under the influence of the church.

Another writer whose name is unknown to me illustrates what Jesus' words suggest:

> "An angel passed in his onward flight,
> With a seed of love and truth and light,
> And cried, O where shall the seed be sown —
>
> That it yield the most fruit when grown?
> The Saviour heard and He said, as He smiled,
> Place it for Me in the heart of a child!"

I read an old proverb which said "Any fool can count the number of seeds in an apple; only God can count the number of apples in a seed." Teachers and congregations often pass up great opportunities for soul-saving and consequent church growth by their failure to increase their potential of accomplishment. Consideration should be given and Christians able to serve in these areas should make use of any of the various and possible means of bringing children and other prospective converts to Christ. Some such ways are through bus ministries or by individuals making contacts and providing transportation to Bible classes and worship services. Some may devise other effective means.

Of course, all recognize the value of saving even one soul, even a child having no connection to a church member. A lone child, taught through such contacts, may not be considered as worth such intensive efforts, but who can know the potential which that child, who accepts Christ and grows toward Christian maturity, may have to convert countless others? Who, but God, knows the potential of that one person to affect, not only the proclamation of the gospel that souls may be saved, but to assist in the preservation of the true faith and practices of the New Testament church? As the apple seed can multiply a hundred-fold and more, so can the potential fruit-bearing of one child in whose heart the seed of truth and love for God and fellowman is carefully planted, takes root, and is nourished in an atmosphere of love and service. Think of the young child Timothy. When he was full grown, he responded to the call of the gospel message, becoming a dedicated young Christian, who soon joined with Paul in his missionary travels. Later, in writing to Timothy, Paul speaks of Timothy's heritage from a godly home:

"But the end of the charge is love out of a pure heart and a good conscience and faith unfeigned" (I Tim. 1:5).

During Timothy's youth, who but God could have known how many souls would be brought to Christ and be saved eternally through the instruction and influence of Timothy, in whom had been cultivated a heart that provided a fertile field for the growth from that gospel seed planted therein?

If parents and teachers could fully realize their responsibilities and their opportunities, surely they would spend more time and give more attention to sharing their own faith, teaching more about it more often and in more ways, with constant prayer, being always aware of their example before the children, realizing that through them the teachers may transcend far beyond their own abilities through the abilities and opportunities of the children when they reach adulthood. Someone wrote this short meaningful verse entitled:

To Bend The Twig

To save a man —
   The best way is to teach a child!
A few short years — and he's a man,
   Then you can't guide him — now you can.
"If you love Me," the Master said,
   "Then feed My lambs — with Living Bread."

Solomon wrote:

"a time to be born, and a time to die; a time to plant, and a time to pluck up that which is planted" (Eccles. 3:2).

The good farmer knows the proper time to plant the seed for whatever crop he wishes to grow, but all realize that no matter what kind of seed one wishes to plant, the right time is not when the ground is frozen under a blanket of ice and snow.

There is no more valuable seed than that which produces Christians. Luke says "The seed is the word of God" (Luke 8:11). To produce the greatest harvest, the seed must be sown in the right kind of soil and at the right time. The best soil is soft, pliable, warm, and receptive. The mind of the child meets all of these conditions if the seed is sown in an atmosphere of love and concern. It takes much more effort and preparation to plant the seed and produce faith if planted in a mature heart which may already have been infested with the thorns of evil deeds or trodden down by sins influenced by worldly temptation. How much better to teach the child and continue teaching through the years rather than wait until he reaches maturity when it may be too late! When the child is properly taught and therefore continues to grow spiritually through the years, he should have been able to develop into a stalwart soldier ready to dedicate his life and do battle through a lifetime of Christian service.

> The soul of a child is the loveliest flower
> That grows in the garden of God.
> It climbs from weakness to knowledge and power,
> To the sky from the clay and the clod.
>
> To beauty and sweetness it grows under care;
> Neglected 'tis ragged and wild.
> 'Tis a plant that is tender and wondrously rare,
> The sweet wistful soul of a child.
>
> Be tender, O gardener, and give it its share
> Of moisture, of warmth and of light;
> And let not it lack for painstaking care
> To protect it from frost and blight.
>
> A glad day shall come when its bloom shall unfold.
> It will seem that an angel has smiled,
> Reflecting a beauty and sweetness untold
> In the sensitive soul of a child.
>
> — Author Unknown

In my college days, one of my professors in the study of Greek was the author of the beautiful thoughts in the following poem:

Who Sowed the Seed?

> Who sowed the seed? None could recall.
> But somewhere, in the by-gone years,
> A toiler in the ground let fall
> A seed that in the soil took hold,

And through long months of heat and cold
Increased and spread, till now appears
An annual harvest of rich gold.

Who planted the tree? Nobody knew.
But someone, some time set it out,
And it through rain and sunshine grew,
Although no eye was near to see
Till from the little tender sprout
There came a sheltering giant tree.
And many a pilgrim breathed a prayer
Of thanks for him who put it there.

Who sowed Good Seed? Perhaps not now,
But in eternity we'll know;
The Master then will tell us how
Some gentle soul, devoid of fame,
Proclaimed a truth in His Great Name,
Showed some one else the way to go.
And then another, seeing the light,
Turned from the way of doubt and wrong,
And followed the pathway of the right.
And thus the good work moved along.
But only in heaven will it be known
By whom the original seed was sown.

— C.R. Brewer

I do not know who wrote the following article which I read somewhere and whose sentiments I hope you share:

Why I Want to Teach

A little boy grows up wrong and hurts the world. The world can't afford to be hurt any more. This is why I want to teach.

The world cries for wisdom and knowledge. Her sore heart yearns for an antidote, the conquering truth. This is why I want to teach.

A little boy ponders in the humble classroom. A little boy absorbs knowledge there and grows fond of it.

And then he understands what and why he loves liberty and understanding.

And suddenly he is a little boy no longer. He emerges from the classroom as the moth from the pupa, full and ripe and beautiful. He offers himself to the world, behind the shield of truth.

She plucks the fruits from out his mind and soul. The cause of liberty is fed; the cause of freedom, the cause of life, of man, of prosperity, are nourished by his fruits. The world knows he lived and kisses his grave. The fruits were seed that grew in the classroom. This is why I want to teach.

To be a part of the planting, the growing, the harvest! To be myself the gardener! To hold in my heart the love of life and liberty and knowledge and truth! And then to have the love of teaching them.

To see the glow of the harvest, and to work that the world might kiss the grace of my own body for the harvest wrought!

This is why I want to teach.

— Author Unknown

What should be taught in these Bible classes? With these inspiring expressions of motivations for teaching the young, and keeping the importance of this work in mind, the next item of great importance is choosing from the wealth of information and instruction provided in the Bible, and considering the limited time given for instruction, how is the best way to use the limited time of the class period and achieve the greatest good?

I do not have all the answers, but I do know that at least three items are necessary and fundamental:

1. To achieve the goal, much thought, effort and study, accompanied by prayer for guidance, needs to be utilized in preparing an organized curriculum covering all the grades from pre-school through grade 12 of high school.

2. The greatest care should be exercised in making sure that material provided must not digress from the revealed truths of the Bible and still be sufficiently inclusive.

3. A definite goal must be established in order that the chosen curriculum will serve, as far as possible, to reach that goal. In general, that goal should be to provide spiritual instruction and inspiration geared toward preparing young people to learn, grow and develop toward spiritual health and advancement through all the years of childhood, adolescence, and later school years culminating in physical, intellectual and spiritual manhood and womanhood.

It has been my observation, over a long period of years and personal experience among many congregations, that in too many cases Bible classes have not been very effective in accomplishing this goal. Perhaps this is true, to some measure, because insufficient attention has been given to selection of teachers and to provision of proper study materials, as well as too little support from many parents in making sure their children are regular in attendance and that they have given attention at home to preparation before or following the Bible school lessons.

I have seen much evidence that Bible instruction in the past has not accomplished what it should. It has been my experience to come in contact with a great many young adults, who have attended Bible classes continuously through all their school years. These young men and women may have their minds filled with a wide selection of Bible stories and scriptures, yet they seem to have no clear conception of the relationship between these events and the theme of the Bible. They do not understand that it is one long narrative setting forth God's purpose in creating man and of His plan for eternity. There is no recognition of the simple message of the whole Bible for humanity — that Christ is coming, Christ came, and He is coming again, and that man must respond to these facts in the proper way or be eternally doomed.

When the idea of segregating children who attended worship services with their parents and others into classes, the idea met with opposition by some in the church who thought it to be an unscriptural innovation. Some congregations even split because of the issue, but over the following years these reservations were largely withdrawn when seen to be in error and the wisdom of such action was recognized, encouraged, and generally adopted. At first these classes were taught by dedicated Christians with no guide as to subject matter and techniques except for each teacher's choosing Bible stories to be taught, drawing appropriate lessons in whatever way the ingenuity of the teacher chose to do so. There was little or no systematized correlation between subject matter taught to various age groups.

Even when I was a child, there did not exist an organized program of Bible class material available for a systematic study that was prepared by members of the church of Christ. The production of the first graded series produced by members of the church was begun in 1950 with Jesse P. Sewell as editor-in-chief. This series was called "Gospel Treasure." I was one of the three writers that he chose from the Beacon Hill congregation in San Antonio, where my husband was the minister, to write certain portions of the series. My material for one year's instruction was published as the work began, but for personal reasons I decided then to withdraw from the project at the end of that year. Others completed this series.

In 1953, the Chronicle Publishing Co. decided to produce a systemized series of material and I was asked to assist. I did so, but due to financial difficulties of the publishers, the project had to be terminated and was discontinued. I then decided to attempt to produce a complete series myself and continued writing, but this involved much more time than I had to devote to it because of other heavy responsibilities, and progress was slow although I continued working toward this end.

After these two initial efforts to produce such series, other Christians became interested in doing so, the most successful for a while appeared under the directorship of R.B. Sweet. His books were made with use of considerable color, making them more attractive than the earlier books, and therefore more expensive. Although I tried on occasion to use some of them in teaching, I noticed quite a few digressions from biblical truth, but their attractive appearance caused them to gain fairly wide use.

In 1965, Reuel Lemmons, editor of Firm Foundation Publishing Co. at that time, approached me asking if I would be willing to provide material for three years of a graded series of Bible studies, as a part of a twelve-year series. I agreed to do so and contributed twenty-four books, including the pupils' workbooks and teachers' manuals for grades eight, ten and eleven. The first copies came off the press in 1965. The series was called "We Learn to Live." Each book of the series was first printed in lots of ten thousand. Due to the total number of books involved, and the high cost of production, the publisher did not make use of color to add to their attraction, depending on quality of content for appeal to users. As the books were sold, quite a number of reprintings were necessary during the following years. Eventually Firm Foundation Publishing Co. was sold, together with the series. The company's headquarters was moved to Florida and later back to Texas, but the new owner did not long continue to replace the various books of the series with new printings as their supply was depleted. Fairly recently, the remaining incomplete series of books were given to foreign missions and are no longer available. These details of the first productions of graded materials for church use are given here to show how recently such became available. After the introduction of the first "Gospel Treasure" series, it became evident to church leaders that proper materials of this nature could be of great benefit in successful teaching of young people regarding Christian living and understanding of God's word. Consequently, other publishers were able to acquire and risk the considerable financial means necessary for such publications and other series were produced.

The quick acceptance and wide use of such materials that were published indicates the prevalence of the need felt among congregations for direction in choosing appropriate subject matter to be taught in Bible classes, and for assistance in techniques for best accomplishing all the good possible.

In the field of secular education, steps of advancement are expected each year by building on fundamental knowledge and skills learned the previous year. The same principle should apply to biblical and spiritual education. Hence, we have the need for a graded series of studies over twelve years, as in public schools. In theory, when such a system is used, the result at conclusion of the twelve years of Bible school attendance should be a graduate that is well versed as to Bible teaching, and should have developed a well-rounded Christian character, strongly committed to living an exemplary life shining forth the glory of

Christ. Although all of the series contained Bible facts and moral truths, no complete series followed this plan completely and no one accomplished the necessary goal. However, I have not seen the most recently published series and cannot pass judgment on them.

Although we cannot enumerate all of the various contributing factors resulting in the conditions that exist in the church today, some of them are evident: (1) the lack of strong teaching on certain subjects from the pulpit, (2) the choice of materials for study in Bible classes, (3) definite disciplinary influence of parents and church leaders, (4) evangelists who shun controversial but crucial subjects when the scriptures are very clear in their teaching, (5) parents who allow their children to give in to peer pressure in manners of dress and activities biblically condemned, and (6) church leaders who are negligent in failing to shepherd each individual in the flock, and who give too little attention to choice of teachers and choice of materials taught in Bible class.

In addressing the last subject, I would ask elders, or those whom they appoint, to choose a course of study for Bible classes, first to determine among themselves, and perhaps with the counsel of those who have made a study of this issue, the best material available. This is not a task to be accomplished in a one-period discussion. A wise course would be to obtain a complete set of books in each series being considered. It is helpful to read each series carefully and make a chart by which the characteristics of each available series can be charted and compared.

I shall not attempt here to list all of the items that should be considered, but will suggest a few of great importance:

(1) Throughout the series, is there absolute conformity with truths revealed in scripture?

(2) Does each higher grade level build on knowledge set forth in previous years toward progressive continuity in revealing God's ultimate purposes for His people?

(3) Is the subject material well adaptable to the interests and abilities of the age level for which it is planned, and is the material such as to invite further attention?

(4) Is the material such that when first presented, it is attractive or appealing to the initial inspection of the student?

(5) Is material set forth in a way to challenge the attention of the student or to appear difficult or dull?

(6) Is the amount of material provided commensurate with the average amount of time available for its development?

(7) Does the material provide for active participation on the part of each student?

(8) Are teachers supplied additional background information helpful to the presentation of the lesson?

(9) Is the information taught merely as factual, or is it presented in forms applicable to the everyday common experiences of the students?

(10) Does the series plainly instruct the student so that he is given a clear picture of the high points of the complete biblical narrative, so as to aid him in forming a clear conception of how the material studied fits into the whole scheme of God's plan for humanity?

(11) In the course of the various studies, is attention given to each item of the Ten Commandments, as well as to other virtues pronounced by Jesus in the Sermon on the Mount? Are these fully explained, enjoined, emphasized and repeatedly set forth as necessary principles of Christian living?

(12) Are the significance and assurance of the fundamental truths upon which the Christian faith rests clearly set forth: the virgin birth of Christ, His life, death, burial, resurrection and ascension into heaven where He shall remain until He returns to judge the world?

(13) Is teaching introduced, with repeated emphasis, on the manner, need, and significance of obedience to the gospel, being born into the family of God, and is this placed at the proper grade levels?

(14) Is this instruction followed by emphasis of the distinctive characteristics of Jesus' church?

(15) Is it made very clear and emphatic that Jesus' church is not a denomination and why denominationalism is unscriptural?

(16) Does the material suggest other related texts for individual study outside of class, or for homework done later for the purpose of summarizing and emphasizing matters set forth during class periods?

(17) Throughout the series, is the principle thoroughly emphasized that we must do only what the scripture authorizes to be done and that we can add nothing to that or take anything from it, lest we shall suffer dire consequences as promised by God?

(18) Is it constantly evident throughout the series that happiness and success in life are not achieved by approval of our peers, by acquisition of wealth, power or fame? Is it emphasized that true satisfaction comes from the realization of having made the strongest efforts, according to one's ability, to live in conformity with God's teaching, so that one constantly enjoys the expectation of receiving the promise of eternal happiness in the presence of God. This far exceeds satisfaction from any earthly endeavor!

It is not only important that the best and most appropriate study material be selected, but teachers need to be impressed with the importance of their work. Some people look on this field of service as a necessity, but nevertheless a chore to be avoided, if possible. This attitude is reflected in the following comments:

I'm Glad I'm A Teacher

"How many times have I heard a fellow Christian say, 'Oh, you mean you teach a class of little kids? Oh, you poor thing, you're a glutton for punishment.' My mental reaction to such a statement is, 'YOU poor thing, if you haven't ever tried it, you don't know the wealth of blessing you are missing!' Poor thing, indeed!

There are a few moments so precious as to see the dancing eyes of a little child as he sees the big fish (made of a bleach bottle) literally swallow up Jonah (a puppet) and then to see relief come and his whole body relax and settle against his chair when he sees that 'God took care of Jonah and he will take care of me too if I obey him.'

Or, the excited voice of a little one tugging at mother and daddy to 'come see the ten lepers Jesus made well.' To mother, that wall mural may look like a pitiful sight, with ten figures (?) possibly with no necks, or all legs and no bodies, but you will never convince those youngsters that it isn't a work of art.

ME A POOR THING? When I hear three seats back the loud whisper, 'Mommy, that's my teacher,' then I receive the most moving, most blessing-filled hour of the week. No, I wouldn't trade all that for a comfortable chair in a quiet classroom, and who knows but that the Bible class YOU teach may lead some child to heaven who otherwise might not have seen the way. **Sorry, friend, that poor thing isn't me!!"**

— Author Unknown

Adult Bible Classes

Children's classes naturally fall into divisions appropriate to their age levels, and the pupils go to their assigned groups. Adult classes, of course, offer more leeway involving individual choice, but some grouping designated by church leaders' concern for different needs among the membership are necessary. It is wise to have a class designed especially for new converts. Their needs for instruction are quite different from those who have been members over longer periods of time. New converts should be given a thorough understanding of the distinctions between all churches of the denominational world and the church of our Lord, that His church is guided only by the direct authority of His word and by nothing more. Each member of the class should be taught so well that each one may be able to confront any non-believer in such a way as to faithfully and authoritatively defend any criticism of the worship in the public assembly of the church. A detailed study of the book of Acts might well contribute to this need.

A Second Needed Class

A class that should follow that for new converts is one which every member should attend at some time. This is a class which concentrates on evidences verifying the authenticity of faith in God's existence.

Tangible evidences to the divine inspiration of the Bible, undeniable evidence from secular history, archaeological finds etc. regarding Jesus' earthly life and other events as recorded in the Bible, should be taught along with reasonable historical evidence of Jesus' resurrection and other subjects. This course is not only necessary for new converts, but also for many who have been church members since adolescence. This is true because in the church of Christ, as in denominational churches, many adults attend and are members because their parents were members who brought their children up accepting the faith of their parents. Out of respect for their parents' judgment, not even questioning the possibility that their parents might have been misinformed, these church members have only a blind childlike faith. If these are to be strong spiritually and serve God acceptably, their faith must rest on a more firm foundation as evidence of its truth.

A Third Needed Class

Every member should attend a class at some time where the history of the church, as recorded in the New Testament, should be continued by means of secular historical records including the writings of Josephus and others, continuing through a study of the gradual departure of the church from divine revelation, and how as centuries passed, the church was guided by men who had changed and corrupted the doctrines of new Testament faith so that it became a very corrupt apostate body, leading men into unholy superstitious, insincere practices which were in direct opposition to divine truth With the invention of the printing press, the scriptures became much more available to the masses. Each person could read and not have to depend on others to understand God's word. People began to see that they had been mistaught and misled. Soon, the great Reformation Movement began, but although many corrupt beliefs and practices of the medieval church were disclosed, the existing professors of Christianity still held many diverse, conflicting and unscriptural views of the church and Christian life. The study of the Reformation Movement should develop into the study of the Restoration Movement and its successful culmination in the restoration of the church in its purity of doctrine and practice as revealed in the Scriptures. Thus we are blessed today with many congregations subscribing in all respects to the same doctrine as that of the New Testament. These congregations are known as churches of Christ.

Members of this church seek to believe and do only what conforms to positive commands of Christ, given through the Holy Spirit to His apostles, and recorded by them for all future generations. This church refuses to do as worship or service to Christ anything not explicitly commanded by His authority. Its members deny being a denomination and profess only to being members of the church that Jesus established. It desires to be known only as belonging to Him.

A Fourth Needed Class

All members beyond the babes in Christ should be attending at some time a class devoted to the study of Old Testament scriptures as they relate to the church today and to Christian behavior. There are some in the church who fail to see this necessity. They argue that since Christians now live under a new dispensation, and since they are no longer subject to the Mosaic Dispensation of Old Testament times, that the Old Testament is passé, that knowing it serves no special purpose.

However, the scriptures reveal something quite different on this subject. Note the following: If a person does not understand clearly the design of the tabernacle, the details of the manner of tabernacle worship, the sacrifices, the priesthood, etc. as revealed by Old Testament writers, much of the New Testament, particularly the book of Hebrews, as well as many other New Testament writings, could not be understood. Paul said that the law was a tutor to lead or bring us to Christ (Gal. 3:23).

The Hebrew writer said that the law was a shadow, that is an indistinct depiction, a type of that which was to come. He named details of the tabernacle parts, each of which was a foreshadowing, a type or representative of its anti-type, or counterpart in the doctrines of Christ. Read Hebrews, chapter 9, to see the beauty of these similitudes. After briefly noting the particulars of the first tabernacle (verses 1-10), the writer compared it to its counterparts in the system of Christianity.

> "But Christ having come a high priest of the good things to come, through the greater and more perfect tabernacle, not made with hands, that is to say, not of this creation" (Heb. 9:11).

The writer continued, extolling the superior virtues of the new covenant (Christianity) above the first covenant (the Mosaic covenant).

To fully appreciate and understand this beautiful revelation, one must have a background and clear understanding of the Old Testament scriptures.

How much more meaningful is Hebrews, chapter 11, to one familiar with the experience of those named there as these are revealed in the Old Testament!

> "For whatsoever things were written aforetime were written for our learning, that through patience and through comfort of the scriptures we might have hope" (Romans 15:4).

Without the Old Testament, our concept of God would be quite different, as well as incomplete. Although the New Testament contains many warnings concerning the eternal fate of the impenitent wicked, the attitude of many whose knowledge of the Bible is limited to that of the New Testament is that our God, being a God of immeasurable love, could never send a soul to such a place as hell is depicted to be. However, a careful study of the Old Testament reveals much more explicitly and expressly that God is also a jealous God, a God who will not allow any imperfection, a God who is strict in demanding full allegiance and obedience. It emphasizes vividly that

> "For we know him that said, Vengeance belongeth unto me, I will recompense. And again, The Lord shall judge his people. It is a fearful thing to fall into the hands of the living God" (Hebrews 10:30,31).

A Fifth Essential Study

Without a knowledge of the multiplied prophecies of such minute and unexpected unusual happenings, specific names, places and times as were foretold centuries before their fulfillment that are recorded in the Old Testament, the world would be robbed of some of the most valuable evidence of the authenticity of the Bible and the student, who diligently searches for a firm basis of faith in Christ as God's Son, would be bereft of a heritage provided by God for man's benefit.

If every New Testament reference to Old Testament prophecies, names, places, specific times and scripture citations were cut out of the

New Testament, the remaining portions would be entirely bereft of its full meaning, and one would look there in vain for sufficient instruction for living the Christian life.

Reader, please never discount the value of the Old Testament, which is truly the New Testament concealed while the New Testament is the Old Testament revealed. Let us treasure, read, study and heed ALL of God's word!

At some time in the adult curriculum, there should be a study covering the life of Christ.

After an adult has studied all the above-suggested courses, then there is room for variation, but these basic themes should precede studies like the following:

1. Selecting one New Testament epistle and studying verse by verse.
2. Selecting a biblical topic, i.e. prayer, forgiveness, use of money, and innumerable other biblical books and topics.

The suggested classes are not arranged in this writing with reference to sequence, but are named as special studies which should be done by all Christians.

It appears more reasonable to divide classes according to the time individuals have been members of the Lord's church, rather than by chronological age, as the spiritual maturity should correspond more to the former than the latter. Sometimes, the regular Bible classes are divided into men's and women's groups. There can be advantages in dividing teenage classes also between boys and girls, at least for short periods of time and for studying certain topics.

Church leaders have certain obligations toward all of these various groups. It should be made sure that the teachers are qualified, and that the format of the class is such as is likely to result in blessings rather than problems.

It is always advisable that the Bible be the basis of study, not some book of human origin about the Bible. Books of philosophy, psychiatry, self-esteem, or similar topics, are not properly used as texts.

I am not ruling out workbooks, comments on scriptures, or other additional helps, but these should be viewed as helps, not texts. The true text must be scripture along with the helps.

Church leaders should be responsible and aware of what goes on in extra classes, such as youth ministries, ladies' Bible classes, etc. Qualified teachers should be present. I have seen materials prepared for such classes that consisted of taking a given passage, and without prior consideration of the actual message meant to be conveyed to the reader, a series of questions is given, such as:

"What does vs. ... or phrase ... mean to you?"

"How do you think vs. ... applies to you?"

This is a dangerous way to approach a lesson. A scripture must first be studied within its context considering:

1. To whom was this written?
2. What was the situation calling forth this instruction?
3. What other scriptures apply to this situation?
4. Can the same situation exist today? If so, how is this passage applicable?

Only after establishing these truths can the reader make an apt application to himself or others. Unless such a procedure precedes such questions as those first mentioned, they are out of order and a class can become simply a "talk show," fail entirely in its purpose and do more harm than good. It is worthy of note that Paul told Titus that it is the duty of older, mature Christian women to teach the younger women (Titus 2:3-5). Church leaders should encourage these ladies to prepare themselves both in scriptural understanding and by being good role models that they may obey this injunction. Certainly elders' wives and wives of evangelists should consider this, not only as an obligation but a privilege.

Christian women, who long to serve Christ and the church, can find no greater opportunity for accomplishment than in giving dedicated and serious instruction and inspiration to others through efficient and well-informed teaching of God's word to others.

Make Me A Better Teacher

I dreamed the pearly gates were opened wide
    And I had entered in for I had died;
And now must give account of all my acts;
    I saw a book there opened with these facts.
I thought, "My role upon this earth was small
    Just teaching in a Bible school, my call."
For I saw all the saints of God up there
    And mine was, at most, a meager share.

I heard the Master call for my report.
    I stood afraid — for mine was short,
I trembled and felt I would not pass,
    Then whispered, "I just taught a Bible class."
And from the throne I heard His voice, "Well done,
    Come in and share eternal life,
Although your place was humble and obscure,
    You led the thirsty to the waters pure."

And then it seemed that from eternal plains,
    There came the sound of voices in refrain
That rolled across the mighty sea of glass,
    "There are the great — the teachers of a class."
After I awoke, I thought of those I'd taught
    And in their lives what glory God had wrought.
I prayed to God, and all that I could say was
    "Make me a better teacher day by day."

        — Author Unknown.

The Teacher

One woman takes her extra time and knits it into lace,
Another takes her extra time embroideries to trace.
The lace may wear a year or two, perhaps go out of style;
The colors of embroideries fade in just a little while.
But she who twines her extra time in lives of lad and lass
Produces that which shall endure when time and tide have
    passed.

        — Author Unknown

The Measure

The measure of a teacher's work
    Is not what people say,
Nor how much popularity
    May come within his day.
It is not in the flash of wit,
    Nor play of fancy free,
Nor anything that his own, time
    Can never know or see.

The measure of a teacher's work,
    Himself can never know.
It is not evident until
    The tides have time to flow.
It is the number of the lives
    In which he still lives on,
For worth and right and happiness
    After his work is done.

— Clarence Edwin Flynn

The following was not written with reference to teaching Bible students, but it provides much food for thought:

"I have taught in high school for ten years. During that time I have given assignments, among others, to a murderer, an evangelist, a pugilist, a thief, and an imbecile.

"The murderer was a quiet little boy who sat on the front seat and regarded me with pale blue eyes; the evangelist, easily the most popular boy in the school, had the lead in the junior play; the pugilist lounged by the window and let loose at intervals a raucous laugh that startled even the geraniums; the thief was a gay-hearted Lothario with a song on his lips; and the imbecile, a soft-eyed little animal seeking the shadows.

"The murderer awaits death in the state penitentiary; the evangelist has lain a year now in the village churchyard; the pugilist lost an eye in a brawl in Hong Kong; the thief, by standing on tiptoe, can see the window of my room from the county jail; and the once gentle-eyed little moron beats his head against a padded wall in the state asylum.

"All of these pupils once sat in my room, sat and looked at me gravely across worn brown desks. I must have been a great help to those pupils— I taught them the rhyming scheme of the Elizabethan sonnet and how to diagram a complex sentence."

— Selected

Every sincere Christian has the duty to carry the message of salvation to the lost and should realize that in addition to Bible study for self improvement there is another important reason.

Before assuming the responsibility of assuming the role of class teacher, one should carefully consider the warning of James, who wrote:

"Be not many of you teachers, my brethren, knowing that we shall receive heavier judgment. For in many things we all stumble... " (James 3:1,2).

CHAPTER ELEVEN

EVERYBODY IS AT RISK?
YOU DON'T HAVE TO BE!

News items and national TV media have at certain times in the recent past headlined printed articles or usual TV broadcasts with the statement: "Everybody Is At Risk!" The particular subject at hand has been the dreaded disease of AIDS. Such declarations have usually been brought to public attention by the discovery and publicizing of the fact that some widely-acclaimed sports star, adored movie idol, or other nationally popular personality is a victim of AIDS.

The reaction to such news is usually a feeling of regret by all, but also accompanied by one or the other of two very different responses. With some, there is only sorrow and sympathy for the one afflicted, recognizing that much physical suffering awaits and the certainty that early death cannot be avoided.

In the minds of others, there is a far different response. These recognize that in the majority of cases, those contracting this disease have done so as a natural consequence of an infraction against one of the many laws set in motion when this earth was created. These are commonly called the laws of nature. Each of these laws demands that certain causes will bring about certain natural results. For instance, when one plants corn, he expects to harvest a crop of corn, not of oats, rye, or any other grain. These laws of the physical world are no more binding or certain than are the moral laws which God also set in motion. He stated one of these laws in simple and emphatic terms:

> "Be not deceived; God is not mocked: for whatsoever a man soweth, that shall he also reap, For he that soweth unto his own flesh, shall of the flesh reap corruption ..." (Gal. 6:7,8).

One cannot "sow wild oats" and expect a life of roses. In the majority of cases, if not all, where such characters as those mentioned earlier have contracted AIDS, it has been a natural consequence of their own unnatural sexual behavior, in either a homosexual or other promiscuous sexual lifestyle. Recognizing this truth does not rule out sympathy and sorrow for the victim of the disease, but that sorrow is mingled with a deep sadness because this tragic situation is so unnecessary. It didn't have to be this way. It could so easily have been avoided.

In calling attention to this strict law of nature and it's sad results for those who failed to respect it, and therefore must suffer the consequences, we are keenly aware of the fact that there are some innocent victims of AIDS — those who have received the disease through blood transfusions. This risk has been greatly decreased, if not obliterated, by more diligent care in the screening of blood to be used for healing purposes. Also, there are an increasing number of infants who are infected by being born of infected mothers. For all of these innocent victims, there can be no other acceptable response than truly deep sympathy, regret, and a strong resentment toward those who allowed their degenerate behavior to contaminate their own bodies, thus causing inevitable suffering for themselves as well as for other involved individuals.

However, it is true that the number of innocent victims resulting from the suggested causes just mentioned is relatively small compared to the number of those who have deliberately rebelled against the absolute declarations of God. This rebellion is against the God who was the guiding force of those who founded this country for the express reason of providing a sanctuary of freedom, where all could live according to their religious convictions, unhampered by any governmental powers or restrictions. It was by the moral principles of the God revealed in the Bible that the Constitution of the United States was written, and legislation was passed governing unacceptable behavior in this country. The virtues of right living, such as honesty, truthfulness, fidelity in marriage, parental responsibility, respect for property and rights of others, the sanctity of marriage and human life were reflected in these laws. Showing the strength of feeling toward Judeo/Christian moral standards of behavior, this country has always had laws dealing with sexual misbehavior — laws against indecent exposure, bigamy, polygamy, child abuse, pornography and sodomy. Until recent decades, divorce was not easily obtained, and when it was granted, blame was attached. Those bearing children out of wedlock bore a stigma of having committed adultery and have thus committed grave sin in so doing. Until recent decades those who were guilty of breaking any of these civil laws were apprehended as soon as possible and were properly punished. It is sad to note, however, that the courts of today are not properly enforcing some of these laws, particularly those regarding indecent lack of clothing and sodomy.

Sodomy gets its name from the historical destruction of the cities of Sodom and Gomorrah. These cities were so wicked that, at the time when they were destroyed, not even ten righteous people could be found there. The sacred book reveals the unbelievable degree to which homosexuality existed in these cities. God demonstrated His great disapproval of this sin, as well as all sin, by raining upon the cities "brimstone and fire" utterly destroying all inhabitants therein, except righteous Lot and his two daughters.

> "If people knew the practices of homosexuals few if any would approve. Too perverted to even discuss are the things these people do and they want the rest of the nation to give their approval. Michael Swift, in the *Gay Community News,* February 15, 1987 wrote,
>
> "*We shall sodomize your sons, emblems of your feeble masculinity, of your shallow dream and vulgar lies. We shall seduce them in your schools, in your dormitories, in your gymnasiums, in your locker rooms, in your sports arenas, in your seminaries, in your youth groups, in your movie theater bathrooms, in your army bunkhouses, in your truck stops, in your all-male clubs, in your houses of Congress, wherever men are with men together. Your sons shall become our minions and do our bidding. They will be recast in our image. They will come to crave us and adore us...*
>
> "*All laws banning homosexual activity will be revoked. Instead, legislation shall be passed which engenders love between men.*

> "'There will be no compromises. We are not middle-class weaklings. Highly intelligent, we're the natural aristocrats of the human race, and steely-minded aristocrats never settle for less. Those who oppose us will be exiled ...
>
> "'The family unit, which only dampens imagination and curbs free will, must be eliminated. Perfect boys will be conceived and grown in a genetic laboratory. They will be bonded together in communal setting, under the control and instruction of homosexual savants ..'
>
> "If you can stomach more, read chapters 6 and 7 of Steve Farrar's book *Standing Tall*. Not only can we not accept homosexuality but we must speak out against it. God did."
>
> — Bill McDonough in Keynoter
Sixth & Izard Church of Christ,
Little Rock, Arkansas

Many centuries after the destruction of Sodom and Gomorrah, and long after the church had been established, the apostle Peter was writing to Christians and warning them against false teachers who were much like the homosexuals of today who are seeking to gain approval for their degenerative lifestyle in a society which has for centuries respected sexual virtue. These false teachers, against whom Peter warned, had likewise appealed to some Christians, who had learned how to live righteously, but who had been enticed to revert to their former lascivious ways through the deceptive teaching by these teachers of evils as truth. Their teaching was to get followers of righteousness to subscribe to the sins of the fleshly appetite. Of these false teachers of moral corruption, Peter wrote:

> "These are springs without water, and mists driven by a storm; for whom the blackness of darkness hath been reserved. For, uttering great swelling words of vanity, they entice in the lusts of the flesh, by lasciviousness, those who are just escaping from them that live in error; promising them liberty, while they themselves are

bondservants of corruption; for of whom a man is overcome, of the same is he also brought into bondage" (II Peter 2:17-19).

Note that Peter says of these proud preachers of lascivious living, that they seek followers from among "those who are just escaping" living in error. In other words, those who may just recently have heard the gospel message, who had accepted Christ and were just beginning to learn the real meaning of Christian living. These were new-born infants in Christ and therefore lacking the needed development toward spiritual maturity necessary to cope intelligently with those false teachers. For such persons, all those who have entered the family of Christ and then revert to their past life of sin, Peter gave a dire warning:

"For if, after they have escaped the defilements of the world through the knowledge of the Lord and Savior Jesus Christ, they are again entangled therein and overcome, the last state is become worse with them than the first. For it were better for them not to have known the way of righteousness, than, after knowing it, to turn back from the holy commandment delivered unto them" (II Peter 2:20,21).

One cannot afford to take such warnings lightly. Peter's words did not set forth the impossibility of one who has thus sinned to sincerely repent, confess his sin, forsake his evil ways, and receive forgiveness, but Peter's words indicate the severe difficulty of doing so. They also indicate the revulsion and disgust felt on the part of God and dedicated Christians by the following comparison made to such sin and those who partake of it.

"It has happened unto them according to the true proverb, The dog turning to his own vomit again, and the sow that had washed to wallowing in the mire" (II Peter 2:22).

Our God knows how, and He is not only willing but able, to deliver the righteous from among the wicked who will just as surely be punished by God. The apostle Peter plainly made this evident. He reminded those Christians to whom his letter was written of several incidents of the past which proved his point:

1. "... God spared not angels when they sinned, but cast them down to hell, and committed them to pits of darkness, to be reserved unto judgment" (II Peter 2:4).

2. "... Jehovah saw that the wickedness of man was great in the earth, and that every imagination of the thoughts of his heart was only evil continually. And it repented Jehovah that he had made man on the earth, and it grieved him at his heart. And Jehovah said, I will destroy man whom I have created from the face of the ground ..." (Gen. 6:5-7).

   "and spared not the ancient world, but preserved Noah with seven others, a preacher of righteousness, when he brought a flood upon the world of the ungodly" (II Peter 2:5).

3. "and turning the cities of Sodom and Gomorrah into ashes condemned them with an overthrow, having made them an example unto those that should live ungodly; and delivered righteous Lot, sore distressed by the lascivious life of the wicked (for that righteous man dwelling among them, in seeing and hearing, vexed his righteous soul from day to day with their lawless deeds)" (II Peter 2:6-8).

For a graphic depiction of the sinful corruption of Sodom and Gomorrah, read Genesis, chapters 18 and 19:1-29. Peter included these wicked persons of Sodom and Gomorrah among all such persons that he described:

"... them that walk after the flesh in the lust of defilement, and despise dominion. Daring, self-willed, they tremble not to rail at dignities: whereas angels, though greater in might and power, bring not a railing judgment against them before the Lord.

"But these, as creatures without reason, born mere animals to be taken and destroyed, railing in matters whereof they are ignorant, shall in their destroying surely be destroyed, suffering wrong as the hire of wrong-doing; men that count it pleasure to revel in the daytime, spots and blemishes, revelling in their deceivings while they feast with you; having eyes full of adultery, and that cannot cease from sin; enticing unstedfast souls; having a heart exercised in covetousness; children of cursing" (II Peter 2:10-14).

It was not until homosexuality and other permissive sexual lifestyles proliferated so extensively in this country that the disease of AIDS made its appearance and became a common word in American usage. These guilty people must bear the responsibility for the sad state of society in trying to combat this problem.

Homosexuality is a form of sodomy. God has always severely denounced sodomy and other sexual sins of lasciviousness. My dictionary defines sodomy as unnatural sexual intercourse, especially of one man with another or of a human being with an animal. Although all of these types of sin are sometimes practiced by people, attempting to fulfill their inordinate fleshly passions, homosexuality is the sin most widely publicized and most evident because of its association with AIDS. Note a particular biblical injunction against this specific sin:

"And if a man lie with mankind, as with womankind, both of them have committed abomination: they shall surely be put to death; their blood shall be upon them" (Lev. 20:13).

This type of sin was so heinous in God's sight that when He gave the laws to Moses concerning the worship to be given to Him, He even forbade certain persons from entering "the assembly of Jehovah." Among these were the prostitutes and sodomites (Deut. 23:17). Later there came a time in the history of Judah while Rehoboam reigned of which it was written:

"And Judah did that which was evil in the sight of Jehovah, and they provoked him to jealousy with their sins which they committed ... and there were also sodomites in the land: they did according to all the abominations of the nations which Jehovah drove out before the children of Israel" (I Kings 14:22,24).

When Isaiah pleaded with God's people who had become so exceedingly sinful that, rather than feel ashamed, repent of their wickedness, and return to God, they refused to heed and became even more open and defiant in performing those sins. Isaiah's reprimand of these evil-doers well applies to the disgusting, decadent behavior exhibited by the modern practitioners of the same sins, who even now are seeking to force upon society in general the acceptance of homosexual behavior as a legitimate lifestyle. Of such as these, Isaiah declared:

" ... they declare their sin as Sodom, they hide it not. Woe unto their soul! for they have done evil unto themselves" (Isa. 3:9).

These words aptly apply to the homosexuals of our society, who parade their wantonness and irreverence for all that is holy by their perverted public displays of nudity, explicitness of sexual perversion of all kinds, even with mocking and desecrating God and all symbols of holiness.

Jeremiah proclaimed God's wrath against those guilty of these explicit kinds of sin when they were committed by those who caused others to embrace these sins:

"... I have seen folly in the prophets of Samaria; they prophesied by Baal, and caused my people Israel to err. In the prophets of Jerusalem also I have seen a horrible thing: they commit adultery, and walk in lies; and they strengthen the hands of evil-doers, so that none doth return from his wickedness: they are all of them become unto me as Sodom, and the inhabitants thereof as Gomorrah" (Jer. 23:13,14).

In the new Christian Dispensation, God continues to reveal His attitude toward these sinners.

> "For the wrath of God is revealed from heaven against all ungodliness and unrighteousness of men, who hinder the truth in unrighteousness" (Rom. 1:18).

> "For the invisible things of him since the creation of the world are clearly seen, being perceived through the things that are made, even his everlasting power and divinity; that they may be without excuse: because that, knowing God, they glorified him not as God, neither gave thanks; but became vain in their reasonings, and their senseless heart was darkened. Professing themselves to be wise, they became fools" (Rom. 1:20-22).

Paul, the writer, leaves no doubt as to the perverted ways of these sinners, describing them graphically along with the consequences of their deeds:

> "For this cause God gave them up unto vile passions: for their women changed the natural use into that which is against nature: and likewise also the men, leaving the natural use of the woman, burned in their lust one toward another, men with men working unseemliness, and receiving in themselves that recompense of their error which was due" (Rom. 1:26,27).

Is not God's language plain that those who practice homosexual and lesbian behavior are recipients of His just punishment which the world calls AIDS?

As we view homosexuals of our society, we see some who still practice their lifestyle privately and participate in the other activities of life without calling attention to themselves. Among others, however, those who participate in public parades in indecent, suggestive attire, even nudity, displaying placards bearing ugly epithets against those who disapprove of their behavior, we see a graphic fulfillment of God's warnings by the way God has dealt with them.

> "And even as they refused to have God in their knowledge, God gave them up unto a reprobate mind, to do those things which are not fitting; being filled with all unrighteousness, wickedness, covetousness, malicious-

ness; full of envy, murder, strife, deceit, malignity; whisperers, backbiters, hateful to God, insolent, haughty, boastful, inventors of evil things, disobedient to parents, without understanding, covenant-breakers, without natural affection, unmerciful: who, knowing the ordinance of God, that they that practice such things are worthy of death, not only do the same, but also consent with them that practice them" (Rom. 1:28-32).

Sexual sins are at the root of many of the tragic situations now plaguing our nation. The existence of such sin is not new, but the indifferent compromising attitudes toward these sins now prevalent in today's society are a great departure from the history of our country from its very beginning until some three decades ago, when a spirit of rebellion against the moral standards heretofore accepted throughout our society began to make itself widely evident and gradually increased throughout the following years.

One could not truthfully say that life during the earlier history of this country did not have various problems such as have plagued humanity ever since Adam and Eve opened the door allowing Satan, the prince of evil, into a perfect world. Nevertheless, this country from its beginning provided the opportunity for each individual to pursue his dream, whatever it was, in a safe humanitarian society. The pioneer patriots, who founded our nation, had a vision, based on faith in God and personal initiative, of a nation rising out of an untamed wilderness to become a haven for all who desired to pursue their own dreams and ambitions and to worship and promote their religious beliefs, unhampered by any governmental agency.

With the passing years of this nation's history, the dreams of the early pioneers were fulfilled. As the United States entered the 1960s, this nation was recognized by all as the rich and powerful leader of the free world and as the land of opportunity, the place where the underprivileged and down-trodden of the world longed to be. Because of its faith in God and dependence on Him, this was a nation blessed by God according to His promise:

"Blessed is the nation whose God is Jehovah..." (Psalms 33:12).

"Behold, the eye of Jehovah is upon them that fear him ..." (Psalms 33:18).

But as the decade of the '60s advanced, these conditions began to change when the rising generation in open rebellion began to flaunt what came to be called "the new morality." Of course, there was nothing new about it. It was simply rebellion against authority — any authority, including that of God. This generation proclaimed personal freedom and the right to satisfy the desires of the flesh by indulging in those activities which seemed to them to provide the satisfaction and pleasure which were so ardently sought. This was the beginning of an ever-widening sexual revolution growing stronger and stronger as time moved forward through the '70s, the '80s, and '90s. The advocates of these changing lifestyles expressed themselves under various terms. There were those "searching to find self," the "me" generation, the "If it feels good, do it" philosophy, the "situation ethics" answers to problems, and now the value judgment decisions. All of these philosophies repudiate the arbitrary God-given laws including laws against illicit sexual relationships.

The advocates of sexual freedom have turned away from, and many have little knowledge of, the Judeo/Christian ideals which have been espoused by the leaders and citizens of this country since its very beginning. The rising younger generation insisted that the old standards of conduct must be abandoned in favor of greater freedom in personal choice regarding matters of private conduct. This has resulted in moral confusion continuing, especially among younger generations, with a rejection of old accepted values and a frustrating search for substitute values. Refusing the proven values of past generations, newer generations seek to make their own laws depending upon the external material world to supply the "sought-after" Utopia of their dreams. These individuals do not realize that they live merely upon the surface of life by their actions, boasting of being violators of convention. In their outward bravado, they proclaim their emancipation from the laws of morality which long have governed our country. The generation of the '60s and following generations made evident, without realizing it, their sad spiritual poverty.

As a result of this moral restlessness — this spiritual famine, this rejection of "proven to be true" laws of morality — each succeeding generation has continued the unlawful practices of the sexual revolution, indifferent to moral laws set forth by God. The tragic results of this rebellion against God's spiritual laws and even, in some instances against the civil laws of the land, are evidenced in the greatly increased occurrences of the breakdown of families ending in divorce, avoidance of parental responsibility, abused and abandoned children, widespread flaunting of adultery, premarital and extra-marital sexual activity, teen pregnancies, abortion, open practice and promotion of homosexualism and lesbianism, murder, assault, and all types of crime related to sexual sins. There are also all kinds of pressures and demands by those living the homosexual lifestyle to make it totally acceptable to society, even efforts to give such people special consideration above the general public. As unbelievable as it seems, the current president of this country made it a priority immediately after his inauguration to do everything in his power trying to put forward this corrupted lifestyle. How blind, foolish and inconsistent can people who claim intelligence become?

Although the demands of the homosexuals in our society have received much publicity by the media of the press and TV, homosexuals number a very small but growing percentage of our society. They claim to represent ten percent, when they actually are only about one or two percent. Nevertheless, they wormed their way into great influence through powerful organizations such as NEA (National Education Association), Planned Parenthood, ACLU, certain women's organizations, atheists, humanists and other groups. The first three of these present themselves as being advocates of proper causes, but in truth they are promoting in our public schools and elsewhere efforts to destroy all influences of the Judeo/Christian faith, including principles of sexual purity and moral conduct.

Sexuality is a natural and important part of God's creation of mankind. Adam and Eve were created of opposite genders. The act of sexual intercourse was intended, not only for the purpose of procreation of humanity, but as an experience to be shared by man and wife as a sealing of their loving intimacy, drawing tighter the close bond of their relationship. To use this act for any other purpose is a degrading act of moral degeneracy. God gave to Moses the first written code of morals.

Among the "Ten Commandments" were two dealing with sexual activity:

"Thou shalt not commit adultery" (Ex. 20:14)

"...thou shalt not covet thy neighbor's wife.." (Ex. 20:17).

Furthermore, when Moses delivered God's laws that were to be enforced upon His people, "the nation of Israel," these laws dealt with all kinds of sex and perversion, fornication, adultery, incest, bestiality and homosexuality. Read Leviticus, chapter 20. Note the explicitness with which God made clear that all types of illicit sexual relationships are an abomination in His sight and that they will, with certainty, be followed with severe punishment.

The title of this chapter poses a question as to whether or not everybody is at risk of contracting AIDS, or any other sexually transmitted disease, of which there are several, though AIDS is the most severe and the one for which as yet there is no cure.

AIDS first surfaced in our society after the sexual revolution, begun in the 1960s. It became so widespread that those engaging in the homosexual lifestyle, who had formerly done so in secret, gradually became so bold that they not only revealed their conduct openly, but began concerted efforts to force its acceptance by all as nothing more than a different way of life. With the increasing number of homosexuals, some of whom are also bisexuals, the AIDS epidemic has spread also among heterosexuals, but it is a known fact that the homosexual lifestyle, coupled with promiscuous sexual behavior of heterosexuals, has promoted the spread of AIDS, as well as other sexually-spread diseases among heterosexuals as well as among homosexuals.

It is the fact that heterosexuals have also become infected that led to the warnings that everybody is at risk. This warning is completely unfounded. There are multiplied tens of thousands, who live according to Bible instructions about sexual relations between men and women, who are not, never have been, and never will be at risk. This is no mystery. The reason is clear. God has always taught that sexual relations before marriage or outside of marriage are forbidden. The sexual relationship is to be confined to that with one's spouse. Paul taught the Corinthians:

"But, because of fornications, let each man have his own wife, and let each woman have her own husband. Let the husband render unto the wife her due: and likewise also the wife unto the husband. The wife hath not power over her own body, but the husband: and likewise also the husband hath not power over his own body, but the wife" (I Cor. 7:2-4).

AIDS, syphilis, gonorrhea and other sexually-transmitted diseases are spread through illicit relations and multiple partners.

God's commands regarding the sanctity of the marriage relationship are for the individual's own welfare as well as for all of society. They do not rob His followers of any of life's pleasures, but rather add to the richness of life. The key words to being free of risk are **abstinence before marriage** and afterward **fidelity to the marriage vows**. The person who follows the way of life prescribed by Christ is no more at risk of contracting AIDS than for murder, rape, DWI or any other violations of law. His way does not injure others at any time, but rather makes his environment a safer, better place to live.

If the family, the church, and all of those whose responsibilities are to teach our young people these important truths would do so, the nation, the communities, the families, and all the individuals who make up our society would be happier, safer, more prosperous and much more pleasing to God.

The following article, expressing the viewpoint of a thoughtful young person, deserves to be read and contemplated seriously by all the youth of our land.

What Do You Do For Fun?

Several years ago a sweet Christian girl told me about an incident with a young man who had been asking her to date. He was not a member of the church and they just didn't have anything in common. She had turned him down twice and now she had said "no" to attending a rock concert with him.

In a kind of mock exasperation, the young man asked, "What do you do for fun? You don't dance, you don't drink, you don't attend rock concerts ... what do you do for fun?

Though she related her answer to me in a way that made it seem as though it was a simple response, it was actually a classic message from all Christians with convictions. To the young man she had replied, "For fun I get up in the morning without feeling embarrassed, ashamed, and guilty about what I did the night before." The young man had nothing more to say.

It's true! That is fun! Come to think of it, there are many things in her life that are fun. She is married now to a fine Christian man. They have a little girl and are building an outstanding Christian home together. I am thrilled thinking about the fun she is having.

She is having fun every day living with no affliction of deep scars and regrets from her past. It's fun getting all prettied up each afternoon to receive her husband from work, knowing that he won't be stopping off at a local bar for a few with the boys.

It's knowing that while he is away from her, his Christian conduct won't allow infidelity or even flirting. It's fun watching him hold his little girl on his lap with loving, protecting arms.

It's fun knowing that her little girl will never see her father in a drunken stupor or experimenting with drugs. It's fun living with the assurance that the home will be led by a spiritual leader who will guide each family member toward heaven.

The list of fun things for Christians is endless; what do you do for fun?

— Barrackville Church of Christ Bulletin
Barrackville, West Virginia

Although some argue that homosexuals and lesbians are as they are because of some influence received at birth and that they cannot change their attitudes toward their sexual behavior, we know this is not true simply because a great many homosexuals and lesbians have changed their lifestyle and now lead normal lives as heterosexuals. The

Bible also confirms this possibility by showing us examples! Paul had established the church in Corinth, a city so noted for its immorality that to denote one as among the vilest of sinners, he was called a Corinthian. When Paul later wrote to that church, he said:

> "Or know ye not that the unrighteous shall not inherit the kingdom of God? Be not deceived: neither fornicators, nor idolaters, nor adulterers, nor effeminate, nor **abusers of themselves with men**, nor thieves, nor covetous, nor drunkards, nor revilers, nor extortioners, shall inherit the kingdom of God. **And such were some of you**: but ye were washed, but ye were sanctified, but ye were justified in the name of the Lord Jesus Christ, and in the Spirit of our God" (I Cor. 6:9-11).

The gospel of salvation is available for all, regardless of one's past sins. The invitation is to all. There is no sin so great, so heinous in God's sight, that it cannot be forgiven if one accepts Jesus as the divine Son of God, truly repents of evil doings, and is baptized in the name of the Father, the Son and the Holy Spirit, thus having his past sins blotted out, washed away through the atoning blood of Christ. Jesus, Himself, pronounced this truth.

> "Blessed are they that wash their robes, that they may have the right to come to the tree of life, and may enter in by the gates into the city. ..... And the Spirit and the bride say, Come. And he that heareth, let him say, Come. And he that is athirst, let him come: he that will, let him take the water of life freely" (Rev. 22:14-17).

Not only are the past sins forgiven when the sinner responds; He receives the gift of the indwelling Holy Spirit as a Guide, Helper, and Strengthener, thus enabling the forgiven sinner to cope more ably with temptation, than was previously true. Without this aid, the homosexual might be unable to reform his life. This is not to say that reformation may not be a struggle, but to say that the struggle can be victorious.

Although the Christian is repulsed and provoked that one has sunk so law morally as to live as a homosexual or lesbian, it should be remembered that he, himself, was a sinner before being redeemed through God's wondrous grace. The Christian, therefore, must not only condemn the sins, but must also willingly and lovingly seek to appeal to those guilty of this type of sin, as well as to all kinds of sin, and extend all possible aid and kindness to those who will repent and reform their lives.

CHAPTER TWELVE

THE CHURCH AND POLITICS

Is there, or can there be, any scripturally proper relationship between the church and politics? Before attempting to answer this question, there should be a clear delineation defining each of these terms or identities.

It has been clearly explained in previous chapters that the church is the total sum of those believers in Christ, who have been born anew into His family. It is that spiritual body of which He is head. It is that spiritual kingdom over which He reigns as king. The mission of the church is the saving of souls. Its members are (1) to teach the plan of salvation so that, in obedience to its commands, individuals may be saved eternally, and (2) to provide mutual fellowship and encouragement that the growth of each member toward spiritual maturity may be encouraged.

What is meant by politics? According to "The New Merriam-Webster Pocket Dictionary," *politics* means: *the art or science of governmental policy*, holding control over government.

Our government was founded by those who left their native soil, after they and their ancestors endured a thousand years of abuse and restraint perpetrated upon them by a collusion of church and state. In setting up our democratic form of government, these men wisely gave us a Constitution into which were written basic safeguards for religious freedom, unequaled in the history of the world.

The First Amendment to our Constitution of the United States of America reads:

> "Congress shall make no law respecting an establishment of religion, or prohibiting the free exercise thereof; or abridging freedom of speech, or of the press;

or the right of the people peaceably to assemble, and to petition the government for a redress of grievances."

This first amendment provides restraint upon the government from interfering in any religious matters, at the same time permitting free expression and practice by all of such beliefs as do not conflict with the common good. Likewise, the church is to refrain from organized participation in government operations. The church is not to become involved on an institutional level with partisan politics. This arrangement has been very satisfactory and never at risk until very recently.

Even if our legal heritage did not provide for separation of church and state, according to divine instruction, the church has no place as a political body. Jesus designed His church to function apart from whatever political or social culture prevails.

The church is not concerned with secondary matters such as taxes, the price of certain commodities, the building of highways, the source of our oil supply, etc. These may be of interest to individual Christians, but not of the church as a body. The church has no concern over what party is in control, over whether its members are Republican, Democrat, or Independent. It has no proper role to campaign for any particular candidate running for office.

However, when political powers seek to pass legislation which encroaches upon standards of righteousness and morality as set forth in divine law, the church cannot and must not ignore the situation and forfeit its obligation to refute the errors and set forth the truth concerning the issues involved. This statement is not advocating that the church, as a body, set itself in array against the political influences and those exercising power. What is being affirmed is that evangelists, elders and teachers in the church have the duty to teach the church membership, making sure that the wrongs that political powers would impose are plainly and positively shown to be opposed to divinely revealed truth regarding the issues. The result would be that individual Christians are prepared to participate as citizens of the state in preventing or reversing wrong decisions of the political powers.

As in all matters, Christians should look to New Testament teaching and example to learn how to handle any situation, whether it pertains to social, personal, or legal relationships. We note that when Jesus lived on the earth and continuing through the years during which the church was established, its teachings were first proclaimed throughout the world. God's people were under the control of the Roman Empire, headed by the Emperor Caesar. Although they deeply resented and chafed under this subservience, they did not try to throw off its restraints. They complied with its demands. Setting the proper example, Jesus paid the taxes required, making no complaint (Matt. 17:24-27). And when the Pharisees, seeking to trap Jesus, asked "Is it lawful to give tribute unto Caesar?" He answered:

> "... Render therefore unto Caesar the things that are Caesar's; and unto God the things that are God's" (Matt 22:21).

> "Let every soul be in subjection to the higher powers: for there is no power but of God; and the powers that be are ordained of God" (Rom. 13:1).

This does not mean, necessarily, that God approves of everything done by the rulers over the nations, or that He approves of the particular persons in power. It does mean that His people are to respect the office of those who rule because God ordained order, not chaos, among the nations; and without some higher direction and recognized authority, chaos would prevail. However when the civil authorities oppose the authority of Christ, the Christian must obey the higher authority. This principle was set forth through the actions of Peter and John soon after the church was established. In an effort to prevent growth of the church, those preaching the gospel became the objects of persecution by the Jewish high court of the Sanhedrin. Peter and John were arrested and charged not to speak at all or teach in the name of Jesus, but they answered:

> "... Whether it is right in the sight of God to hearken unto you rather than unto God, judge ye: for we cannot but speak the things which we saw and heard" (Acts 4:19,20).

Continuing through the recorded history of the church during the apostolic period, we can see the limited extent to which Christians were involved with civil government.

When Paul was arrested in Jerusalem, he offered no physical resistance, but when it was ordered that he be beaten, he offered in self-defense the fact that he was a Roman citizen. By so doing, he averted that cruel punishment (Acts 22:25,26). And when Festus wanted Paul to leave Caesarea and go back to Jerusalem for judgment, he again appealed to the authority of the Roman law by saying:

> "... I am standing before Caesar's judgment-seat, where I ought to be judged: to the Jews have I done no wrong, as thou also very well knowest. ... I appeal unto Caesar" (Acts 25:10,11).

It is evident then that Christians, like all other citizens of the nation, have the right to appeal to legal authorities in their defense against mistreatment. However, Paul taught that Christians should choose to suffer hardship rather than appeal to the law if offended by a brother in Christ.

> "Dare any of you, having a matter against his neighbor, go to law before the unrighteous, and not before the saints?" (I Cor. 6:1).

> "Nay, already it is altogether a defect in you, that ye have lawsuits one with another. Why not rather take wrong? why not rather be defrauded?" (I Cor. 6:7).

As indicated by Jesus instructions to "render unto Caesar the things that are Caesar's and unto God the things that are God's," it is evident that the Christian has a two-fold citizenship. He is a citizen of Christ's spiritual kingdom and also a citizen of the nation. Each citizenship involves one in definite responsibilities. As a citizen of Christ's kingdom, one must seek to emulate Him and follow His teachings. As a citizen of the nation, the Christian must be bound by its national laws, but if those laws and the principles of Christianity are in conflict, it is evident that both cannot be obeyed. In such cases, obedience to God-given law must take precedence over obedience to civil law.

The Christian's efforts in seeking to eliminate the wrong influences of bad legislation are not made for his own sake, but for the sake of other citizens who may be influenced to accept as proper the immoral legislation. Christians must themselves be fully indoctrinated with true moral and spiritual values of Christ through personal study and as a result of proper preaching and teaching in order that they may recognize error when it is set forth and promoted by political influence and proposed legislation. It is only through efforts to promote these moral principles and refute opposing influence by those who understand and adhere in their personal lives to these divine instructions that the world comes to know and be influenced by them. This enables the light of Christ to shine forth enlightening the world and exercising the preserving quality of the salt of Christianity.

No, the church is not to be engaged in politics, but its individual members have a heavy obligation to use their political rights to affect politics when the government seeks to control or legislate in any way regarding each citizen's freedom to choose and exercise religious choice and advancement of its cause. When the government imposes or seeks to control matters of righteousness and morality, Christians must exercise their right as citizens to resist and to prevent further impingement upon the freedom declared by our Constitution. Christians must proclaim biblical truth relevant to moral issues involved. Christians must actively work against legislation and administration which is opposed to moral truths.

There are those who chafe at the idea that the United States was meant to be a Christian nation, but by so doing they reveal their ignorance of the historical facts which show that it was the intention of our founding fathers to set up a nation where every individual has the right to worship as his conscience directs with no infringement upon his right to practice and promote his beliefs.

Our nation has a great spiritual heritage, based on the fundamental principles of Judeo/Christian faith. In the Mayflower Compact, the Pilgrims upon their arrival to this land stated their motive in coming to this new part of the world:

"In the name of God, Amen ... having undertaken for the glory of God and the advancement of the Christian faith ..."

After the Pilgrims had settled and God had provided them an abundant harvest, they celebrated that first thanksgiving by recognizing God as the provider of their blessings.

Those who framed our Constitution and first governed our nation were not ashamed of their faith in God, but gladly and humbly portrayed it. This is evident in examining some of their affirmations.

"Without an humble imitation of the characteristics of the Divine Author of our blessed religion ... we can never hope to be a happy nation." — George Washington

"It is impossible to rightly govern the world without God and the Bible." — George Washington

"It cannot be emphasized too strongly or too often that this great nation was founded, not by religionists, but by Christians; not on religions, but on the gospel of Jesus Christ!" — Patrick Henry

"It is the duty of nations as well as of men to own their dependence upon the overruling power of God, to confess their sins and transgressions in humble sorrow ... and to recognize the sublime truth, announced in the Holy Scriptures and proven by all history: that those nations only are blessed whose God is the Lord." — Proclamation Appointing a National Fast Day, 1863, Abraham Lincoln

"Those who will not be governed by God will be ruled by tyrants." — William Penn

"He who shall introduce into public affairs the principles of primitive Christianity will change the face of the world." — Benjamin Franklin

"We have staked the whole future of American civilization, not upon the power of government, far from it. We have staked the future of all our political institutions ... upon the capacity of each and all of us to govern ourselves, to control ourselves, to sustain ourselves according to the Ten Commandments of God." — James Madison

"Whatever makes men good Christians, makes them good citizens." — Daniel Webster

"Whenever the pillars of Christianity shall be overthrown, our present republican forms of government, and all the blessings which flow from them, must fall with them." — Jedediah Morse

And from the first Chief Justice of the United States Supreme Court:

"Providence has given to our people the choice of their rulers, and it is the duty as well as the privilege and interest of our Christian nation to select and prefer Christians for their rulers." — John Jay

In answer to the question as to whether or not the United States continued to be a Christian nation, after reviewing thousands of documents on America's founding, the Supreme Court concluded in 1892:

"This is a religious people ... these and many other matters which might be noted, add a volume of unofficial declarations to the mass of organic utterances that this is a Christian nation."

These attestations, and a host of others that could be cited, make it clearly evident that from its beginning, this nation has professed to be, and has been recognized as being, a Christian nation. No longer ago than during the presidency of Ronald Reagan, our leaders have proclaimed the dependence of our nation upon God.

"Without God there is not virtue because there is no prompting of the conscience ... without God there is a coarsening of society; without God democracy will not and cannot long endure ... If we ever forget that we are

One Nation Under God, then we will be a nation gone under." — Ronald Reagan

Nevertheless, the decade of the 1960s ushered into our society, especially among the younger generations, the beginning of a rapid decline of interest in and guidance by those principles of morality so long cherished by our forefathers. This change in our culture and general society began with a sexual revolution wherein respect for the monogamous family decreased. Free love, living together out of wedlock, frequency of extra-marital affairs, increased numbers of divorces, promiscuity among singles, open revelations of homosexuality and lesbianism, shameless disclosure of children born out of wedlock, teen pregnancies, and near nudity, became more and more common and acceptable to many members of our society.

All of these situations increased to alarming proportions during the years between the 1960s and the present. Added to these have been other infractions against the long-recognized guiding moral principles of the past.

Evidences of the growing moral degeneracy are seen in the continuing slaughter of millions of unborn infants, the rapidly increasing numbers of neglected or abandoned children as well as those displaced through divorce, numbers of homeless on the streets, multiplied welfare recipients, street gangs, reckless shooting at random, car-jacking, suicides among the young and assisted suicides among the older, the acceptance or indifference of society toward vulgarity in speech and action, flaunted obscenity and irreverence toward God and holiness, pornography, and explicitness of sexual activities in movies, TV and in talk shows where the most shameful and debasing behavior is defiantly portrayed, schools where teachers or others are attacked by students with guns, daily murders throughout the nation, robbery, drunk driving with innocent victims, decreasing quality of education in public schools, and wide use of alcohol and drugs. AIDS has made its appearance and, along with other sexually transmitted diseases, has increased to alarming proportions.

These conditions are evidence to all intelligent and reasonable adults in our nation that immoral chaos reigns, especially among the younger generations. This poses a real threat which might easily be compared to a time in the distant history of Israel. This was during the period described in the book of "Judges." Sacred history reveals that after the death of Joshua and those of his generation,

> "... all that generation were gathered unto their fathers: and there arose another generation after them, that knew not Jehovah, nor yet the work which he had wrought for Israel" (Judges 2:10).
>
> "And they forsook Jehovah, and served Baal and the Ashtaroth" (Judges 2:13).

The moral situation among today's younger generations is very similar to that existing in Israel during the times described. A generation, strikingly ignorant of the Bible and its influence throughout this country's past history, is exercising its influence in the leadership of our country's government and cultural institutions. Even the highest governmental powers admit that this nation is experiencing a condition heretofore nonexistent in its history; but those who are making our laws and financing federally-supported projects either refuse to admit, or they purposely deny that the founding fathers, as they wrote The Declaration of Independence, as well as the Constitution, were guided by the following principles of Judeo/Christian ethics.

1. The principle of dignity of human life (Ex. 20:13; Matt. 5:21).

2. The principle of monogamous marriage only (Gen. 2:24; Matt. 5:32).

3. The principle of common decency (Gen. 3:7, 21; Matt. 5:28; Eph. 5:3-5).

4. The principle of work (Gen. 3:19; Ex. 20:9; II Thess. 3:10).

5. The principle of God-centered education (Det. 6:6-9; Eph. 6:4).

6. The principle of divinely ordered institutions:

    a. The home (Gen. 2:21-24; Eph. 5:22,23).

    b. The church (Matt. 16:18; Acts 2:2).

    c. Civil government (Rom. 13:1).

Rather than admit that it is the departure from, and lack of respect for, these principles that has brought about the widespread moral deterioration and consequently the tragic social conditions of today, the government is seeking to correct these devastating conditions by treating the symptoms. This is just as wise as trying to bail water with a teacup from a rapidly sinking boat during a rainstorm.

It is claimed that by spending more and more money to deal with the homeless, abused and neglected children, the spread of AIDS, dysfunctioning of schools, divorce, gang activities, bulging prisons, thievery, serial-killers, street crime, and other moral corruption, these problems can be solved. While trying all sorts of schemes to cope with these conditions, the government is spending vast sums on activities that actually increase what it professes to try to reduce.

More and more money is appropriated to treat the victims and to find a cure for the killer disease of AIDS. More money is spent to fight crime by putting increased numbers of police on the streets, midnight basketball leagues, housing projects, policing schools, sex education in schools, distribution of condoms and instruction for their use. All of these fail to attack the causes of the conditions now threatening the very survival of our nation.

Those in control of affairs of state who legislate our laws stubbornly refuse to admit the basic cause of all the deteriorating conditions in our society which, simply stated, is that a large segment of our society, including those who are in high governmental positions, has chosen to act in defiance of the principles which heretofore have always been our guides. Many of these leaders have knowingly forsaken heretofore recognized principles, choosing to walk according to their own personal desires and judgment. In so doing, their decisions have affected not only their own personal behavior, but also the entire nation. It should be understood that **every** deteriorating social problem has resulted indirectly and largely from the activities of certain organizations which made it their aim to impose a social form of government upon this nation by destroying the influence of Bible-based religion. Among these organizations are the American Civil Liberties Union (ACLU), Planned Parenthood, certain feminist organizations and National Education Association (NEA). Others with similar aims are contributing toward the same end. Among these are atheists, humanists, occult practitioners and those proclaiming New-Age religions.

These agencies, all of whom are Satan's emissaries, have gone a long way toward accomplishing their goal, to destroy every vestige of biblical moral influence on the behavior of our people. These destructive forces knew that their most fertile field for accomplishing their goal would be the minds of our children, so it was in the classrooms of the nation that the attack was begun. Never mind that the public schools of this nation were started primarily to promote the biblical principles of morality upon which our society was built. Never mind that the Bible had been the first textbook used in the public schools. Never mind that from their very beginning, it was mandated that in order to teach in the public schools, one must believe in God as the Creator of our world and in the Bible as His inspired word. Never mind that from the beginning of the public school system, and until some thirty or so years ago, teachers freely read Bible passages in the classroom and prayer was often said. God's name was respected and obedience to His teaching was enjoined. The importance of building character was taught, and children learned to discipline their actions.

As a result of the activities and deceitful workings of the organizations which set out to destroy the favorable social conditions of the past, beginning over three decades ago, these conditions favorable to building characters, representative of the moral values of our forefathers, have gradually been withdrawn from the public schools. One by one the underpinnings supporting the development of these characteristics have been removed, these actions drawing minimal attention by the public at large. These removals from the curriculum did not come about by the will of the teachers, students, or general parental request, but rather because of lawsuits filed because of objections by those identified as belonging to or in sympathy with one or more of the organizations that set out with the avowed purpose of destroying the influence of biblical concepts of morality. The sequence of court decisions which have so drastically changed our public schools is listed here:

In 1962 —   Prayer was removed from public schools, <u>Engel v. Vitale</u>.

In 1963 — Reading from the Bible was removed from public schools, <u>Abington v. Schempp</u>.

In 1973 — Abortion was declared legal, <u>Roe v. Wade</u>.

In 1980 — The Ten Commandments were removed from public schools, <u>Stone v. Gramm</u>.

In 1985 — Benedictions and invocations were removed from public school, <u>Graham v. Central</u>.

These destroyers of character-building provisions in our schools have also been successful in removing from school textbooks every trace of the fully-documented historical facts of our forefathers battling to preserve our Christian heritage, the knowledge of which would inspire an appreciation of that heritage and the basis of true patriotism.

Not only have these destructive workers removed the desirable character-building processes from our public school system, but in their place have been substituted, in an insidious manner, the concepts of atheism, humanism, dependance on the occult, and New-Age religions. Pupils are asked to make value judgments without any background basis for making such decisions. Often there are instructions from teachers for secrecy because, "although parents may mean well, they don't know the truth about this subject," or "They don't understand."

Coupled with the loss of value-teaching in the schools, another contributing factor to the outrageous moral conduct exhibited in today's society has been the decrease and often entire lack of such parental teaching of values as was common in the homes of past generations. One reason for this is the increase in numbers of divorce, leaving children in one-parent homes in which, due to the necessity of the parent to work outside the home, the children are deprived of time and energy needed by the parent for such instructions. Still another contributing factor is that today's children often have parents who were themselves deprived of such instruction.

Is it any wonder that we are experiencing the terrible moral corruption now seen in our society?

The governmental powers are making various kinds of assaults upon the freedom proclaimed through the first amendment for the individual's right to practice religion according to his own conscience and to utilize the freedom of speech to proclaim, unhampered, his beliefs and religious principles.

Although each session of the Supreme Court opens with a call to order with a short prayer, prayer is now forbidden in the public schools. The Supreme Court allowed a lower court ruling of a Georgia court which banned posting of the Ten Commandments from a display at a Georgia County Courthouse, even though there is on the walls of the Supreme Court chamber a list of the Ten Commandments. Although biblical messages and scriptures are on state buildings in Washington, D.C. bearing evidence of the Christian faith of our forefathers, the Ten Commandments have been outlawed in public schools. Dozens of instances such as the following could be cited where individuals have been penalized because of references to Christian beliefs:

> In Jackson, Mississippi, a school principal was fired for allowing prayers led by students over the school intercom. — Associated Press, Nov. 25, 1993.

> A student in Austin, Texas could not have her essay printed in the school newsletter unless she deleted a reference to Christ. — Christianity Today, Oct. 25, 1993.

> In Texas, a student was denied permission to write a paper on the life of Jesus, even though other students wrote on reincarnation, the occult and spiritualism. — Los Angeles Times, Aug. 24, 1991.

> In Oklahoma, an 11-year-old-girl was ordered to stop reading the Bible and talking to other pupils about God during recess. — Washington Post, April 12, 1991.

> In California, students were not allowed to establish a Christian Bible study and prayer group on campus. — Los Angeles Times, June 5, 1991.

> A judge in North Carolina was ordered to stop opening each day's proceedings with prayer. — UPI, Oct. 25, 1991.

In North Carolina, a radio commentator was banished from the air because he quoted Bible passages upon which he based his comments. — Charlotte Observer, Sept. 17, 1993.

In Pennsylvania, a high school pupil was ordered to stop giving religious tracts to fellow students. — Philadelphia Enquirer, June 2, 1991

Our society today is becoming more and more like the nation of God's people shortly before they were carried away into captivity because of their refusal to give up their evil ways and serve Him faithfully. The prophet Hosea rebuked them and foretold their impending punishment unless they would repent. He spoke to them God's message:

"My people are destroyed for lack of knowledge" (Hosea 4:6).

He was not speaking of knowledge of worldly wisdom. Our nation is rich in the knowledge and development of technology, science, medicine and many other subjects, but God spoke of a different kind of knowledge, of that kind of which Solomon wrote:

"The fear of the Lord is the beginning of knowledge" (Prov. 1:7).

"Where there is no vision, the people perish" (Prov. 29:18).

A more accurate translation of this passage is:

"Where there is no revelation, the people cast off restraint" (NRSV).

Revelation refers to God's word. Where the knowledge and respect of His word are lacking, behavior deteriorates. Principles, unrecognized, are violated. Restraints are absent. Every person becomes his own lawmaker. This situation now prevails among many of our younger generation. The inevitable has happened and the result is infidelity, broken homes, hurt and rebellious children. Anxiety, instability, pain and suffering permeate many lives. On the other hand, those whose lives have been governed by Christian principles and instruction for living find satisfaction, hope, fulfillment, and happiness. How sad that that which is within reach of every individual is so often ignored, belittled, rejected!

From the very beginning when our nation began under direction of the founding fathers until recent years, in spite of our failings, most of our people had faith in God and gave Him honor and reverence. God has blessed and protected this nation just as promised in His word:

> "Blessed is the nation whose God is the Lord" (Psalms 33:12).

As a nation, God is still honored by the majority but that majority is decreasing. Our coins still bear the inscription, "In God We Trust," but many today do not have this trust in their hearts and lives. All need to hear and properly respond to this warning:

> "beware lest you forget Jehovah your God, in not keeping his commandments, and his ordinances, and his statutes, which I command you this day" (Deut. 8:11).

God gave man certain moral laws and warned that when they are broken, the penalty will be imposed on individuals or on nations. Paul gave the Roman Christians dire warnings of the consequences of rejecting Him:

> "For the wrath of God is revealed from heaven against all ungodliness and unrighteousness of men, who hinder the truth in unrighteousness" (Rom. 1:18).

> "because that, knowing God, they glorified him not as God, neither gave thanks; but became vain in their reasonings, and their senseless heart was darkened. Professing themselves to be wise, they became fools" (Rom. 1:21,22).

> "Wherefore God gave them up in the lusts of their hearts unto uncleanness, that their bodies should be dishonored among themselves" (Rom. 1:24).

> "For this cause God gave them up unto vile passions: for their women changed the natural use into that which is

against nature: and likewise also the men, leaving the natural use of the woman, burned in their lust one toward another, men with men working unseemliness, and receiving in themselves that recompense of their error which was due. And even as they refused to have God in their knowledge, God gave them up unto a reprobate mind, to do those things which are not fitting" (Rom. 1:26-28).

The rise and spread of AIDS is a prime example of God keeping His word. Primarily, those affected are receiving in themselves "that recompense of their error which was due." The rejection, rebellion and disobedience against God's law, in recent years, have been openly and blatantly flaunted by those guilty. God has begun to assess the rightful penalty on individuals and the nation. Yet our government refuses to recognize these evident facts and continues to encourage homosexualism and lesbianism by attempting through legislation to legitimize those deviant behaviors as natural and unpreventable. No steps are taken to confine those having the contagious disease, as would be done with some other highly dangerous and communicable disease. No assistance is prescribed to help the homosexual and lesbian to overcome their evil and pernicious habit. Instead, the powers in Washington continue to appropriate more money to treat the ill and to experiment to find a cure rather than make efforts to remove the need for that by teaching the truth and by making no concessions granting favors to these people.

Instead of programs to teach our youth the need and beauty of sexual abstinence except in a monogamous marriage, millions of dollars are appropriated for Planned Parenthood, an organization claiming to work toward decreasing teenage pregnancies and abortions. Instead, it promotes promiscuous sexual activity and abortions through its school clinics and its claims to teach "safe sex."

In spite of the spiritual corruption growing on every hand and the indifference manifested by many, all must be assured that God ultimately rules in this world and the guilty will receive their just and promised penalty.

Of those various organizations which are attacking and trying to remove every trace of Christianity from our society, the ACLU is perhaps more active in the public view. It is likely that relatively few realize the extremes of moral depravity advocated by this group, and the depths of degradation that make up the agenda of its members. Among other things,

1. They denounce the death penalty, regardless of how horrendous the crime committed.
2. They call flag-burning, pornography, and desecration of things sacred simply expressions of free speech.
3. They think it is unfair to expect those on welfare to work.
4. They would allow homosexual couples to adopt children.
5. They favor reverse discrimination in favor of minorities.
6. They oppose airport searches to catch violent terrorists, who blow up planes.
7. They are willing to allow homosexuals special privileges and the opportunity to bind their manner of life on every school child, beginning at a young age.

History of the world, both religious and secular, confirms the fact that although unseen and unrecognized, God rules in the affairs of men. Secular history reveals that there have been four world empires: Babylonian, Medo-Persian, Grecian, and Roman. God's foreknowledge of these was prophetically revealed to His servant Daniel as recorded in the biblical record (Daniel, chapter 2).

The rich and powerful kingdom of Babylon was ruled by Nebuchadnezzar. It was allowed to flourish for a time, being used by God to discipline the nation of Israel for its faithlessness to God. The armies of King Nebuchadnezzar crushed Israel and carried its people into captivity, never to be reinstated as God's chosen nation. Later these armies destroyed the great temple in Jerusalem and carried the remaining Jews of the nation of Judah into captivity in Babylon. This was as God had planned and foretold through warnings of His prophets. God allowed Babylon to prosper as a nation for a time. But when Babylon had accomplished God's purposes, the wickedness of Babylon's kings and the consequent wickedness of its people brought its demise, as is so graphically described when King Belshazzar and his guests, in the midst of drunken revelry, saw the handwriting on the wall depicting God's message that Belshazzar had been weighed in God's balances and was found unsatisfactory and that His kingdom was to come to an end (Daniel, fifth chapter). That very night, the invading Medes entered the city of Babylon. Belshazzar was slain and the Babylonian kingdom fell, to be succeeded by the reign of the Medo-Persian Empire.

God's hand was still ruling to work out His purposes. The Jews were still captive, but had repented of their idolatry never more to engage in it. It was now time for God's prophecies, foretold by Isaiah and Jeremiah many years previously, to be fulfilled. Therefore the Lord moved the Persian King Cyrus to issue a proclamation allowing the captives to return to Judah.

According to the prophecy given through Daniel, the Persian Empire fell eventually to the Greek, Alexander the Great. This Grecian Empire later gave way to the even more extended Roman Empire. Although conditions were far from desirable for the Jews under Roman rule, God had brought about suitable conditions to promote the spread of Christianity which began with the establishment of the church in Jerusalem under Roman rule, about 33 or 34 A.D. The world was comparatively peaceful. The system of good roads and commerce through much of the empire was advantageous to travel, and the Greek language became the language understood over most of the empire. Although trade and commerce flourished and the higher classes in Rome lived lavishly in luxury, a sad case of extreme moral decadence finally brought the fall of this last great empire. It is sad to note that the conditions contributing to the fall were much like conditions that have developed in our nation which once ranked highest in the world for its living standard and advantages of personal freedom and opportunities for happiness and success. History asserts that the following devastating conditions were the primary reasons that Rome fell:

1. The sanctity of the home was undermined by the high percentage of divorces.

2. Taxes were exorbitant and the money was misused by the government.

3. The people were preoccupied with worldly pleasures. Sporting events excited much attention, becoming increasingly more brutal and dehumanizing.

4. Great armaments were provided for physical protection with little attention given to declining morals.

5. Religious faith, as a vital force for character development and good citizenship, was generally lacking in society.

6. Respect for the dignity of human life was largely lost. Unwanted babies were cast out.

These same characteristics have traditionally preceded the fall of all great nations. Therefore, it behooves all those who love this country, and hope to preserve for their posterity living conditions under which freedom to practice and preach their religious convictions may be assured, to take all possible measures to improve the moral status of our society lest God soon will see fit to discipline this country as He always has done eventually under such conditions.

Christians must realize that the warfare is already in array in this nation. Its enemies are those who hope to destroy life in this country, as it has been enjoyed since its establishment, and to replace it with a secular socialistic society totally directed by the powers in Washington. The enemy is already entrenched in the White House at the time of this writing. We have a president who openly endorses the homosexual agenda, aligning himself with these profligate people, and who made it legal to perform abortions on demand through the full term of pregnancy. He is assisted in his endeavors by over one hundred and fifty known homosexuals and lesbians in the federal governing body of the land. Recently a group of Christians, in an effort for which they had already obtained permission to film a video from Washington near the White House, was harassed by White House police and forced to go elsewhere. Nevertheless, there was no objection made by the authorities when in celebration of the president's inauguration, homosexuals and lesbians paraded before the White House openly flaunting near nudity and all kinds of obscenity. All of this occurred in spite of the fact that sodomy, the practices of homosexual activity, is contrary to the laws of the land as well as strongly condemned by the commands of God.

This nation is a democracy. It professes to have a government "of the people, by the people, and for the people." Our government is what our society has made it. It is what it is because too many Christians have abrogated their responsibility to safeguard the ruling powers by withdrawing and leaving its conduct to those who have appropriated it for their own selfish and private interests. Because the church has recognized that, as a body, it cannot officially participate in the secular conduct of the government, individual church members have for too long assumed that position as their own guide. But in this they have made a completely wrong assumption. As a citizen of the nation, every Christian has the same responsibility as every other citizen of the nation to have a voice in guiding this ship of state. In fact, the Christian has an even greater interest when the matter being considered is a moral issue. Moral issues threatening our country today concern government support for the traditional family unit, abortion, victims of AIDS, obscene so-called art, pornographic literature, and homosexuality, as well as various kinds of criminal activity.

Those who make our laws must be made to realize that certain issues are not matters to be controlled by the government because they represent areas where moral principles inherent in our national Constitution have already been established. It must be made clear that laws and taxes should not conflict with the enforcement of moral principles on which our national Constitution rests, and which represent the traditional values of our citizens since this nation was established. Lawmakers need to realize that abortion is directly opposed to the concept of the sanctity of human life, to civil laws as well as God's laws against murder, and against personal abuse of others. Furthermore, laws and taxes should not support homosexuality. This is a deviant lifestyle corrosive to personal and national welfare and destructive of every principle of spiritual purity and well-being. This nation must return to traditional values and by so doing will be strengthened and once again attain its position of superiority and supremacy in the world. Christians, all Christians, must make their voices heard by those who conduct governmental affairs.

The moral and political conflict in which this nation is now embroiled is a violent attack against Christianity, against the basic fundamental values upon which our nation and its great institutions were founded. The attitude prevailing among those who wrote our Constitution was well stated by James Madison, a leading framer of this great document when he said:

> "We have staked the whole of all our political institutions upon the capacity of mankind for self-government, upon the capacity of each and all of us to govern ourselves, to sustain ourselves according to the Ten Commandments of God."

This is no longer the prevailing sentiment among the men and women who make up our government in Washington.

Today in the political circles of our land there is no mention or indication of reliance upon God, or even any recognition of His standards of conduct. In fact, legislation considered and actions of the courts are in defiance of this standard. The principles of respect for the sanctity of human life were ignored in the court case of Roe v. Wade. Efforts have been and are being made to legislate in favor of homosexuals and lesbians above the rights of others, in spite of civil laws against sodomy.

The homosexuals are left alone not only to pursue their degrading conduct, but to accuse any who oppose them of being bigoted, prejudiced homophobics, seeking to bind their beliefs on others. The laws of the country place strenuous penalties on murderers. Yet, the courts are failing to mete out proper justice. In defense of the criminals in case after case it is argued that they are not really criminals; the killers were themselves victims of mistreatment so great that they are not now responsible. Even after the guilty are sentenced, few serve their full time in prison. Daily, dangerous criminals are released because of bulging prison walls. More and more money is appropriated to build prisons. While citizens cringe under the load of heavy taxes, our nation is still plagued with poverty-stricken families, hungry and homeless children. Yet our government continues to appropriate millions for ridiculous projects.

To cite a few examples, refer to the July 1993 issue of Readers Digest:

It's A Hard Life

Six small defense contractors charged the Pentagon for perks such as liquor, lottery tickets, caviar and trips to the Caribbean. The Pentagon picked up the tab because a vaguely written federal regulation allowed contractors to collect for costs that benefit employee morale and welfare. Among the bills found in an audit by the General Accounting Office:

- $14,000 for Boston Red Sox and Celtics tickets, including parking.
- $5800 for running shoes to improve employees' health.
- $12,000 for cable TV for retired workers.
- $62,000 to maintain a 46-foot sport-fishing boat.
- $24,000 for liquor.
- $383,000 for management conferences in Bermuda, the Grand Cayman islands, Jamaica, Hawaii and Mexico.

— Mark Thompson in Knight-Ridder/Tribune News Service

The reader is probably aware of some recent publicity objecting to the appropriation of government-funding for "the arts" including nauseating pornography and various irreverent and degrading depictions of that which is holy and sacred to Judeo/Christian concepts. These examples could be multiplied. In our society, any sort of unusual behavior seems to be permissible as it is being publicized by the media in the daily news reports. All seem to have lost any concept of a clear-cut standard between what is right and what is wrong, and no one dares to mention God's standards. This nation is truly living on borrowed time. Only a national revival and broad recognition of a standard of conduct based on definite moral principles, together with a change in course of action, can prevent this nation's ultimate downfall like that of every great nation before it.

Where have Christians been while these conditions have been developing? During the past three decades, they have, in the main, gone about their business as usual, although they have become increasingly aware of the younger generations' rebellions against the moral restrictions which prevailed previously throughout this nation. As this movement away from Christian morality developed and the quality of life in this country continued to decrease year by year, too many Christians have continued activities in their own little sphere, perhaps critical of developing conditions and bemoaning the moral decline, but failing to assume an active role in overcoming the enemies of everything that is good, those who are waging war against all that is holy. Too many Christians have abrogated unthinkingly their civil and moral responsibilities to others — others too willing to set forth their evil agenda to overthrow all that has been accomplished in building a great democracy where all have enjoyed complete personal freedom to pursue their dreams and ambitions without governmental restraint.

Fellow-Christians, our Lord gave each of us a commission to let His light shine through us, to proclaim the gospel to all sinners. We cannot merely continue complacently going about our business as usual. Our first obligation is to get the message of salvation to all possible, including homosexuals who are one of the threats to society. We must not simply condemn, but must realize that not all who live that lifestyle are the ones who vociferously and savagely attack Christian standards. Many homosexuals and lesbians are uncomfortable and unhappy, thinking that there is no other alternative for them. Christians must hold out to them the message that God loves them, extends to them the same offer of forgiveness and the divine help of His indwelling Spirit that they may renounce their sinful ways, turn to Jesus, be comforted and be saved eternally. Our world can be improved by changing the sinners — one by one. But Christians cannot stop there.

Preaching the gospel has always been the chief work of Christians individually and of the church as a body. Now even more attention must be given to this activity, but individual Christians must reach out and find additional ways to fight for the continuation of complete personal liberty for all and for the preservation of Christian moral standards as the foundation of peace and prosperity throughout our land.

In addition to those church activities for promoting the spread of Christianity, Christians must lend their support to the many other groups and organizations that are working to uphold those traditional American concepts of moral propriety. These can be strengthened by increased support of many more individuals. By actively and continually supporting all of those who take the lead in opposing evil and harmful threats to decency and moral behavior, much can be accomplished. One alone likely fails, but there is power in numbers. All who love God and want to see this nation restored to its former glory and to see once more a nation whose society can live a peaceful existence free to serve God and fellow-man, must stand up now and be counted among those willing to do battle for these causes. Christians should take the time and spend the energy necessary to acquaint themselves with the issues and the persons supporting or opposing these issues. All should be prepared on election days to make use of the privilege and opportunity to vote. Those who refuse to do this have no right to complain about the outcome and could be held responsible in the final day for failure to do their duty.

When Christians refrain from active involvement to perpetuate their Christian heritage, they are virtually turning affairs over to those whose selfish and worldly interests overrule their regard for humanity. Edmund Burke said:

> "All that is necessary for evil to triumph is for good men to do nothing."

We have seen this simple logic tragically demonstrated within our nation. Too many good men have done nothing, and others haven't done enough. God still hears the calls of His people and when, through their actions, they use those powers available to accomplish His purposes and call on Him, the greatest benefactor of all, He stands ready to help. Paul instructed Timothy, and through Timothy encourages us all:

> "I exhort therefore, first of all, that supplications, prayers, intercessions, thanksgivings, be made for all men; for kings and all that are in high place; that we may lead a tranquil and quiet life in all godliness and gravity" (I Tim. 2:1,2).

The foregoing writing was completed immediately prior to the November 8, 1994, election, the result of which indicates that the previous lethargic attitude of many God-fearing citizens of our nation has been supplanted by an awakening realization of the threat hanging over our destiny. Many, who previously had left it up to others to direct the affairs of our country, assumed their personal responsibility as citizens of this great nation, studied the issues, the character of those involved in the government and of others who might help to make the changes necessary to reclaim the rightful place of morality in our society, went to the polls and voted. Thus, there occurred one of the most phenomenal events in our political history — a massive display of public dissatisfaction with the "status quo" and a thundering demand for changes and the restoration of decency and order. The hand of Providence is clearly seen. Untold numbers of prayers were answered. Christians, continue your prayers and your efforts for the revival of reverence for all things holy, for the rebuilding of family values, for the return of school curriculum teaching basic fundamental moral values, and the removal of all the factors leading to moral deterioration.